THE BOOK
OF EULOGIES

A Collection of Memorial Tributes,
Poetry, Essays, and Letters of Condolence

EDITED WITH COMMENTARY BY
PHYLLIS THEROUX

SCRIBNER

SCRIBNER
1230 Avenue of the Americas
New York, NY 10020

DESIGNED BY ERICH HOBBING

Set in Palatino

Manufactured in the United States of America

1   3   5   7   9   10   8   6   4   2

Library of Congress Cataloging-in-Publication Data

The book of eulogies : a collection of memorial tributes, poetry, essays, and letters of
condolence / edited with commentary by Phyllis Theroux.
p. cm.
Includes index.
1. Eulogies.   2. Bereavement.   3. Grief.   4. Biography.
I. Theroux, Phyllis.
CT105.B66   1997
920.02—dc21   97-2197
CIP

ISBN 0-684-82251-2

For my mother,

PHYLLIS HOLLINS GRISSIM,

whose life reminds me of what is possible.

Whatever is true or good in this book

can be found in her.

ᏬᏜᏜᎧ

CONTENTS

ᚼᛜᚼ

CONTENTS

CONTENTS

CONTENTS

CONTENTS

CONTENTS

INTRODUCTION

For the past two years, I have been consorting with the dead, which has dramatically widened my historical context and my circle of available friends (say this about the dead, they are never too busy). In time, the curtain that divided the living from those who had lived became quite thin and then immaterial. I easily passed back and forth as if I were already dead myself. I attribute this phenomenon to the power of the words in which I had been immersed. Great eulogies instantly and effortlessly brought into my room the past and a host of people I had been born too late to meet.

The eulogy, or "funeral praise," is the oldest and, in some ways, least valued of our literary forms. It is practiced by amateurs. When someone dies, it is customary for a member of the family or a friend to "say a few words," composed under great duress, about the deceased. Mourners are not literary critics; we will accept any words at all, as long as they are not mean-spirited or self-serving, and if a particularly moving or graceful tribute is delivered, we are grateful for the balm.

But for such a neglected literary form, the eulogy is surprisingly elastic, stretching beyond the pulpit to embrace memorial tributes, reminiscences, newspaper and magazine appreciations. As a powerful container for human feeling, it may not be surpassed. Robert Louis Stevenson's tribute to his friend James Ferrier is at once an essay on friendship, a meditation upon the meaning of failure, and a story about a gifted boy who threw his life over his shoulder. Rev. Theodore Parker's eulogy for Daniel Webster is a history lesson and the tale of a broken heart—Parker's—when Webster betrayed the abolitionists' cause.

We don't usually think of Lincoln's Gettysburg Address as a eulogy, although it was. But if eulogies can be used to bind wounds, they have also been used to inflict them. Irish revolutionary Patrick Pearse's graveside lament for O'Donovan Rossa at Glasnevin Cemetery in Dublin in 1915 was nothing less than a call for the Irish to revolt against seven centuries of British rule. Eulogies are also ideal vehicles for philosophical ruminations, character sketches, and short stories. That being said, when one encounters a great eulogy, all the categories collapse as they always do in the presence of great literature. For what else does great literature reflect except a great ability to create life out of a skein of words.

"I remember," wrote William Makepeace Thackeray in his tribute to novelist Charlotte Brontë, "the trembling little frame, the little hand, the great honest eyes. . . . I fancied an austere little Joan of Arc marching in upon us and rebuking our easy lives, our easy morals."

"He smiled, not with the mouth but with his mind—" reminisced Helen Keller of Mark Twain, "a gesture of the soul rather than of the face."

"I can see him now," wrote W. E. B. Du Bois of his infant son, "changing like the sky from sparkling laughter to darkening frowns, and then to wondering thoughtfulness as he watched the world. He knew no color-line, poor dear,—and the Veil, though it shadowed him, had not yet darkened half his sun."

Eulogies are always double portraits, which deepens the pleasure of reading them. Jefferson's assessment of Washington's intellect ("It was slow in operation . . . but sure in conclusion") enables us to assess Jefferson's. Diana Trilling's essay on the death of Marilyn Monroe ("Even while she symbolized an extreme of experience, of sexual knowingness . . . in some vital depth, she had been untouched by it") reveals Trilling's understanding of the psyche that is not, we sense, academic. Winston Churchill's analysis of Lawrence of Arabia could just as easily have described Churchill:

> He was not in complete harmony with the normal. . . . The multitudes were swept forward till their pace was the same as his. In this heroic period he found himself in perfect relation both to men and events.

We are aware as much of the eulogist as the eulogized, for to praise or characterize the traits of another human being, the eulogist must possess these same traits, at least in embryonic form, too. And because the occasion is death, which strips the eulogists of their customary reserve, we are given glimpses into the recesses of their minds and hearts that under ordinary circumstances are concealed.

As a ritual, the delivering of eulogies dates back to the first time one person stood above the body of another and tried to say, in so many words, who that person was and what his or her life signified. As a form, it has at various times been a vehicle for the practice of rhetoric, the glorification of royalty (as in the French *eloges*), and the imparting of religious instruction.

In Dr. Samuel Johnson's eulogy for his wife—and he was by every account extremely fond of her—she is barely mentioned except to remind the mourners that paradise is not for shirkers and that her place in heaven is far more assured than their own.

Most of the selections in *The Book of Eulogies* are culled from the last two centuries. The elaborate prose of the great nineteenth-century stylists, such as Robert Ingersoll and Frederick Douglass, reminds us how stark the language has become. But each age has its own style and the simplicity of the late twentieth century makes up in directness what it has lost in metaphor. We are, in other words, no less moved.

The voices vary. A husband does not speak in the same tones as a president paying tribute to a field of fallen soldiers. A senator reminiscing over the career of a colleague has a different cadence from that of a cardinal mourning the passing of a pope. But whispered or roared, eulogies have a natural majesty to them, reflecting both the force of the event and the struggle of the eulogist to come to terms with it.

"The light has gone out of our lives," exclaimed Nehru when Gandhi was assassinated.

"When it came, that last breath," wrote author Richard Selzer of his mother, Gertrude, "it was as though a lamp in whose circle of light I had lived all my life had been extinguished. Now I was free to live anywhere. In the dark."

The eulogist is the first person to step forward, in a formal way, to hold a lantern above the loss.

"It is one of the mysteries of our nature," wrote Mark Twain after receiving word that his elder daughter, Susy, had died, "that a man, all unprepared, can receive a thunderstroke like that and live." But live he did, to write one of the most moving tributes to a daughter in modern literature. Susy Clemens is vividly portrayed, but the interior of Twain's mind is even more exposed.

In one of the most remarkable eulogies, John Conrad begins his eulogy for his son, John Jr., with questions: "How do you celebrate a tragic life and death? How do you find any redeeming value to the life of a retarded boy who suffered from severe and bizarre emotional problems? How do you celebrate a life of dead expectations?"

It is in the questions, judgments, and attempts to understand a completed life that a eulogy can speak to us all.

Life is not fair, even in death. It was distressing to discover how few women were accorded the honor of having eulogies given for them—and most by husbands who, like Theodore Roosevelt, regarded their wives as rare and delicate edelweiss. But even fewer women deliver eulogies. If one had no other record, one would not know that women have lived and died in such equal numbers.

It is interesting to note that, with few exceptions, the physical attributes of the deceased are rarely mentioned in a tribute. Whether he or she had radiant coloring or a splendid physique, or eyes that reminded one of lakes or oceans, is not terribly important. While not exactly a proof for the soul's immortality, there is nothing like reading a sizable number of eulogies to realize that the soul is real—and all that matters.

One of the reasons for compiling *The Book of Eulogies* was the conviction that learning how other souls had negotiated the trip between birth and death would be instructive to those of us striding toward the finish line. Reading eulogies filled with so many tales of courage, faith, and synchronicity was exhilarating, rather like having everybody else's life pass before my eyes.

Voltaire, whose pen never stopped moving, was thrown in and out of prison for attacking the injustices of eighteenth-century French society. Illinois governor John Peter Altgeld's decision to pardon three anarchists ruined his career. The blind orphan Annie Sullivan was tossed like refuse into a Massachusetts almshouse. Through the eyes of the eulogist, one gains a glimpse of how people confronted with pain, sorrow, and crushing circumstances nevertheless endured.

Winston Churchill attributed Lawrence of Arabia's ability to surmount many disappointments to his being "a man, solitary, austere, to whom existence is no more than a duty, yet a duty to be faithfully discharged."

"Time and again," wrote Hannah Arendt of the poet W. H. Auden, "when to all appearances he could not cope any more . . . he would begin to kind of intone an utterly idiosyncratic, absurdly eccentric version of 'count your blessings.' . . . It took me years to realize that in his case appearance was not deceptive."

John Steinbeck's analysis of his friend Ed Ricketts's gift for friendship centered upon Ricketts learning to like himself. "Once Ed was able to like himself he was released from the secret prison of self-contempt. Then he did not have to prove superiority any more by any of the ordinary methods, including giving. He could receive. . . ."

After I had stared at them long enough, individual lives began to bump into one another. That Beethoven still composed music when Ralph Waldo Emerson was at Harvard brought the hem of time up short. That Helen Keller's funeral received so little press coverage because it was held on the same day Robert Kennedy was assassinated joined two disparate lives at the seams. Eventually, I came to see them not as discrete lives but as streams of life, braiding their currents together, affecting and carrying one another forward. Working on the book was giving me a context that my own life could not provide.

Not all eulogies are complimentary. H. L. Mencken's final swat at William Jennings Bryan has so much acid in it that the paper can barely hold the print. The sketch of Queen Anne by Sarah, Duchess of Marlboro, is grounds for beheading. These are not loving eulogies but skillful demolitions. This raises the question of veracity. What reason do we have for believing what any of the eulogists are saying, other than the natural persuasiveness of the words themselves? Short of knowing the deceased personally, we have none. But if the eulogist is wrong about the deceased, he or she can be quite right about a larger truth that the death of the person being eulogized brings to light.

What was also brought to light, as my search lengthened, were numerous essays, letters, and poems on the subject of death, sorrow, and loss that seemed too good to leave out. I revised my original plan to make room for them. They seem an important counterweight and companion to the eulogies themselves.

I had assumed at the outset that the most inspiring eulogies would be attached to the most inspiring lives. This was only partially proved out. Some of the most soaring spirits were not eulogized at all, while an unremarkable or tragic life often gave the eulogist an occasion to say something profound. In *The Book of Eulogies* it is the excellence of the eulogy, not the life, that is the connecting thread.

Some of the people are famous. Others are obscure. But all of them have one thing in common.

When they died, someone wrote about them uncommonly well.

PHYLLIS THEROUX
Ashland, Virginia, 1997

PART I

PUBLIC TREASURES

⟨ɷɯɯɷ⟩

CHAPTER ONE

THE CREATORS

If there is any one reason to single out artists as being more necessary to our lives than any others, it is because they provide us with light that cannot be extinguished. They go into dark rooms and poke at their souls until the contours of our own are familiar to us. They stare at flowers until their secrets unfold, wrestle with angels that the rest of us are terrified to disturb.

They are a diverse lot, genteel ladies tapping out nightmares on manual typewriters, patresfamilias filling up cathedrals with sound. And to lay the completed lives of a number of artists end to end is to realize how little time so many of them had to work. Henry David Thoreau died at forty-five, Robert Louis Stevenson at forty-four. Flannery O'Connor had only ten years to produce a lifetime of work. But the brevity of the artist's life bears little relationship to the fruitfulness of it. Neither does creativity necessarily diminish at the end.

With age some of the greatest artists increased in depth and strength, oftentimes under crushing adversity. Beethoven created his most beautiful music after he went completely deaf. Milton was blind when he dictated *Paradise Lost* to his daughter. Yeats battled mental illness and the specter of poverty, the artist's most frequent companion beside the muse. In a sarcastic letter to Lord Chesterfield, Samuel Johnson defined a "patron" as "one who looks with unconcern on a man struggling for life in the water and, when he has reached the ground, encumbers him with help."

We live in a culture that assumes an artist must have a massive ego to maintain creative momentum. But Bach was unconcerned with posterity, Emily Dickinson scribbled poetry behind a curtain, and Renoir, who did not underestimate his worth, was nonetheless always a learner. His words on the last day of his life, which was spent painting, were "I think I am beginning to understand something about it."

One of the most touching tributes is by Hannah Arendt for W. H. Auden. "What made him a poet," she writes, "was his extraordinary facility with, and love for, words, but what made him a great poet was the unprotesting willingness with which he yielded to the 'curse.' " But she wonders whether he realized what was going to be involved.

"It seems . . . very unlikely that young Auden, when he decided that he was going to be a great poet, knew the price he would have to pay. I think it entirely possible that in the end . . . he might have considered the price too high."

Speaking of Auden, Arendt sums up the debt we owe to all great artists: "We . . . his audience, readers and listeners, can only be grateful that he paid his price up to the last penny."

"The music of Bach disturbs human complacency because one can't readily understand finiteness in its presence."

JOHANN SEBASTIAN BACH
(1685–1750)

by

WILLIAM F. BUCKLEY
(1925–)

Bach brought the polyphonic baroque tradition in music to its highest peak of excellence, but he had no idea of his own greatness, except as a performer, and most of his works were not published before he died. A deeply religious man, Bach served as music director for the Church of St. Thomas in Leipzig, Germany, from 1723 until his death.

William F. Buckley, the noted conservative author, critic, television personality, and newspaper columnist, is an amateur performer of Bach's piano works. This tribute is excerpted from one of his columns.

. . . Bach has the impact of a testimonial to God's providence not because he wrote the most searingly beautiful church music ever heard (about "The Passion According to St. Matthew" one can say only that it does credit to the Gospel according to St. Matthew), but because he wrote the most beautiful music ever written. If one were to throw away the three hundred cantatas, the hundred-odd chorale preludes, the three oratorios, the passions, and the Mass (which would be the equivalent of destroying half of Shakespeare), still the other half would sustain Bach as a creature whose afflatus is inexplicable, for some of us, in the absence of a belief in God.

If it is true, as the poet says, that one can't look out upon a sunset without feeling divinity, then it is also true that one can't close the door on the sunset and, entering the darkened chapel, listen to the organist play one of Bach's toccatas and fugues without sensing divinity.

It is not necessary to believe in God in order to revel in Bach. It is not necessary, for that matter, to love one's country in order to fight for it, nor even to love one's family in order to protect it. And there is no need to make heavy weather over the point, though there is a need for such human modesty as Einstein expressed when he said that the universe was not explicable except by the acknowledgment of an unknown mover. The music of Bach disturbs human complacency because one can't readily understand finiteness in its presence.

Carl Sagan, who sometimes sounds like the village atheist, reports that the biologist Lewis Thomas of the Sloan-Kettering Institute answered, when asked what message he thought we should send to other civilizations in space in that rocket we fired up there a few years ago with earthly jewels packed in its cone, "I would send the complete works of Johann Sebastian Bach." Then he paused and said, "But that would be boasting." There are those who believe it is not merely to boast, but to be vainglorious to suggest that the movements of Bach's pen could have been animated by less than divine impulse.

There are sobering lessons to contemplate. One of them is that when he lived, he was almost entirely unnoticed. True, he was renowned as a virtuoso at the harpsichord and the organ. When he died, one of his biographers notes, there were something on the order of ninety obituaries written, only three of which, however, mentioned him as a composer. This is tantamount to remembering Shakespeare as a great actor.

The thought reminds us of what it is that we almost let slip through our fingers—and reminds us, even more darkly, of what it is that we have irreversibly let slip through our fingers. We are reluctant to believe that anyone else ever existed of such artistic eminence as JSB; but we can never know, can we? Nor can we ever understand how it was that so musically minded a culture as that of what we now know as East Germany could have greeted so indifferently a genius so overpowering.

And it reminds us, too, that there are among us men and women who will not drink from this most precious vessel of our cultural patrimony. To some he does not speak. If we understand that, then we understand, surely, what the problems are in Geneva, where grown men are actually talking to each other as if it were a challenge to formulate arrangements by which the world should desist from the temptation to destroy itself. If a human being exists who is unmoved by the B minor Mass, it should not surprise that human beings exist who are unmoved by democracy, or freedom, or peace. They have eyes but they do not see, ears but they do not hear. Well, Bach tended to end his manuscripts with the initials S.D.G.—*Soli Deo Gloria*, to

God alone the glory. But God shares that glory, and did so three hundred years ago when Johann Sebastian was born.

ᘓᘏᘏᘙ

"As the behemoth storms through the seas, so he strained the boundaries of his art."

LUDWIG VAN BEETHOVEN
(1770–1827)

by

FRANZ GRILLPARZER
(1791–1872)

Beethoven, the towering musical genius who bridged the classical and romantic eras, enjoyed one luxury beyond his talent—it was recognized during his lifetime. But at the age of thirty-one his hearing began to deteriorate, and for the last ten years of his life he was entirely deaf. During that time he composed the Hammerklavier sonata, the monumental Ninth Symphony, and five string quartets considered by some authorities to be the greatest music ever created. He never married, although he had a number of heartbreaking romances with unattainable women, and his personal life was a lonely one.

Franz Grillparzer was the leading Austrian playwright of his time. He was asked to compose a eulogy, which was then delivered by the actor and orator Heinrich Anschutz on March 29, 1827.

As we stand here at the grave of the deceased, we are, as it were, the representatives of a whole nation, of the German people in its entirety, grieving at the fall of the one, highly celebrated half of the remaining vanished glory of indigenous art, of the nation's flourishing spirit. To be sure, the hero of German poesy, Goethe, still lives—and may he live long!—but the last master of sonorous song, of music's sweet voice, the heir to Handel's immortal fame and Bach's, the heir to Haydn and Mozart, has passed away, and we stand weeping by the torn strings of faded harmony.

Of faded harmony! Let me call him so! For here was an artist, and what he was, he was only through art. The thorns of life had wounded him deeply; as a shipwrecked man clings to the shore, so he fled into your arms, O Art, equally glorious sister of the good and the true, comforter of suffering, begotten on high. He held fast to you, and even when the gate was closed through which you had gained entrance to him and spoke to him; when his deaf ear made him blind to your features, still he carried your image in his heart, and when he died, it still lay upon his breast.

He was an artist, and who has arisen beside him? As the behemoth storms through the seas, so he strained the boundaries of his art. From the cooing of the dove to the rolling of thunder, from the most intricately woven of idiosyncratic artistic devices to the terrifying point where achieved form becomes the lawless clashing forces of nature, he had reckoned everything, grasped everything. Those who come after him will not be able to continue, they will have to begin, for the predecessor halted only where art itself halts. . . .

He was an artist, but also a human being. A human being in the word's fullest meaning. Because he shut himself off from the world, they called him hostile, and because he avoided emotion, unfeeling. Oh, he who knows himself to be hard does not flee! It is precisely the excess of emotion that shuns emotion. When he fled the world, it was because in the depths of his loving heart he found no weapon to resist it; when he withdrew from people, it occurred after he had given them his all and received nothing in return. He remained lonely because he found no other. But until his death he retained a humane heart toward all people, a fatherly one to his family, devoted his talent and life to the whole world!

So he was, so he died, so he shall live for all time.

You, however, who have followed our lead thus far, govern your pain! You have not lost him, you have gained him. Not until the gates of our life close behind us do the gates to the temple of immortality spring open. There he stands among the great of all times, untouchable, forever. Therefore depart from his place of rest, mourning but composed, and whenever in life the power of his creations overwhelms you like a gathering storm, whenever your tears flow in the midst of a still unborn generation, remember this hour and think: we were there when they buried him, and when he died, we wept.

"I saw her first just as I rose out of an illness from which I had never thought to recover. I remember the trembling little frame, the little hand, the great honest eyes. An impetuous honesty seemed to me to characterize the woman."

CHARLOTTE BRONTË
(1816–1855)

by

WILLIAM MAKEPEACE THACKERAY
(1811–1863)

Charlotte Brontë, the English novelist most well known for Jane Eyre, *was the daughter of an impoverished, widowed Anglican clergyman and the sister of novelists Emily and Anne Brontë. Self-publishing their first work under the names "Currer, Ellis and Acton Bell," they became the faceless toast of literary London. In 1854, Charlotte married her father's curate, Arthur Bell Nichols, but died of pregnancy toxemia only a year after her marriage.*

Novelist William Makepeace Thackeray is best known today for his novel Vanity Fair *and its wily, albeit winning, heroine, Becky Sharp, who must make her unsupported way in society. It was a task that fell to Charlotte Brontë as well.*

Of the multitude that has read her books, who has not known and deplored the tragedy of her family, her own most sad and untimely fate? Which of her readers has not become her friend? Who that has known her books has not admired the artist's noble English, the burning love of truth, the bravery, the simplicity, the indignation at wrong, the eager sympathy, the pious love and reverence, the passionate honor, so to speak of the woman? What a story is that of that family of poets in their solitude yonder on the gloomy northern moors! At nine o'clock at night, Mrs. Gaskell tells us, after evening prayers, when their guardian and relative had gone to bed, the three poetesses—the three maidens Charlotte and Emily and Anne—Charlotte being the "motherly friend and guardian to the other two"—"began, like restless wild animals, to pace up and down their parlors," making out "their wonderful stories, talking over plans and projects, and thoughts of what was to be their future life."

One evening at the close of 1854, as Charlotte Nichols sat with her husband by the fire, listening to the howling of the wind about the house, she suddenly said to her husband, "If you had not been with me, I must have been writing now." She then ran upstairs and brought down and read aloud the beginning of a new tale. When she had finished, her husband remarked, "The critics will accuse you of repetition." She replied, "Oh! I shall alter that. I always begin two or three times before I can please myself." But it was not to be. The trembling little hand was to write no more. The heart, newly awakened to love and happiness, and throbbing with maternal hope, was soon to cease to beat; that intrepid outspeaker and champion of truth, that eager, impetuous redresser of wrong, was to be called out of the world's fight and struggle, to lay down the shining arms. . . .

I saw her first just as I rose out of an illness from which I had never thought to recover. I remember the trembling little frame, the little hand, the great honest eyes. An impetuous honesty seemed to me to characterize the woman. Twice I recollect she took me to task for what she held to be errors in doctrine. Once about Fielding we had a disputation. She spoke her mind out. She jumped too rapidly to conclusions. . . . She formed conclusions that might be wrong and built up whole theories of character upon them. New to the London world, she entered it with an independent, indomitable spirit of her own; and judged of contemporaries, and especially spied out arrogance or affectation, with extraordinary keenness of vision. She was angry with her favorites if their conduct or conversation fell below her idea.

Often she seemed to be judging the London folk prematurely: but perhaps the city is rather angry at being judged. I fancied an austere little Joan of Arc marching in upon us and rebuking our easy lives, our easy morals. She gave me the impression of being a very pure and lofty and high-minded person. A great and holy reverence of right and truth seemed to be with her always. Such, in our brief interview, she appeared to me. As one thinks of that life so noble, so lonely—of that passion for truth—of those nights and nights of eager study, swarming fancies, invention, depression, elation, prayer; as one reads the necessarily incomplete, though most touching and admirable, history of the heart that throbbed in this one little frame—of this one amongst the myriads of souls that have lived and died on this great earth—this great earth?—this little speck in the infinite universe of God—and with what wonder do we think of today, with what awe await tomorrow, when that which is now but darkly seen shall be clear! . . .

How well I remember the delight and wonder and pleasure with which I read *Jane Eyre*, sent to me by an author whose name and sex were then alike to me; the strange fascinations of the book; and how with my own work pressing upon me, I could not, having taken the volumes up, lay them down until they were read through! Hundreds of those who, like myself, recognized and admired that masterwork of a great genius will look with a mournful interest and regard and curiosity upon this, the last fragmentary sketch from the noble hand which wrote *Jane Eyre*.

⟡

"To her, life was rich, and all aglow with God and immortality."

EMILY DICKINSON
(1830–1886)

by

SUSAN GILBERT DICKINSON
(D. 1913)

Emily Dickinson, one of the great American poets, was virtually unknown during her lifetime beyond her circle of family and friends in Amherst, Massachusetts. Around the age of thirty, she began to live the life of a recluse, eventually not leaving the house or seeing friends or family visitors. At her death, over a thousand poems were found in her bureau drawers. Susan Dickinson was her sister-in-law. She wrote this editorial for the Springfield Republican *newspaper.*

The death of Miss Emily Dickinson, daughter of the late Edward Dickinson, at Amherst on Saturday, makes another sad inroad on the small circle so long occupying the old family mansion. . . . Very few in the village, except among the older inhabitants, knew Miss Emily personally, although the facts of her seclusion and her intellectual brilliancy were familiar Amherst traditions. . . . As she passed on in life, her sensitive nature shrank from much personal contact with the world, and more and more turned to her own large wealth of individual resources for companionship. . . . Not disappointed with the world, not an invalid until within the past two years, not from any lack of sympathy, not because she was insufficient for any mental work or social career—her endowments being so exceptional—but the "mesh of her soul" . . . was too rare, and the sacred quiet of her own home proved the fit atmosphere for her worth and work. . . .

To her, life was rich, and all aglow with God and immortality. With no creed, no formulated faith, hardly knowing the names of dogmas, she walked this life with the gentleness and reverence of old saints, with the firm step of martyrs who sing while they suffer.

⟲⟳

"One of the greatest lines in our literature is his. Speaking of an outcast—'Not until the sun excludes the earth will I exclude you.'"

WALT WHITMAN
(1819–1892)

by

ROBERT GREEN INGERSOLL
(1833–1899)

On the Fourth of July, 1855, an anonymous book of poems arrived in the mail for Ralph Waldo Emerson. Emerson found the work astounding and, upon learning who the poet was, quickly wrote to him saying, "I rubbed my eyes a little to see if this sunbeam were no illusion; but the solid sense of the book is a sober certainty." A grateful Walt Whitman immediately had Emerson's note duplicated and used to advertise his Leaves of Grass.

Illinois politician Robert Ingersoll delivered the following eulogy at Whitman's funeral in Camden, New Jersey. One of the most eloquent orators in the nineteenth century, Ingersoll was called "the great agnostic" because he expressed doubt in an afterlife, and while he was greatly admired by the more liberal-minded, he was much maligned by orthodox churchmen, who considered him a poisoner of impressionable minds. When he died, one newspaper wrote: "Robert Ingersoll died yesterday. Perhaps he knows better now."

Again we in the mystery of life are brought face-to-face with the mystery of death. A great man, a great American, is dead before us, and we have met to pay a tribute to his greatness and to his worth. His fame is secure. He laid the foundation of it deep in the human heart. He was, above all that I have known, the poet of humanity, of sympathy. Great he was—so great that he rose above the greatest that he met without arrogance; and so great that he stooped to the lowest without conscious condescension. He never claimed to be lower or greater than any other of the sons of man. He came into our generation a free, untrammeled spirit, with sympathy for all. His arm was beneath the form of the sick; he sympathized with the imprisoned and the despised; and even on the brow of crime he was great enough to place the kiss of human sympathy. One of the greatest lines in our literature is his. Speaking of an outcast—"Not until the sun excludes the earth will I exclude you." A charity as wide as the sky! And whenever there was human suffering, human misfortune, the sympathy of Whitman bent above it as the firmament bends above this earth. He was the poet of that divine democracy that gives equal rights to all the sons and daughters of men. He uttered the great American voice, uttered a song worthy of the great Republic.

He was the poet of life. He loved the clouds. He enjoyed the breath of morning, the twilight, the wind, the winding streams. He loved to look at the sea when the winds and waves burst into the whitecaps of joy. He loved the fields, the hills. He was acquainted with trees, with birds, with all the beautiful objects on the earth; and he understood their meaning and used them that he might exhibit his heart to his fellowmen. He was also the poet of love. He was not ashamed of the divine passion that has built every home in the world; that divine passion that has painted every picture and given us every real work of art—that divine passion that has made the world worth living in and gives value to human life. He was the poet of the human race everywhere. His sympathy went out over the seas to all the nations of the earth. And above genius, above all the snowcapped peaks of intelligence, above his art, rises the man—greater than all.

He was true absolutely to himself. He was frank, candid, pure, serene, and noble. And for years he was maligned and slandered, simply because he had the candor of nature. He will be understood yet, and that for which he was condemned will add to the glory and the greatness of his name. He wrote a liturgy for humanity—the greatest gospel that can be preached.

He was not afraid to live, not afraid to speak his thoughts. Neither was he afraid to die. Cheerful every moment, the laughing nymphs of day remained that they might clasp the hand of the veiled and silent sisters of the night when they should come. And when they did come, Walt Whitman stretched his hand to both. And so, hand in hand, between smiles and tears, he reached his journey's end.

Today we give back to Mother Nature, to her clasp and kiss, one of the bravest, sweetest souls that ever lived in human clay. Since he has lived, death is less fearful than it was before, and thousands and millions will walk down into the dark valley of the shadow, holding Walt Whitman by the hand, long after we are dead.

And so I lay this poor wreath upon this great man's tomb. I loved him living and I love him still.

⚬⚬⚬

"Like a prince he would enter a room. . . ."

RUPERT BROOKE
(1887–1915)

by

SIR IAN HAMILTON
(1853–1947)

In 1915, the poet Rupert Brooke volunteered to join the British army. Less than a year later, he died of an infection off the Isle of Skyros in the Aegean. In his most famous poem, "The Soldier," he prophesied the circumstances of his death abroad. Brooke was not only brilliant but he looked the way people thought a poet ought to look, with patrician features, golden, loose-flowing locks, and bright blue eyes. When he died, all of England mourned as if everything that was best and brightest about itself had sunk into the sea.

At the unveiling of a memorial to Brooke at Rugby School, Sir Ian Hamilton, who had been the British military leader of the Mediterranean forces in World War I, remarked upon the effect Brooke had upon others.

I have seen famous men and brilliant figures in my day, but never one so thrilling, so vital, as that of our hero. Like a prince he would enter a room, like a prince quite unconscious of his own royalty, and by that mere act put a spell upon everyone around him. In the twinkling of an eye gloom was changed into light; dullness sent forth a certain sparkle in his presence. . . . Here was someone who was distinguished by a nameless gift of attraction, head and shoulders above the crowd; and it is the memory of this personal magnetism more even than the work his destiny permitted him to fulfill that adds strength to the roots of his ever-growing fame.

⟳

"He now dominated Nature, which all his life he had served as a worshiper. In return, she had finally taught him to see beyond surface appearances; and, like herself, to create a world out of almost nothing."

PIERRE-AUGUSTE RENOIR
(1841–1919)

by

JEAN RENOIR
(1894–1979)

The French painter and sculptor Pierre-Auguste Renoir, one of the leading impressionists, learned how to make light explode upon the canvas. At the end of his life he was cruelly afflicted with arthritis and unable to walk. But when a doctor helped Renoir regain the use of his legs, Renoir pronounced the success too great a drain upon his waning energies. "I give up," he said. "It takes all my willpower and I would have none left for painting." He sat down in his wheelchair and never walked again.

In this excerpt from My Father, Renoir, *his son, Jean, writes of his father's last days, when, despite excruciating pain, he painted one of his greatest works,* The Women Bathers, *which his son called "the tremendous cry of love he uttered at the end of his life."*

Jean Renoir became a filmmaker, director of Grand Illusion, La Bête Humaine, Rules of the Game, *and many other films.*

The more intolerable his suffering became, the more Renoir painted. Some friends in Nice had found a young model for him, Andrée, whom I was to marry after his death. She was sixteen years old, red-haired, plump, and her skin "took the light" better than any model that Renoir had ever had in his life. She sang, slightly off-key, the popular songs of the day; told stories about her girlfriends; was gay; and cast over my father the revivifying spell of her joyous youth. Along with the roses, which grew almost wild at Les Collettes, and the great olive trees with their silvery reflections, Andrée was one of the vital elements which helped Renoir to interpret on his canvas the tremendous cry of love he uttered at the end of his life. . . .

While he was being put into his wheelchair, the model went outside and took her place on flower-spangled grass. The foliage of the olive trees sifted the rays of light and made an arabesque on her red blouse. In a voice still weak from his suffering during the night, Renoir had the adjustable windows opened or closed, as he wished; and material hung up, to provide him with a protection against the intoxication of the Mediterranean morning. While one of us prepared his palette, he could not help groaning once or twice. Adjusting his stricken body to the hard seat of the wheelchair was painful. But he wanted this "not too soft" seat, which helped him to keep upright and allowed him a certain amount of movement. . . . My father's suffering devastated all of us. The nurse, Grand Louise, the model—often it was Madeleine Bruno, a young girl from the village—and I, all felt a lump in our throats. Whenever we would try to talk in a cheerful voice, it sounded false.

One of us would put the protecting piece of linen in Renoir's hand, pass him the brush he had indicated with a wink of the eye. "That one, there. . . . No, the other one."

The flies circled in a shaft of sunlight. . . . "Oh, these flies!" he would exclaim in a rage as he brushed one off the end of his nose. "They smell a corpse." We made no answer. After the fly had ceased to bother him, he sank back into his somnolence, hypnotized by a dancing butterfly or by the distant sound of a cicada. The landscape was a microcosm of all the riches in the world. His eyes, nose, and ears were assailed by countless contradictory sensations. "It's intoxicating," he kept repeating. He stretched out his arm and dipped his brush into the turpentine. But the movement was painful. He waited a few seconds, as if asking himself, "Why not give up? Isn't it too hard?" Then a glance at the subject restored his courage. He traced on the canvas a mark, in madder red, that only he understood. "Jean, open the yellow curtain a little more." Another touch of madder. Then, in a stronger voice, "It's divine!" We watched him. He smiled and winked, as he called us to witness this conspiracy which had just been arranged between the grass, the olive trees, the model, and himself. After a minute or two he would start humming. And a day of happiness would begin for Renoir, a day as wonderful as the one which preceded it, and the one which was to follow. . . . It was under these conditions that he painted his *Women Bathers*, now in the Louvre. He considered it the culmination of his life's work. . . .

Renoir had succeeded in fulfilling the dream of his whole life: "to create riches with modest means." From his palette, simplified to the last degree, and from the minute "droppings" of color lost on its surface, issued a splendor of dazzling golds and purples, the glow of flesh filled with young and healthy blood, the magic of all-conquering light, and towering above all these material elements, the serenity of a man approaching supreme knowledge. He now dominated Nature, which all his life he had served as a worshiper. In return, she had finally taught him to see beyond surface appearances; and, like herself, to create a world out of almost nothing. With a little water, a few minerals, and invisible radiations, Nature creates an oak tree, a forest. From a passionate embrace beings are born. Birds multiply, fish force their way upstream, the rays of the sun illumine and quicken all this stirring mass. "And it costs nothing!" If it were not for man, "this destructive animal," the equilibrium of a world in ceaseless movement would be assured.

This profusion of riches which poured forth from Renoir's austere palette is overwhelming in the last picture he painted, on the morning of his death. An infection which had developed in his lungs kept him to his room. He asked for his paintbox and brushes, and he painted the anemones which Nenette, our kindhearted maid, had gone out and gathered for him. For several hours he identified himself with these flowers and forgot his pain. Then he motioned for someone to take his brush and said, "I think I am beginning to understand something about it." . . . He died in the night.

CRULD

**"Earth, receive an honoured guest;
William Yeats is laid to rest. . . ."**

WILLIAM BUTLER YEATS
(1865–1939)

by

WYSTAN HUGH AUDEN
(1907–1973)

William Bulter Yeats, who won the Nobel Prize in 1923, is considered the greatest lyric poet Ireland has ever produced. This tribute to him by a fellow poet is considered one of Auden's most masterful works, not only because of what he wrote, but because of the way in which he employed the numerous poetic forms Yeats used so well, within the body of the tribute.

IN MEMORY OF W. B. YEATS
(D. JAN. 1939)

1

*He disappeared in the dead of winter:
The brooks were frozen, the airports almost deserted,
And snow disfigured the public statues;
The mercury sank in the mouth of the dying day.
O all the instruments agree
The day of his death was a dark cold day.*

*Far from his illness
The wolves ran on through the evergreen forests,
The peasant river was untempted by the fashionable quays;*

By mourning tongues
The death of the poet was kept from his poems.

But for him it was his last afternoon as himself;
An afternoon of nurses and rumours;
The provinces of his body revolted,
The squares of his mind were empty,
Silence invaded the suburbs,
The current of his feeling failed: he became his admirers.

Now he is scattered among a hundred cities
And wholly given over to unfamiliar affections;
To find his happiness in another kind of wood
And be punished under a foreign code of conscience.
The words of a dead man
Are modified in the guts of the living.

But in the importance and noise of tomorrow
When the brokers are roaring like beasts on the floor of the Bourse,
And the poor have the sufferings to which they are fairly accustomed,
And each in the cell of himself is almost convinced of his freedom;
A few thousand will think of this day
As one thinks of a day when one did something slightly unusual.
O all the instruments agree
The day of his death was a dark cold day.

2

You were silly like us: your gift survived it all;
The parish of rich women, physical decay,
Yourself; mad Ireland hurt you into poetry.
Now Ireland has her madness and her weather still,
For poetry makes nothing happen: it survives
In the valley of its saying where executives
Would never want to tamper; it flows south
From ranches of isolation and the busy griefs,
Raw towns that we believe and die in; it survives,
A way of happening, a mouth.

3

Earth, receive an honoured guest;
William Yeats is laid to rest:
Let the Irish vessel lie
Emptied of its poetry.

Time that is intolerant
Of the brave and innocent,
And indifferent in a week
To a beautiful physique,

Worships language and forgives
Everyone by whom it lives;
Pardons cowardice, conceit,
Lays its honours at their feet.

Time that with this strange excuse
Pardoned Kipling and his views,
And will pardon Paul Claudel,
Pardons him for writing well.

In the nightmare of the dark
All the dogs of Europe bark,
And the living nations wait,
Each sequestered in its hate;

Intellectual disgrace
Stares from every human face,
And the seas of pity lie
Locked and frozen in each eye.

Follow, poet, follow right
To the bottom of the night,
With your unconstraining voice
Still persuade us to rejoice;

With the farming of a verse
Make a vineyard of the curse,
Sing of human unsuccess
In a rapture of distress;

In the deserts of the heart
Let the healing fountain start,
In the prison of his days
Teach the free man how to praise.

⚭

"One would think . . . that she could not look so steadily, so drily, and so long at so much false respect without herself dying of despair."

FLANNERY O'CONNOR
(1925–1964)

by

THOMAS MERTON
(1915–1968)

On the brink of her writing career, at the age of thirty, the Catholic writer Flannery O'Connor was diagnosed with lupus, a degenerative disease, which forced her return to her mother's farm near Milledgeville, Georgia. As Sally Fitzgerald, O'Connor's friend and editor, wrote, "Her return was for good, in more ways than one." O'Connor's disease got worse, but during this last decade of her life, she produced most of her best work.

Thomas Merton, a convert to Catholicism, became a Trappist monk in Gethsemane, Kentucky. It was said that the door shutting behind him was a noise heard round the world. His autobiography, The Seven Storey Mountain, *triggered a wave of applications to monasteries in the 1950s. His essays, poetry, and books of spiritual reflection continue to be widely read.*

Now Flannery is dead and I will write her name with honor, with love for the great slashing innocence of that dry-eyed irony that could keep looking the South in the face without bleeding or even sobbing. Her South was deeper than mine, crazier than Kentucky, but wild with no other madness than the crafty paranoia that is all over the place, including the North! Only madder, craftier, hung up in wilder and more absurd legends, more inventive of more outrageous lies! And solemn! Taking seriously the need to be respectable when one is an obsolescent and very agile fury.

The key word to Flannery's stories probably is *respect*. She never gave up examining its ambiguities and its decay. In this bitter dialectic of half-truths that have become endemic to our system, she probed our very life—its conflicts, its falsities, its obsessions, its vanities. Have we become an enormous complex organization of spurious reverences? Respect is continually advertised, and we are still convinced that we respect "everything good"—when we know too well that we have lost the most elementary respect even for ourselves. Flannery saw this and saw, better than others, what it implied.

She wrote in and out of the anatomy of a word that became genteel, then self-conscious, then obsessive, finally dying of contempt, but kept calling itself *respect*. Contempt for the child, for the stranger, for the woman, for the Negro, for the animal, for the white man, for the farmer, for the country, for the preacher, for the city, for the world, for reality itself. Contempt, contempt, so that in the end the gestures of respect they kept making to themselves and to each other and to God became desperately obscene.

But respect had to be maintained. Flannery maintained it ironically and relentlessly with a kind of innocent passion long after it had died of contempt—as if she were the only one left who took this thing seriously. One would think (if one put a Catholic chip on his shoulder and decided to make a problem of her) that she could not look so steadily, so drily, and so long at so much false respect without herself dying of despair. She never made any funny faces. She never said, "Here is a terrible thing." She just looked and said what they said and how they said it. It was not she that invented their despair, and perhaps her only way out of despair herself was to respect the way they announced the gospel of contempt. She patiently recorded all they had got themselves into. Their world was a big, fantastic, crawling, exploding junk pile of despair. I will write her name with honor for seeing it so clearly and looking straight at it without remorse. Perhaps her way of irony was the only possible catharsis for a madness so cruel and endemic. Perhaps a dry honesty like hers can save the South more simply than the North can ever be saved.

Flannery's people were two kinds of very advanced primitives: the city kind, exhausted, disillusioned, tired of imagining, perhaps still given to a grim willfulness in the service of doubt, still driving on in fury and ill will, or scientifically expert in nastiness; and the rural kind: furious, slow, cunning, inexhaustible, living sweetly on the verge of the unbelievable, more inclined to prefer the abyss to solid ground. . . .

The way Flannery made a story: she would put together all these elements of unreason and let them fly slowly and inexorably at one another. Then sometimes the urban madness, less powerful, would fall weakly prey to the rural madness and be inexorably devoured by a superior and more primitive absurdity. Or the rural madness would fail and fall short of the required malice and urban deceit would compass its destruction, with all possible contempt, cursing, superior violence, and fully implemented disbelief. For it would usually be wholesome faith that left the rural primitive unarmed. So you would watch, fascinated, almost in despair, knowing that in the end the very worst thing, the least reasonable, the least desirable, was what would have to happen. Not because Flannery wanted it so, but because it turned out to *be* so in a realm where the advertised satisfaction is compounded of so many lies and of so much contempt for the customer. . . .

. . . She respected all her people by searching for some sense in them, searching for truth, searching to the end and then suspending judgment. To have condemned them on moral grounds would have been to connive with their own crafty arts and their own demonic imagination. It would have meant getting tangled up with them in the same machinery of unreality and of contempt. The only way to be saved was to stay out of it, not to think, not to speak, just to record the slow, sweet, ridiculous verbalizing of Southern furies, working their way through their charming lazy hell.

That is why when I read Flannery I don't think of Hemingway or Katherine Anne Porter or Sartre, but rather of someone like Sophocles. What more can be said of a writer? I write her name with honor, for all the truth and all the craft with which she shows man's fall and his dishonor.

◦⟨∞∞⟩◦

"Now, with the sad wisdom of remembrance, he seems to me to have been an expert in the infinite varieties of unrequited love

among which the infuriating substitution of admiration for love
surely must have loomed large."

WYSTAN HUGH AUDEN
(1907–1973)

by

HANNAH ARENDT
(1906–1975)

*Along with Christopher Isherwood and Sir Stephen Spender, Auden was a
leader in a left-wing literary group that lived in England during the thirties. In 1939, he moved to the United States, becoming a citizen in 1946. A
professor of poetry at Oxford from 1956 to 1961, he was awarded the
National Medal for Literature in 1967. In 1971 he returned for good to
England, where he lived until his death.*

*Political scientist, writer, and philosopher, Hannah Arendt is best
known for her writings on Jewish affairs and the rise of nineteenth-century
anti-Semitism and imperialism. She became an established intellectual
power with her 1951 book* The Origins of Totalitarianism. *In this excerpt
from her tender tribute to Auden, she explores what it was that accounted
for both his misery and his greatness.*

I met Auden in the autumn of 1958, but I had seen him before, in the
late forties at a publisher's party. Although we did not exchange a word
on that occasion, I still remembered him quite well—a nice-looking,
well-dressed, very English gentleman, friendly and relaxed. I would
not have recognized him more than ten years later, for now his face was
marked by those famous deep wrinkles as though life itself had
delineated a kind of face-scape to make manifest the "heart's invisible
furies." If you listened to him, nothing could be more deceptive than
this appearance. Time and again, when to all appearances he could not
cope any more, when his slum apartment was so cold that the water
no longer functioned and he had to use the toilet in the liquor store at
the corner, when his suit—no one could convince him that a man
needed at least two suits so that one could go to the cleaner or two pairs
of shoes so that one pair could be repaired, a subject of an endlessly
ongoing debate between us throughout the years—was covered with

spots or worn so thin that his trousers would suddenly split from top to bottom, in brief, whenever disaster hit before your very eyes, he would begin to kind of intone an utterly idiosyncratic, absurdly eccentric version of "count your blessings." Since he never talked nonsense or said something obviously silly, and since, moreover, I always remained aware that this was the voice of a very great poet, it took me years to realize that in his case appearance was not deceptive and that it was fatally wrong to ascribe what I saw and knew to the harmless eccentricity of a typically English gentleman.

I finally saw the misery, somehow realized vaguely his compelling need to hide it behind the "count your blessings" litany, and still found it difficult to understand fully what made him so miserable, so unable to do anything about the absurd circumstances that made everyday life so unbearable for him. It certainly could not be lack of recognition. He was reasonably famous and anyhow ambition in this sense could not have counted for much, since he was the least vain of all authors I ever met. . . . Not that he was humble; in his case it was self-confidence that protected him against flattery, and this self-confidence was prior to recognition and fame, prior also to achievement. ("I am going to be a great poet," he told his Oxford tutor, Nevill Coghill.) . . . In other words, he was blessed with that rare self-confidence that does not need admiration and the opinions of others and can even withstand self-criticism and self-examination without falling into the trap of self-doubt. This has nothing to do with arrogance but is easily mistaken for it. Auden was never arrogant except when provoked by some vulgarity, in which case he protected himself with the rather abrupt rudeness characteristic of English intellectual life.

Stephen Spender, who knew him so well, has stressed that "throughout the whole development of [Auden's] poetry . . . his theme had been love." . . . And he tells, at the end of the address he gave in memory of the dead friend at the Cathedral Church in Oxford how he had asked Auden about a reading he had given in America: "His face lit up with a smile that altered its lines, and he said, 'They loved me!' " They did not admire him, they *loved* him—here I think lies the key both to his extraordinary unhappiness and to the extraordinary greatness, intensity, of his poetry. Now, with the sad wisdom of remembrance, he seems to me to have been an expert in the infinite varieties of unrequited love among which the infuriating substitution of admiration for love surely must have loomed large. And beneath these emotions, there must have been from the beginning a certain animal *tristesse* which no reason and no faith could overcome:

> *The desires of the heart are as crooked as corkscrews,*
> > *Not to be born is the best for man;*
> *The second-best is a formal order,*
> > *The dance's pattern; dance while you can.*

When I knew him, he would not have mentioned the best any longer so firmly had he opted for the second-best, the "formal order," and the result was what Chester Kallman so aptly has named—"the most disheveled child of all disciplinarians." . . .

What made him a poet was his extraordinary facility with, and love for, words, but what made him a great poet was the unprotesting willingness with which he yielded to the "curse"—the curse of vulnerability to "human unsuccess" on all levels of existence; the crookedness of the desires, the infidelities of the heart, the injustices of the world. . . .

It seems, of course, very unlikely that young Auden, when he decided that he was going to be a great poet, knew the price he would have to pay. I think it entirely possible that in the end, when not the intensity of his feelings and not the gift to transform them into praise, but the sheer physical strength of the heart to bear them and live with them gradually faded away, he might have considered the price too high. We, at any event, his audience, readers and listeners, can only be grateful that he paid his price up to the last penny for the everlasting glory of the English language. And his friends may find some consolation in Stephen Spender's beautiful joke beyond the grave—that "his wise unconscious self chose a good day for dying"—for more than one reason. The wisdom to know "when to live and when to die" is not given to mortals; but Wystan, one would like to think, may have received it as the supreme reward that the cruel gods of poetry bestowed on the most obedient of their servants.

"His was a granite passion ... rooted in the conviction that writing was a vocation in the most humble sense of that word...."

JOHN HERSEY
(1914–1993)

by

BERNADINE CONNELLY
(1964–)

An American writer, John Hersey was the son of missionaries to China. His work, both fiction and nonfiction, centered on man's inhumanity to man. Notable among his many works is his first novel, A Bell for Adano, *which won the Pulitzer Prize, and* Hiroshima, *a nonfiction account of the effect of the bombing of that city.*

Bernadine Connelly is a short-story writer and novelist.

My name is Bernadine Connelly, and I was one of John's students during his last semester at Yale. John was a great and a passionate teacher. He did not jump on desks or chain-smoke himself into feverish monologues. He did not hide fifths of bourbon in his file drawers or carry on any of the eccentricities that one might envision when linking the words *passion, writing,* and *teaching.* Because those are the trappings of ego, not passion, and in John's teaching there was none of that. His was a granite passion, a constant passion, a passion rooted in the conviction that writing was a vocation in the most humble sense of that word, a calling, and that great writing can and should try to improve the world.

John did not write in the semesters he taught. In addition to teaching his classes, each week he met individually with every student to review the previous week's papers. Every student, every week. He critiqued your paper in pencil and in conference would file through his comments patiently, making sure you understood them, and then would neatly erase the marks he'd made, as if to say, I'm gone now, it's up to you, get back to work.

John taught his course by using models. We studied and wrote from these models the way art students draw from the Old Masters. We wrote personal essays based on the wondrous depiction of

Achilles' shield in Robert Fitzgerald's translation of *The Iliad*, and profiles of Yale professors based on Gorky's portrait of Tolstoy. But there is no question that the model we clung to was his. We wanted to know about Hiroshima, about May Day, about how he was going about writing *The Call*. A few students even took to speaking in that Hersey cadence, the soft but sure footfalls on every word, and that little twitch at the back of the neck when he was making an important point. But, in the tradition of truly great teaching he shook off the copycats and sent us all out to find our own voices, and our own calling.

He made sure we understood the difference between striving for fame and striving for excellence, a near impossible task considering that most of us were convinced that in any minute we would be receiving the first Pulitzer for college reporting or perhaps the first O. Henry awarded to a short story published in a campus quarterly. He rid us of our desire for fads and left us with the universals: that when language breaks down, violence enters, and that a writer speaks for those who have no voice.

⊙⥲⥲⥲⊙

"Who will take my father's place ... in this daily practice of the language of the tribe? Anyone who wishes. He said once the field of writing will never be crowded—not because people can't do important work, but because they don't think they can."

WILLIAM STAFFORD
(1914–1993)

by

KIM R. STAFFORD
(1949–)

Poet William Stafford was the consultant to the Poetry Division of the Library of Congress in 1970–1971. Stafford's son, Kim, is also a poet and director of the Northwest Writing Institute at Lewis and Clark College in Portland, Oregon.

MY FATHER'S PLACE

A few days after my father, poet William Stafford, died, I was sleeping alone at the house of my parents when something woke me at around 4 A.M. My mother, who was away, had told me of this effect, for she, too, had been wakened since his death at my father's customary writing time. As I opened my eyes, the moon was shining through the bedroom window. But that wasn't it. The house was still, the neighborhood quiet. The house wanted me to rise. It was the hour, a beckoning. There was a soft tug. Nothing mystical, just a habit to the place. The air was sweet, life was good, it was time.

I dressed and shuffled down the hall. In the kitchen, I remembered how he would make himself a cup of instant coffee and some toast. I followed the custom, putting the kettle on, slicing some bread my mother had made, letting the plink of the spoon stirring the coffee be the only sound, then the scrape of a butter knife. And then I was to go to the couch and lie down with paper. I pulled the green mohair blanket from the closet, turned on a lamp, and settled in the horizontal place where my father had greeted maybe ten thousand mornings with his pen and paper. I put my head on the pillow just where his head had worn through the silk lining.

What should I write? There was no sign, only a feeling of generosity in the room. A streetlight brightened the curtain beside me, but the rest of the room was dark. I let my gaze rove the walls—the fireplace, the dim rectangle of a painting, the hooded box of the television cabinet, a table with magazines. It was all ordinary, suburban. But there was this beckoning. In the dark of the house it felt as if my father's death had become an empty bowl that was filled from below, like the stone cavern of a spring that brimmed cold with water from a deep place. There was grief, and also this abundance. So many people had written to us saying, "Words cannot begin to express how we feel . . ." They can't? I honored the feeling, for I, too, am sometimes mute with grief. But words *can* begin to express how it is, especially if they can be relaxed, brimming in their own plain way.

I looked for a long time at the bouquet of sunflowers on the coffee table beside the couch. I remembered sunflowers are the state flower of Kansas. I remembered my father's poem about yellow cars. I remembered how, the night before, we had eaten the last of his third summer planting of green beans. For a time, I thought back to the last writing my father had done at this place, the morning of August 28. As often, he had begun with a line from an ordinary experience, a stray call from an insurance agent trying to track down what turned out to be a different William Stafford. The call had amused him, the words had stayed with him. And that morning, he had begun to write:

"Are you Mr. William Stafford?"

"Yes, but . . ."

As often, he started with the recent daily news from his own life, and came to deeper things:

> *Well it was yesterday.*
> *Sunlight used to follow my hand.*
> *And that's when the strange*
> *siren-like sound flooded*
> *over the horizon and rushed*
> *through the streets of our town . . .*

But I wasn't delving into his writing now, only his writing life. I was inhabiting the cell of his habit: earlier than anyone, more ordinary in this welcome, simply listening.

The house was so quiet, I was aware distinctly of my breathing, my heart, how sweet each breath came into me, and the total release of each exhalation. I felt as if my eyes, too, had been "tapered for braille." The edge of the coffee table held a soft gleam from the streetlight. The jostled stack of magazines had a kind of sacred logic, where he had touched them. Then I saw how each sunflower had dropped a little constellation of pollen on the table. The pollen seemed to burn, so intense in color and purpose. But the house—the house didn't want me to write anything profound. The soft tug that had wakened me, the tug I still felt, wanted me to be there with myself, awake, awake to everything ordinary, to sip my bitter instant coffee, and to gaze about and to remember. I remembered how my father had said once that such a time alone would allow anyone to go inward, in order to go outward. Paradoxically, he said, you had to go into yourself in order to find the patterns that were bigger than your own life.

I started to write ordinary things. And then I came to the sun-flowers, and the spirit of the house warned me this could be told wrong if I tried to make something of it. It's not about trying. It's not about writing poems. It's not about achievement, certainly not fame, importance. It's about being there exactly with the plain life of a time before first light, with breath, the streetlight on one side of the house and the moon on the other, about the worn silk, the blanket, and that little dusting of pollen from the sunflowers.

My head fit the dent in the pillow, the blanket warmed my body, my hand moved easily, carelessly with the pen. I heard the scratch on paper. If this was grieving, it was active in plain things. I found myself relishing the simplest words, mistrusting metaphor, amused by my own habits of verve with words, forgiving myself an occa-sional big thought:

> *. . . to pause at the gate to take*
> *off the one big shoe*
> *of his body and step forward light*
> *as wind . . .*

I could forgive myself because there was this abundance in time and place and habit. And then I had a page, I closed my notebook, and I rose for the day. There was much to do, but I had done the big thing already.

Who will take my father's place in the world of poetry? No one. Who will take his place in this daily practice of the language of the tribe? Anyone who wishes. He said once the field of writing will never be crowded—not because people can't do important work, but because they don't think they can. This way of writing beckons to anyone who wishes to rise and listen, to write without fear of either achievement or failure. There is no burden, only a beckoning. For when the house beckons, you will wake easily. There is a stove where you make something warm. There is a light that leaves much of the room dark. There is a place to be comfortable, a place you have worn with the friendly shape of your body. This is your own breath, the treasuries of your recollection, the blessings of your casual gaze.

What is this way of writing, of listening easily and telling simply? There is the wall, the table, and whatever stands this day for Kansas pollen in your own precious life.

⟨∞⟩

CHAPTER TWO

A NATION'S HEROES
AND MARTYRS

In Eric Sevareid's tribute to the three American astronauts who perished in 1967, he defines a hero as one who goes first. Few of us are
given that privilege or seek out that responsibility. "Going first"
means going alone.

In Jules Michelet's famous account of Jeanne d'Arc at the stake, he
marvels at her steadfastness once it was too late to escape the fire.
"That all her uncertainty should have ceased in the flames," he
writes, "gives us ample reason to believe that . . . she no longer
understood safety, salvation *(salut)* in the judaic sense, as till then she
had done. . . ."

On a biographical level, the men and women assembled here
have little in common with each other, but they were none of them
preoccupied with their own safety. This is not to imply that they
were reckless or inopportune, but unlike most human beings, for
whom safety is a prerequisite, even a goal, these men and women
had something else to accomplish that made the instinct for safety
counterproductive. In a profound sense, they viewed themselves as
disposable assets to be used, not hoarded.

There are strong ties between these eulogists and their subjects:
Michelet—the most passionate of French historians—was clearly in
love with Jeanne d'Arc as the purest symbol his country had ever
produced; Pearse and Rossa were fellow Irish revolutionaries;
Nehru was Gandhi's protégé; and Noa Ben-Artzi Philosof was
Rabin's grandchild. Between Churchill and Lawrence of Arabia are
similarities of temperament and talent. And the Reverend Henry

Ward Beecher, if not a moral peer of General Grant's, was similarly insecure and understood Grant's nature well enough to speak to it.

"He was," wrote Beecher of Grant, "of all men the least likely to attain eminence, and absolutely unfitted, apparently, for pre-eminence; yet God's providence selected him."

Grant rose to the occasion. So did they all.

"To retain mildness and benevolence amidst so many keen disputes, to run the range of experience without allowing it to impair that innate treasure, this is divine. Those who continue thus to the end are the real elect. And even though they have sometimes tripped upon the difficult path of the world, still amidst their lapses, their weaknesses and childishnesses, they will remain not the less God's children!"

JEANNE D'ARC
(1412?–1431)

by

JULES MICHELET
(1798–1874)

Nowhere has the story of France's most famous soldier saint, Jeanne d'Arc, who was burned at the stake, been more passionately told than by the nineteenth-century French historian Jules Michelet. In his greatest work, Histoire de France, *he recalls the essence of France's greatness as exhibited in the fifteenth-century peasant girl whose visions led her to defend the dauphin (Charles VII) against the English pretender (Henry VI) to the French throne. "A woman," writes Michelet, "had obscured this great question of right, and by a woman it was cleared up."*

After winning the crown for France, Joan was captured by some French sympathizers of the English, put on trial for heresy, and after recanting the voices that had told her to save the dauphin, reconfessed that her voices were true. She was then tried before a secular court, in Rouen, and sentenced to burn at the stake. In this final passage of his account, Michelet writes of her death and significance.

She was bound beneath the infamous inscription, and on her head was placed a miter, on which was written: "Heretic, relapsed, apostate, idolator." Then the executioner applied the fire. She saw it from above and shrieked. The monk who was exhorting her did not pay attention to the flames; and she, forgetting herself, became alarmed for him and made him go down. . . .

Meanwhile, the flames were ascending. At the moment they reached her the poor creature started and called out for holy water;

water, the natural exclamation of terror. But immediately collecting herself she uttered no names but those of God, her angels, and her saints. She testified her faith in them: "Yes, my voices were of God; my voices have not deceived me!" That all her uncertainty should have ceased in the flames gives us ample reason to believe that she accepted death as the promised deliverance, that she no longer understood safety, salvation (*salut*) in the judaic sense, as till then she had done, that she at last saw clearly, and that emerging from the shadows that enveloped her, she attained that measure of light and holiness which was yet wanting to her.

The grand expression of hers is attested by the compulsory and sworn witness of her death, the Dominican who ascended the pile with her, whom she sent down from that dangerous post, but who continued speaking with her from below, listened to her words, and held up the cross to her sight.

We have yet another witness of this holy death, a witness of very grave character, who was himself doubtless a saint. This man, whose name history ought to preserve, was the Augustine monk already mentioned, brother Isambart de la Pierre. He was near perishing in the course of the prosecution for having given counsel to the Maid, and yet though so conspicuously obnoxious to the English, he voluntarily ascended the cart with her, procured her the parish cross, and stood by her in the midst of the furious crowd, both on the platform and at the stake.

Twenty years after the event the two venerable men, humble monks, devoted to poverty and with nothing to gain or to fear in this world, depose as follows: "We heard her in the fire invoking her saints and her archangel; she repeated the Savior's name. . . . At last dropping her head, she cried aloud, 'Jesus.' "

"Ten thousand men wept." Some English alone laughed or tried to laugh. One of the most violent among them had sworn to fling a fagot on the pile; she was expiring at the moment he deposited it, and he was taken ill. His comrades carried him off to a tavern to revive his spirits with drink, but he could not recover his equanimity. "I saw," he cried distractedly, "I saw a dove escape from her mouth with her last sigh." Others had read in the flames the word *Jesus*, which she repeated. The executioner went that evening in utter dismay to Brother Isambart and confessed, but could not believe that

God would ever forgive him. One of the King of England's secretaries said openly as he returned from the horrid scene, "We are undone; we have burned a saint!" . . .

Martyrs there have been many; history has innumerable lists of them, more or less pure, more or less glorious. Pride, too, and hatred and the spirit of disputation have had their own. No age has been without pugnacious martyrs, who died no doubt with a good grace, when they were not able to kill. But there was nothing in common between such fanatics and this saintly girl; she was not of them, but was signed with a different token: goodness, charity, meekness.

She had the meekness of the martyrs of old, but with a difference. The first Christians retained the gentleness and purity only by shunning action, and sparing themselves the struggles and the trials of the world. Joan was meek in the keenest conflict, good amongst the bad, pacific in war itself; into war, that triumph of the devil, she carried the spirit of God.

She took up arms when she knew "the pity there was in the realm of France." She could not bear to see "French blood flow." This tenderness of heart she displayed towards all men; she used to weep after her victories and bestow her care on the wounded English.

Purity, gentleness, heroic goodness; that this supreme beauty of soul should have been found in a daughter of France may surprise foreigners, who are fond of judging of our nation only from the levity of its manners. Let us tell them (and with partiality, now that all this is so remote from our day) that with all this levity, with its follies and its vices even, old France was not without cause denominated the most Christian nation. It was certainly the people of love and grace; whether the words be understood in the human or in the Christian acceptation, in both cases is the proposition true.

It was fit the Savior of France should be a woman; France herself was a woman; she had the fickleness of the sex, but also its amiable gentleness, its facile and charming pity, and the excellence of its first impulses. Even when it took delight in vain elegancies and outward overrefinements, at core it remained nearer to nature. The Frenchman, even though vicious, retained more than any other man good sense and a good heart.

May new France not forget the saying of old France: "None but great hearts know how much glory there is *in being good*." To be, and continue so, under the injustices of man and the severities of Providence, is not only the gift of a happily constituted nature, it is strength and heroism. To retain mildness and benevolence amidst so many keen disputes, to run the range of experience without allowing it to impair that innate treasure, this is divine. Those who continue thus to the end are the real elect. And even though they have sometimes tripped upon the difficult path of the world, still amidst their lapses, their weaknesses, and childishnesses, they will remain not the less God's children!

⟲⟳

"Men without faults are apt to be men without force. A round diamond has no brilliancy. Lights and shadows, hills and valleys, give beauty to the landscape."

ULYSSES S. GRANT
(1822–1885)

by

REV. HENRY WARD BEECHER
(1813–1887)

The eulogy to Ulysses S. Grant, the brilliant military leader and lackluster president, was written by the Reverend Henry Ward Beecher, one of the most popular preachers in the late nineteenth century. That the flamboyant Beecher should have had such a grasp of the plain, self-deprecating Grant is nevertheless understandable. Both were insecure men, which led Grant to drink and Beecher to tireless self-promotion. This excerpt from Beecher's eulogy dwells upon Grant's real calling, which was to lead the Union to victory in the Civil War.

Another name is added to the roll of those whom the world will not willingly let die. A few years since storm clouds filled his heaven, and obloquy, slander, and bitter lies rained down upon him.

The clouds are all blown away, under a serene sky he laid down his life, and the nation wept. The path to his tomb is worn by the feet of innumerable pilgrims. The mildewed lips of Slander are silent,

56

and even Criticism hesitates lest some incautious word should mar the history of the modest, gentle, magnanimous Warrior.

. . . Grant made no claim to saintship. He was a man of like passions, and with as marked limitations, as other men. Nothing could be more distasteful to his honest, modest soul while living, and nothing more unbecoming to his memory, than lying exaggerations and fulsome flatteries.

Men without faults are apt to be men without force. A round diamond has no brilliancy. Lights and shadows, hills and valleys, give beauty to the landscape. The faults of great and generous natures are overripe goodness, or the shadows which their virtues cast.

Three great elements enter into the career of a great citizen:

That which his ancestry gives;

That which opportunity gives;

That which his will develops.

Grant came from a sturdy New England stock; New England derived it from Scotland; Scotland bred it, at a time when Covenanters and Puritans were made—men of iron consciences hammered out upon the anvil of adversity. From New England the stream flowed to the Ohio, where it enriched the soil, it brought forth abundant harvests of great men. When it was Grant's time to be born, he came forth without celestial portents, and his youth had in it no prophecy of his manhood. His boyhood was wholesome, robust, with a vigorous frame. With a heart susceptible of tender love, he yet was not social. He was patient and persistent. He loved horses and could master them. That is a good sign.

Grant had no art of creating circumstance; opportunity must seek him, or else he would plod through life without disclosing the gifts which God hid in him. The gold in the hills cannot disclose itself. It must be sought and dug.

A sharp and wiry politician, for some reason of Providence, performed a generous deed, in sending young Grant to West Point. He finished his course there, distinguished as a skillful and bold rider, with no inclination to mathematics, with little taste for the theory and literature of war. . . . After leaving the Academy he saw service in Mexico and afterwards in California, but without conspicuous results.

Then came a clouded period, a sad life of irresolute vibration between self-indulgences and aspiration, through intemperance. He resigned from the army, and at that time one would have feared that his life would end in eclipse. . . .

At length he struck at the root of the matter. Others agreed not to drink, which is good; Grant overcame the *wish* to drink—which is better. . . . Of all his victories, many and great, this was the greatest, that he conquered himself. His will was stronger than his passions.

Poor, much shattered, he essayed farming. Carrying wood for sale to St. Louis did not seem to be that for which he was created; neither did planting crops, nor raising cattle.

Tanning is an honorable calling, and, to many, a road to wealth. Grant found no gold in the tan vat.

Then he became a listless merchant—a silent, unsocial, and rather moody waiter upon petty traffic.

He was a good subaltern, a poor farmer, a worse tanner, a worthless trafficker. Without civil experience, literary gifts, too diffident to be ambitious, too modest to put himself forward, too honest to be a politician, he was of all men the least likely to attain eminence, and absolutely unfitted, apparently, for preeminence; yet God's providence selected him.

When the prophet Samuel went forth to anoint a successor to the impetuous and imperious King Saul, he caused all the children of Jesse to pass before him. He rejected one by one the whole band. At length the youngest called from the flock came in, and the Lord said to Samuel, "Arise, this is *he*," and Samuel took the horn of oil and anointed him in the midst of his brethren, and the spirit of the Lord came upon him from that day forward.

Ordained was Grant with the ointment of war—black and sulphurous.

Had Grant died at the tan-yard, or from behind the counter, the world would never have suspected that it had lost a hero. He would have fallen as an undistinguishable leaf among the millions cast down every year. His time had not come. . . . It was coming!

"I hold it a Christian thing, as O'Donovan Rossa held it, to hate evil. . . ."

JEREMIAH O'DONOVAN ROSSA
(D. 1915)

by

PATRICK HENRY PEARSE
(1879–1916)

Jeremiah O'Donovan Rossa was an early 1850s member of the rebel Irish Republican Brigade. Upon his death in America in 1915, his body was returned for burial in Ireland at Glasnevin Cemetery in Dublin. Patrick Pearse intended his graveside eulogy to Rossa to be a call to arms for the Irish to rebel against the English. In 1916, Pearse led the Easter Rebellion in Dublin, which resulted in his capture, court-martial, and execution in England. It was the beginning of the revolt against seven centuries of British rule.

We stand at Rossa's grave not in sadness but rather in exultation of spirit. O'Donovan Rossa was splendid in the proud manhood of him, splendid in the Gaelic strength and clarity and truth of him. In a closer spiritual communion with him now than ever before, we pledge to Ireland our love, and we pledge to English rule in Ireland our hate.

This is a place of peace sacred to the dead, where men should speak with all charity and with all restraint; but I hold it a Christian thing, as O'Donovan Rossa held it, to hate evil, to hate untruth, to hate oppression, and hating them to strive to overthrow them. . . . Life springs from death; and from the graves of patriot men and women spring living nations.

The Defenders of this Realm have worked well in secret and in the open. They think they have pacified Ireland. They think they have purchased half of us and intimidated the other half. They think that they have foreseen everything and provided against everything. But the fools, the fools, the fools! They have left us our Fenian dead, and while Ireland holds these graves, Ireland unfree shall never be at peace.

ᏀᎢᎢᎢᏒᏀ

"The world naturally looks with some awe upon a man who appears unconcernedly indifferent to home, money, comfort, rank, or even power and fame."

LAWRENCE OF ARABIA
(1888–1935)

by

SIR WINSTON CHURCHILL
(1874–1965)

Thomas Edward Lawrence (known as Lawrence of Arabia) was a British adventurer, soldier, and scholar who in World War I left a British intelligence unit in Egypt to lead Arab forces against the Turks. After seeking in vain to secure Arab independence following the war, he developed a passion for anonymity and assumed a variety of new names (T. E. Shaw, J. H. Ross) and occupations. The Seven Pillars of Wisdom, *a narrative of his Arab adventures, is considered a masterpiece.*

Winston Churchill, who was not yet prime minister when he delivered this eulogy, writes prophetically of the man he himself would become—the leader who "flew best and easiest in the hurricane" of World War II and the Nazi bombardment of England, which Churchill held together by the strength of his will. He spoke these words at a memorial unveiling at Oxford High School in 1936.

Although more than a year has passed since Lawrence was taken from us, the impression of his personality remains living and vivid upon the minds of his friends, and the sense of his loss is in no way dimmed among his countrymen. All feel the poorer that he has gone from us. In these days dangers and difficulties gather upon Britain and her Empire, and we are also conscious of a lack of outstanding figures with which to overcome them. Here was a man in whom there existed not only an immense capacity for service, but that touch of genius which everyone recognizes and no one can define. Whether in his great period of adventure and command or in these later years of self-suppression and self-imposed eclipse, he always reigned over those with whom he came in contact. They felt themselves in the presence of an extraordinary being. They felt that his latent reserves of force and willpower were beyond measurement. If he roused himself to action, who should say what crisis he could not surmount or quell? If things were going very badly, how glad one would be to see him come round the corner.

Part of the secret of this stimulating ascendancy lay of course in his disdain for most of the prizes, the pleasures, and comforts of life. The world naturally looks with some awe upon a man who appears unconcernedly indifferent to home, money, comfort, rank, or even power and fame. The world feels not without a certain apprehension that here is someone outside its jurisdiction; someone before whom its allurements may be spread in vain; someone strangely enfranchised, untamed, untrammeled by convention, moving independently of the ordinary currents of human action; a being readily capable of violent revolt or supreme sacrifice; a man, solitary, austere, to whom existence is no more than a duty, yet a duty to be faithfully discharged. He was indeed a dweller upon the mountaintops where the air is cold, crisp, and rarefied, and where the view on clear days commands all the kingdoms of the world and the glory of them.

Lawrence was one of those beings whose pace of life was faster and more intense than what is normal. Just as an aeroplane only flies by its speed and pressure against the air, so he flew best and easiest in the hurricane. He was not in complete harmony with the normal. The fury of the Great War raised the pitch of life to the Lawrence standard. The multitudes were swept forward till their pace was the same as his. In this heroic period he found himself in perfect relation both to men and events.

I have often wondered what would have happened to Lawrence if the Great War had continued for several more years. His fame was spreading fast and with the momentum of the fabulous throughout Asia. The earth trembled with the wrath of the warring nations. All the metals were molten. Everything was in motion. No one could say what was impossible. Lawrence might have realized Napoleon's young dream of conquering the East; he might have arrived at Constantinople in 1919 or 1920 with most of the tribes and races of Asia Minor and Arabia at his back. But the storm wind ceased as suddenly as it had arisen. The skies were clear; the bells of Armistice rang out. Mankind returned with indescribable relief to its long-interrupted, fondly cherished ordinary life, and Lawrence was left once more moving alone on a different plane at a different speed.

In this we find an explanation of the last phase of his all too brief life. It is not the only explanation. The sufferings and stresses he had undergone, both physical and psychic, during the War had left their scars and injuries upon him. These were aggravated by the distress which he felt at which he deemed the ill-usage of his Arab friends and allies to whom he had pledged the word of Britain, and the word of Lawrence. He was capable of suffering mental pain in an exceptional degree. I am sure that the ordeal of watching the helplessness of his Arab friends in the grand confusions of the Peace Conference was the main cause which decided his renunciation of all power, and so far as possible of all interest in public affairs.

In this premature retirement he had to lay hold of detailed tasks wherewith to fill the days and the hours. The writing of his book, *The Seven Pillars*, was a powerful solace to him. To all of us it is one of the treasures of English literature. *The Seven Pillars* as a narrative of war and adventure, as a portrayal of all that the Arabs mean in the world, is unsurpassed. It ranks with the greatest books ever written in the English language. It is not, I think, excessive to class it in interest and charm with *Pilgrim's Progress, Robinson Crusoe,* and *Gulliver's Travels.* If Lawrence had never done anything except write this book as a mere work of the imagination, his fame would last, in Macaulay's familiar phrase, "as long as the English language is spoken in any quarter of the globe." But this was a book of fact, not fiction, and the author was also the commander. When most of the vast literature of the Great War has been sifted and superseded by the epitomes, commentaries, and histories of future generations, when the complicated and infinitely costly operations of ponderous armies are the concern only of the military student, when our struggles are viewed in a fading perspective and in truer proportion, Lawrence's tale of the revolt in the desert will gleam with immortal fire.

When the literary masterpiece was written, lost, and written again; when every illustration had been profoundly considered and every incident of typography and paragraphing settled with meticulous care; when Lawrence on his bicycle had carried the precious volumes to the few—the very few—he deemed worthy to read them, happily he found another task to his hands which cheered and comforted his soul. He saw as clearly as anyone the vision of airpower and all that it would mean in traffic and war. He found in the life of an aircraftsman that balm of peace and equipoise which no great station or command could have bestowed upon him. He felt that in living the life of a private in the Royal Air Force he would dignify that honorable calling and help to attract all that is keenest in our youthful manhood to the sphere where it is most urgently needed. For this service and example, to which he devoted the last twelve years of his life, we owe him a separate debt. It was in itself a princely gift.

If on this occasion I have seemed to dwell upon Lawrence's sorrows and heart-searchings rather than upon his achievements and prowess, it is because the latter are so justly famous. He had a full measure of the versatility of genius. He held one of those master keys which unlock the doors of many kinds of treasure-houses. He was a savant as well as a soldier. He was an archaeologist as well as a man of action. He was an accomplished scholar as well as an Arab partisan. He was a mechanic, as well as a philosopher. His background of somber experience and reflection only seemed to set forth more brightly the charm and gaiety of his companionship, and the generous majesty of his nature. Those who knew him best miss him most; but our country misses him most of all, and misses him most of all now. . . .

⌒⫶⌔

"If, as I believe, his spirit looks upon us and sees us, nothing would displease his soul so much as to see that we have indulged in any small behavior or any violence."

MAHATMA MOHANDAS K. GANDHI
(1869–1948)

by

JAWAHARLAL NEHRU
(1889–1964)

Mahatma *means "great soul," an honorific Gandhi earned by his powerful nonviolent political and spiritual leadership in India before and after it achieved independence. Gandhi differed from other leaders in that he*

63

refused to profit from the misfortunes of the oppressor, insisting that his adversaries be won over by the moral rightness of his position. A Hindu opposed to the partitioning of India and the creation of a separate Muslim state (Pakistan), he was assassinated by a fanatic Hindu enraged at Gandhi's solicitude for the Muslims.

Jawaharlal Nehru was a protégé of Gandhi's, the leader of the Indian National Congress, and eventually, prime minister of the country.

Friends and comrades, the light has gone out of our lives and there is darkness everywhere. I do not know what to tell you and how to say it. Our beloved leader, Bapu as we called him, the father of the nation, is no more. Perhaps I am wrong to say that. Nevertheless, we will not see him again as we have seen him for these many years. We will not run to him for advice and seek solace from him, and that is a terrible blow, not to me only, but to millions and millions in this country, and it is a little difficult to soften the blow by any other advice that I or anyone else can give you.

The light has gone out, I said, and yet I was wrong. For the light that shone in this country was no ordinary light. The light that has illumined this country for these many years will illumine this country for many more years, and a thousand years later that light will still be seen in this country, and the world will see it and it will give solace to innumerable hearts. For that light represented the living truth . . . the eternal truths, reminding us of the right path, drawing us from error, taking this ancient country to freedom.

All this has happened when there was so much more for him to do. We could never think that he was unnecessary or that he had done his task. But now, particularly, when we are faced with so many difficulties, his not being with us is a blow most terrible to bear.

A madman has put an end to his life, for I can only call him mad who did it, and yet there has been enough of poison spread in this country during the past years and months, and this poison has effect on people's minds. We must face this poison, we must root out this poison, and we must face all the perils that encompass us and face them not madly or badly but rather in the way that our beloved teacher taught us to face them. The first thing to remember now is that no one of us dare misbehave because we're angry. We have to behave like strong and determined people, determined to face all the perils that surround us, determined to carry out the mandate that our great teacher and our great leader has given us, remembering always that if, as I believe, his spirit looks upon us and sees us, nothing would displease his soul so much as to see that we have indulged in any small behavior or any violence.

So we must not do that. But that does not mean that we should be weak, but rather that we should in strength and in unity face all the troubles that are in front of us. We must hold together, and all our petty troubles and difficulties and conflicts must be ended in the face of this great disaster. A great disaster is a symbol to us to remember all the big things of life and forget the small things, of which we have thought too much.

⊙ɯɯ9

"The men who go first are accounted heroes, and rightly so, whatever the age, whatever the new element and horizon."

ASTRONAUTS VIRGIL GRISSOM,
EDWARD WHITE, AND ROGER CHAFFEE
(D. JANUARY 27, 1967)

by

ERIC SEVAREID
(1912–1992)

On January 27, 1967, a fire aboard the Apollo 1 *spacecraft on the ground at Cape Kennedy, Florida, killed the three astronauts Grissom, White, and Chaffee. They were buried on January 31. That evening, on the* CBS Evening News, *commentator Eric Sevareid delivered the following statement.*

Grissom and White and Chaffee—mortals who aspired to the moon and eternal space—were returned to the earth today from which they came and to which we all belong.

They had lived life more intensely in a very few years than most of us do in our lifetimes, and they shall be remembered far longer.

They were among the men who wield the cutting edge of history, and by this sword they died.

65

Grissom and Chaffee were buried near the grave of Lt. Thomas Selfridge, the first American military pilot to be killed in an airplane crash, nearly sixty years ago. Then, the air above the ground was as unfamiliar as the space above the air.

The men who go first are accounted heroes, and rightly so, whatever the age, whatever the new element and horizon. Space, said the late President Kennedy, is our new ocean and we must sail upon it.

It was truly the hazards of the unknown oceans and territories that took the lives of earlier heroes, like Magellan or Captain Cook, men who went first and were killed by inhabitants of the Pacific.

It was not precisely the unknown hazards of space that killed our astronauts; it was the hazards of fallible man's calculations. It was not a technical failure: all technical failures are human failures. It was the familiar, never totally escapable failure of the human brain to cope with the complexities it has arranged.

A slight miscalculation, a single slip, then a spark, a flame, and the end of three remarkable products of those infinitely more complex mysteries, genetic inheritance and environment. The processes that occasionally produce personalities like Grissom and White and Chaffee—men who are brave but not brash; proud but not self-conscious; thoughtful but not brooding. Men of a health, a wholeness we all aspire to but so few attain.

We are told they will be replaced. This only means that other such men will take their places. The three cannot be replaced. There never was a replaceable human being.

☙

"Grandfather, you were the pillar of fire in front of the camp and now we are left in the camp alone, in the dark; and we are so cold and so sad."

YITZHAK RABIN
(1922–1995)

by

NOA BEN-ARTZI PHILOSOF
(1978–)

Prime minister of Israel Yitzhak Rabin was assassinated at a peace rally in Tel Aviv by a right-wing Israeli enraged at Rabin's conciliatory policies toward the Palestinians. A onetime hawk whose famous handshake with Yasir Arafat at the White House Rose Garden had signaled a new beginning for peace in the Middle East, Rabin had earned the respect of both his enemies and allies. Kings and presidents delivered moving eulogies, but it was Rabin's seventeen-year-old granddaughter, Noa Ben-Artzi Philosof, whose words, spoken directly to her grandfather, went directly to the heart.

Please excuse me for not wanting to talk about the peace. I want to talk about my grandfather.

You always awake from a nightmare, but since yesterday I was continually awakening to a nightmare. It is not possible to get used to the nightmare of life without you. The television never ceases to broadcast pictures of you, and you are so alive that I can almost touch you—but only almost, and I won't be able to anymore.

Grandfather, you were the pillar of fire in front of the camp and now we are left in the camp alone, in the dark; and we are so cold and so sad.

I know that people talk in terms of a national tragedy, and of comforting an entire nation, but we feel the huge void that remains in your absence when grandmother doesn't stop crying.

Few people really knew you. Now they will talk about you for quite some time, but I feel that they really don't know just how great the pain is, how great the tragedy is; something has been destroyed.

Grandfather, you were and still are our hero. I wanted you to know that every time I did anything, I saw you in front of me.

Your appreciation and your love accompanied us every step down the road, and our lives were always shaped after your values. You, who never abandoned anything, are now abandoned. And here you are, my ever-present hero, cold, alone, and I cannot do anything to save you. You are missed so much.

Others greater than I have already eulogized you, but none of them ever had the pleasure I had to feel the caresses of your warm, soft hands, to merit your warm embrace that was reserved only for us, to see your half-smile that always told me so much, that same smile which is no longer, frozen in the grave with you.

I have no feelings of revenge because my pain and feelings of loss are so large, too large. The ground has been swept out from below us, and we are groping now, trying to wander about in this empty void, without any success so far.

I am not able to finish this; left with no alternative, I say good-bye to you, hero, and ask you to rest in peace, and think about us, and miss us as down here we love you so very much. I imagine angels are accompanying you now and I ask them to take care of you, because you deserve their protection.

കൗ

CHAPTER THREE

PUBLIC SERVANTS

∽

Represented in this chapter are four presidents, one vice president, and one presidential candidate called by an eminent journalist of the day "the right man for the wrong time." All six men were public servants of great talent and integrity, which is not to say that they were universally admired while alive.

Washington, the land surveyor who became the founding father of the country, seems to have incurred the least criticism, although Jefferson concedes that he was not a man of the first intellectual rank and that when he got mad—which was seldom—it was not a pretty sight. Jefferson, who is approaching deification in this century, died within hours of another president, John Adams, on a day of astonishing synchronicity—July 4, 1826.

That two signers of the Declaration of Independence should die on Independence Day was, one eulogist remarked, to "feel that these illustrious men had rather been translated than died." But when Jefferson defeated John Adams for the presidency in 1800, a disgruntled New Jersey legislature passed laws to deny the vote to New Jersey women of property, who, it turned out, had put Jefferson over the top. The part of Nicholas Biddle's eulogy excerpted here is a scolding to the nation, which had allowed Jefferson to sink so deeply into poverty before he died.

By the time Lincoln was assassinated, the country knew his worth. All of the greatest minds and orators of the day stepped forward to express themselves: Robert Ingersoll, Rev. Henry Ward Beecher, Phillips Brooks, and Ralph Waldo Emerson, the latter confessing his shortsightedness. Only a half dozen years before, Emerson observed, the news that Lincoln had been nominated for president by the Republican Party had been received "coldly and sadly. It seemed too rash, on a purely local reputation, to build so grave a trust in such anxious times." Included here is Carl Sandburg's eulogy, for his description of Lincoln weeping.

In Sean Quinlan's essay on the death of Kennedy, he observes "a great death quickens all life." And legend. Americans eagerly followed the story of Camelot on the Potomac, when the impossibly handsome president and his grave-eyed, beautiful wife brought Pablo Casals to play at the White House and the lawn was strewn with rocking horses and hope. The broad outlines of the Kennedy story retain their legendary quality—the sacrifice of sons to assassins; the valor that was demanded of the privileged, in payment for their gifts; and the suspicion, when the slain president was laid to rest, that Daniel Webster was right, "there's a divinity which shapes our ends."

There is also a divinity that thwarts our ends. In Senator Eugene McCarthy's affectionate tribute to Hubert Humphrey he writes "his not being elected to the presidency was just short of tragedy." But he adds, "he who preaches the crusade may not be called to lead it, at least not to Jerusalem." The former governor of Illinois, Adlai Stevenson, was also denied the prize. The tribute by Richard Goodwin to Adlai Stevenson, the governor from Illinois, is perhaps the most endearing—a portrait of a thoughtful, witty man who made public service seem like the natural and human thing to do. An intellectual who poked fun at himself, Stevenson once remarked that in campaigns "people might be better served if a party purchased a half hour of radio and TV silence during which the audience would be asked to think quietly for themselves." In his 1952 concession speech he said that he "felt like a little boy who had stubbed his toe in the dark; that he was too old to cry, but it hurt too much to laugh."

Stevenson once remarked that history can't be hurried. Neither can it be delayed. In the 1960 election, he bowed to John Kennedy, who won the presidency—and beat him to the grave.

"His mind was great and powerful, without being of the very first order; his penetration strong, though not so acute as that of a Newton, Bacon, or Locke; and as far as he saw, no judgment was ever sounder."

GEORGE WASHINGTON
(1732–1799)

by

THOMAS JEFFERSON
(1743–1826)

In this posthumous analysis of Washington, fellow Virginian Thomas Jefferson gives us a sustained glimpse into the mind and character of America's first president. Jefferson, who was Washington's first secretary of state, was not always in agreement with Washington, but he appreciated his virtues, and in this excerpt from a letter to Dr. Walter Jones, who was preparing a history of the new American republic, he paints a portrait of a cautious, courageous, and incorruptible man of action.

Monticello, January 2, 1814

Dear Sir— . . .

You say that in taking General Washington on your shoulders, to bear him harmless through the federal coalition, you encounter a perilous topic. I do not think so. . . . I think I knew General Washington intimately and thoroughly; and were I called on to delineate his character, it should be in terms like these.

His mind was great and powerful, without being of the very first order; his penetration strong, though not so acute as that of a Newton, Bacon, or Locke; and as far as he saw, no judgment was ever sounder. It was slow in operation, being little aided by invention or imagination, but sure in conclusion. Hence the common remark of his officers, of the advantage he derived from councils of war, where hearing all suggestions, he selected whatever was best; and certainly no general ever planned his battles more judiciously. But if deranged during the course of the action, if any member of his plan was dislocated by sudden circumstances, he was slow in readjustment. The consequence was that he often failed in the field, and rarely against an enemy in station, as at Boston and York. He was incapable of fear, meeting personal dangers with the calmest unconcern. Perhaps the strongest feature in his character was prudence, never acting until every circumstance, every consideration, was maturely weighed; refraining if he saw a doubt, but, when once decided, going through with purpose, whatever obstacles opposed. His integrity was most pure, his justice the most inflexible I have ever known, no motives of interest or consanguinity, or friendship or hatred, being able to bias his decision. He was indeed, in every sense of the word, a wise, a good, and a great man. His temper was naturally high toned; but reflection and resolution had obtained a firm and habitual ascendancy over it. If ever, however, it broke its bonds, he was most tremendous in his wrath. In his expenses he was honorable, but exact; liberal in contributions to whatever promised utility; but frowning and unyielding on all visionary projects and all unworthy calls on his charity. His heart was not warm in its affections; but he exactly calculated every man's value, and gave him a solid esteem proportioned to it. His person, you know, was fine, his stature exactly what one would wish, his deportment easy, erect, and noble; the best horseman of his age, and the most graceful figure that could be seen on horseback. Although in the circle of his friends, where he might be unreserved with safety, he took a free share in conversation, his colloquial talents were not above mediocrity, possessing neither copiousness of ideas, nor fluency of words. In public, when called on for a sudden opinion, he was unready, short, and embarrassed. Yet he wrote readily, rather diffusely, in an easy and correct style. This he had acquired by conversation with the world, for his education was merely reading, writing, and common arithmetic, to which he added surveying at a later day. His time was employed in action chiefly, reading little, and that only in agriculture and English history. His correspondence became necessarily extensive, and, with his journalizing his agricultural proceedings, occupied most of his leisure hours within doors. On the whole, his character was, in its mass, perfect, in nothing bad, in few points indifferent; and it may truly be said that never did nature and fortune combine more perfectly to make a man great, and to place him in the same constellation with whatever worthies have merited from man an everlasting remembrance. For his was the singular destiny and merit of leading the armies of his country successfully through an arduous war, for the establishment of its independence; of conducting its councils through the birth of a government, new in its forms and principles, until it had settled down into a quiet and orderly train; and of scrupulously obeying the laws through the whole of his career, civil and military, of which the history of the world furnishes no other examples.

How, then, can it be perilous for you to take such a man on your shoulders? I am satisfied that the great body of republicans think of him as I do. . . . For he was no monarchist from preference of his judgment. The soundness of that gave him correct views of the rights of man, and his severe justice devoted him to them. He has often declared to me that he considered our new constitution as an experiment on the practicability of republican government, and with what dose of liberty man could be trusted for his own good; that he was determined the experiment should have a fair trial, and would lose the last drop of his blood in support of it. . . . I do believe that General Washington had not a firm confidence in the durability of our government. He was naturally distrustful of men, and inclined to gloomy apprehensions; and I was ever persuaded that a belief that we must at length end in something like a British constitution had some weight in his adoption of the ceremonies of levees, birthdays, pompous meetings with Congress, and other forms of the same character, calculated to prepare us gradually for a change which he believed possible, and to let it come on with as little shock as might be to the public mind.

These are my opinions of General Washington, which I would vouch at the judgment seat of God, having been formed on an acquaintance of thirty years. I served with him in the Virginia legislature from 1769 to the Revolutionary war, and again, a short time in Congress, until he left us to take command of the army. During the war and after it we corresponded occasionally, and in the four years of my continuance in the office of Secretary of State, our intercourse was daily, confidential, and cordial. After I retired from that office, great and malignant pains were taken by our federal monarchists, not entirely without effect, to make him view me as a theorist, holding French principles of government, which would lead infallibly to licentiousness and anarchy. And to this he listened the more easily from my known disapprobation of the British treaty. I never saw him afterwards, or these malignant insinuations should have been dissipated before his just judgment, as mists before the sun. I felt on his death, with my countrymen, that "verily a great man hath fallen on this day in Israel."

∽〰〰∾

"As the shades of age and infirmity were gathering round him, there came in and sat down beside his hearth the cold and spectral form of poverty."

THOMAS JEFFERSON
(1743–1826)

by

NICHOLAS BIDDLE
(1786–1844)

On July 4, 1826, the two most important signers of the Declaration of Independence, John Adams and Thomas Jefferson, died within hours of each other. Adams's last words were "Thomas Jefferson still survives." But Jefferson did not last the night. It was not generally known that near the end of Jefferson's life he had come upon hard times. In a letter to James Madison he confided that he might not be able to afford "ground for burial." Bad crops, needy and debt-ridden relatives, and a lifetime of public service that did not allow him time to secure a fortune had reduced Jefferson to asking the state of Virginia to allow him to organize a lottery to sell all his land, so that he might liquidate his debts. Failing that, he would vacate Monticello.

In his eulogy, delivered a year after Jefferson's death, Philadelphia financier Nicholas Biddle details the extent of his poverty and expresses his admiration for the uncomplaining way Jefferson, in his eighties, in wretched health and without resources, faced his end.

. . . This is an unwelcome theme, but the history of [Jefferson's] life were imperfect without it, and perhaps his country, which so often profited by his successes, may yet learn something from his misfortunes. The long career of public employment, which separated him from his domestic concerns, the incompetency of the emoluments annexed to his stations, the distinction which compelled him to the exercise of a simple yet costly hospitality, these with accidental disasters had so impaired his fortunes, that, as the shades of age and infirmity were gathering round him, there came in and sat down beside his hearth the cold and spectral form of poverty. In the luxuries of abundance men disregard that stern but distant being, whose invasion they think should be repelled by economy or disarmed by resignation. But these salutary truths cannot always repress the terrors of this startling intruder. They who have not known prosperity may go on unrepining till life is exhausted in the habitual struggle with their destiny. But to those who were born to affluence, whose habits have softened under its influence, and whose cultivated minds render them doubly sensitive to the happiness of all around them, the change comes with an almost overwhelming reality. They see the weakness to whose wants they once ministered, yet feel the decay of their power to relieve it, they mark one by one the silent abstraction of those enjoyments which soothed the infirmities of our nature, till at length they are left to brood in despair over the wrecks of fallen fortunes, to gaze on the widening circle of domestic sorrow, and to witness that ruin which they did not make yet cannot repair. This affliction in all its acuteness, not for himself, but for those who depended on him, seems to have been the lot of Jefferson. But the philosophy which he had cultivated teaches men to make their own destiny, to be unmoved by prosperous or adverse events, and to bear the ills of life, as incidents to its nature, sent to warn but not to subdue us. He was faithful to these principles, and as success had never disturbed his equanimity, adversity only displayed in him the dignity of misfortune. His descent from power into poverty attested his purity, and his devotion to the public service, which in generous minds naturally inspires a disregard of personal interests. He therefore neither desponded nor complained, but prepared with a scrupulous fidelity to surrender his earnings and his patrimony, his chosen home, the scene of his attachments and his enjoyments, and then to retreat to some possession which would still survive the claim of justice, and furnish a last refuge and grave. The knowledge of it aroused his countrymen to efforts which but for his death might have relieved him. But it is not less worthy of his country to consider whether this inadequate provision for public services should continue, in hostility to all the principles of our institutions, by proscribing from service of the state men of humble fortunes, and rendering the life of a statesman a perpetual struggle between his domestic duties and the impulses of a generous ambition. We may hereafter outgrow this weakness of our youth, but it is a subject of melancholy instruction that the last days of Jefferson were clouded by anxieties which the country for its own glory should have averted or relieved.

The time however had arrived when his cares and his existence were to end. His health had been through life singularly robust, as the vigorous frame which nature had bestowed on him was preserved by habits of great regularity and temperance. But for some months previous to his death he was obviously declining, and at length the combination of disease and decay terminated his life on the fourth day of July 1826 in the eighty-fourth year of his age. He died with the firmness and self-possession native to his character, and the last hours of his existence were cheered and consecrated by the return of that day when of all others it was most fit that he should die—the birthday of his country. He felt that this was his appropriate resting place, and he gave up to God his enfeebled frame and his exhausted spirit on the anniversary almost of that hour which half a century before had seen him devoting the mature energies of his mind and the concentered affections of his heart to the freedom of his country.

So lived and died Thomas Jefferson, a name illustrious in our day and destined to an enduring fame hereafter.

✑

"In the mixed shame and blame of the immense wrongs of two crashing civilizations, often with nothing to say, he said nothing, slept not at all, and on occasions he was seen to weep in a way that made weeping appropriate, decent, majestic."

ABRAHAM LINCOLN
(1809–1865)

by

CARL SANDBURG
(1878–1967)

When Lincoln was assassinated in 1865, the eulogies began to pour forth in an abundance that has not ceased to this day. But the hoarse and elderly voice of Carl Sandburg, the eighty-one-year-old populist poet and historian from Galesburg, Illinois, was one of the most powerful. Sandburg, whose six-volume biography of Lincoln was his most monumental work, was invited in 1959 to address a joint session of the House and Senate, to speak about Lincoln's life.

Not often in the story of mankind does a man arrive on earth who is both steel and velvet, who is as hard as rock and soft as drifting fog, who holds in his heart and mind the paradox of terrible storm and peace unspeakable and perfect. Here and there across the centuries come reports of men alleged to have these contrasts. And the incomparable Abraham Lincoln, born 150 years ago this day, is an approach if not a perfect realization of this character.

In the time of the April lilacs in the year 1865, on his death, the casket with his body was carried north and west a thousand miles; and the American people wept as never before; bells sobbed, cities wore crepe, people stood in tears and with hats off as the railroad burial car paused in the leading cities of seven states, ending its journey at Springfield, Illinois, the hometown.

During the four years he was president he at times, especially in the first three months, took to himself the powers of a dictator; he commanded the most powerful armies till then assembled in modern warfare; he enforced conscription of soldiers for the first time in American history; under imperative necessity he abolished the right of habeas corpus; he directed politically and spiritually the wild, massive, turbulent forces let loose in civil war. . . .

In the month the war began he told his secretary, John Hay, "My policy is to have no policy." Three years later, in a letter to a Kentucky friend made public, he confessed plainly, "I have been controlled by events." His words at Gettysburg were sacred, yet strange with a color of the familiar: "We cannot consecrate—we cannot hallow—this ground. The brave men, living and dead, who struggled here, have consecrated it, far beyond our poor power to add or detract."

He could have said "the brave Union men." Did he have a purpose in omitting the word *Union*? Was he keeping himself and his utterance clear of the passion that would not be good to look at when the time came for peace and reconciliation? Did he mean to leave an implication that there were brave Union men, and brave Confederate men, living and dead, who had struggled there? We do not know, of a certainty.

Was he thinking of the Kentucky father whose two sons died in battle, one in Union blue, the other in Confederate gray, the father inscribing on the stone over their double grave, "God knows which was right"? We do not know. . . .

Among his bitter opponents were such figures as Samuel F. B. Morse, inventor of the telegraph, and Cyrus H. McCormick, inventor of the farm reaper. In all its essential propositions the Southern Confederacy had the moral support of powerful, respectable elements throughout the North, probably more than a million voters believing in the justice of the Southern cause.

While the war winds howled, he insisted that the Mississippi was one river meant to belong to one country, that railroad connection from coast to coast must be pushed through and the Union Pacific Railroad made a reality. While the luck of war wavered and broke and came again, as generals failed and campaigns were lost, he held enough forces of the North together to raise new armies and supply them, until generals were found who made war as victorious war has always been made, with terror, frightfulness, destruction, and on both sides, North and South, valor and sacrifice past words of man to tell.

In the mixed shame and blame of the immense wrongs of two crashing civilizations, often with nothing to say, he said nothing, slept not at all, and on occasions he was seen to weep in a way that made weeping appropriate, decent, majestic.

As he rode alone on horseback near Soldiers' Home on the edge of Washington one night, his hat was shot off; a son he loved died as he watched at the bed; his wife was accused of betraying information to the enemy, until denials from him were necessary.

An Indiana man at the White House heard him say, "Voorhees, don't it seem strange to you that I, who could never so much as cut off the head of a chicken, should be elected, or selected, into the midst of all this blood?" . . .

To Gov. Michel Hahn, elected in 1864 by a majority of the eleven thousand white male voters who had taken the oath of allegiance to the Union, Lincoln wrote:

"Now you are about to have a convention which, among other things, will probably define the elective franchise, I barely suggest for your private consideration, whether some of the colored people may not be let in—as for instance, the very intelligent and especially those who have fought gallantly in our ranks."

Among the million words in the Lincoln utterance record, he interprets himself with a more keen precision than someone else offering to explain him. His simple opening of the House Divided speech in 1858 serves for today:

"If we could first know where we are, and whither we are tending, we could better judge what to do, and how to do it."

To his Kentucky friend Joshua F. Speed he wrote in 1855:

"Our progress in degeneracy appears to me to be pretty rapid. As a nation we began by declaring that 'all men are created equal, except Negroes.' When the Know-Nothings get control, it will read, 'All men are created equal except Negroes and foreigners and Catholics.' When it comes to this, I shall prefer emigrating to some country where they make no pretense of loving liberty."

Infinitely tender was his word from a White House balcony to a crowd on the White House lawn, "I have not willingly planted a thorn in any man's bosom," or to a military governor, "I shall do nothing through malice; what I deal with is too vast for malice."

He wrote to Congress to read on December 1, 1862:

"In times like the present men would utter nothing for which they would not willingly be responsible through time and eternity."

Like an ancient psalmist he warned Congress:

"Fellow citizens, we cannot escape history. We will be remembered in spite of ourselves. No personal significance or insignificance can spare one or another of us. The fiery trial through which we pass will light us down in honor or dishonor to the latest generation."

Wanting Congress to break and forget past traditions, his words came keen and flashing: "The dogmas of the quiet past are inadequate for the stormy present. We must think anew, we must act anew, we must disenthrall ourselves." They are the sort of words that actuated the mind and will of the men who created and navigated that marvel of the sea, the *Nautilus*, and her voyage from Pearl Harbor and under the North Pole ice cap.

The people of many other countries take Lincoln now for their own. He belongs to them. He stands for decency, honest dealing, plain talk, and funny stories. "Look where he came from—don't he know all us strugglers and wasn't he a kind of tough struggler all his life right up to the finish?" Something like that you can hear in any nearby neighborhood and across the seas.

Millions there are who take him as a personal treasure. He had something they would like to see spread everywhere over the world. Democracy? We can't find words to say exactly what it is, but he had it. In his blood and bones he carried it. In the breath of his speeches and writings it is there. Popular government? Republican institution? Government where the people have the say-so, one way or another telling their elected leaders what they want? He had the idea. It's there in the lights and shadows of his personality, a mystery that can be lived but never fully spoken in words.

Our good friend the poet and playwright Mark Van Doren tells us: "To me, Lincoln seems, in some ways, the most interesting man who ever lived. He was gentle, but his gentleness was combined with a terrific toughness, an iron strength."

How did Lincoln say he would like to be remembered? His beloved friend Rep. Owen Lovejoy of Illinois had died in May of 1864, and friends wrote to Lincoln and he replied that the pressures of duties kept him from joining them in efforts for a marble monument to Lovejoy, the last sentence of his letter saying, "Let him have the marble monument along with the well-assured and more enduring one in the hearts of those who love liberty, unselfishly, for all men."

So perhaps we may say that the well-assured and most enduring memorial to Lincoln is invisibly there, today, tomorrow, and for a long time yet to come in the hearts of lovers of liberty, men and women who understand that wherever there is freedom, there have been those who fought, toiled, and sacrificed for it.

⚭

"He and Jacqueline brought a glow like Canaletto's London to Washington. There was a poet at the inauguration and there was a breath of festival, a pause for beauty, poetry, and song at the White House."

JOHN FITZGERALD KENNEDY
(1917–1963)

by

SEAN QUINLAN

John Fitzgerald Kennedy, the thirty-fifth president of the United States, was assassinated on November 22, 1963, by a gunman in Dallas, Texas. A young and handsome man, with a beautiful wife and two small children, Kennedy was the first Irish American to become president, and he captivated the imagination of the world with his wit, intelligence, and charm.

In this tribute, Irish poet Sean Quinlan writes of the visit Kennedy paid to Ireland not long before he died.

They told us when we were boys how Cuchulain died: "And he went to a pillar-stone which is in the plain, and he put his breast-girdle round it that he might not die seated nor lying down, but that he might die standing up." Remembering now-ancestral precedents, I know that in my people instinctive prompting will ask America to grant us the right to number John Fitzgerald Kennedy among the heroes of our race.

I think of the hearts he warmed in my Irish homeland those few months ago. For heart spoke to heart when he came to us to end the great hunger and to redeem us not a little from our brooding on the past. We believe that we gave him something, too, some richer awareness that he shared with his Jacqueline, who summoned the jackets green across the "bowl of bitter tears" from the plains by the Liffey to a shield's length of earth at Arlington.

We remember the litany of the names of battles as he uncovered the flag of the Irish Brigade in the Irish Parliament.

We remember, distressed for our brother, that stripling's dash in Dublin back from the helicopter to kiss gently the gracious Sinead De Valera. That was on the lawn of what was the Vice-Regal Lodge in the days when a Kennedy sailed downstream from New Ross, going west "to find the sun-tree growing."

We remember the ancient manuscript we gave him with its memories of Dalcassian land. One day may his son, grown strong and handsome, hear the love song from another Irish manuscript of the eighth century:

> *He is a heart,*
> *An acorn from the oakwood.*
> *He is young,*
> *A kiss for him.*

We remember the old priest watching television in the cancer hospital in Dublin and saying, "It's the people. They have taken him to their heart for pride. *Securus judicat orbis terrarum.*"

And when his daughter blossoms, her days of playing with a Connemara pony in the sunlit fields of Virginia over, may she, remembering "O'Donnell Abu" at her father's funeral, see one day the tomb of Nuala O'Donnell, last of Gaelic princesses, at Louvain.

We remember, too, how he and Jacqueline brought a glow like Canaletto's London to Washington. There was a poet at the inauguration and there was a breath of festival, a pause for beauty, poetry, and song at the White House.

He told us there are no permanent enemies. Who knows what impulses went through his death to the great Council which is renewing the gospel in Rome. Who knows how many hearts were purified of hate as they saw new Arimatheans, Negro and white, bear his casket to its shield's length of earth. A great death quickens all life.

Someone has quoted Camus. That is well. When history places an immortal comma to one of its mysterious phrases, all literature and every archetype echo. His exemplary death adds a new dimension to the foundations of love, and so he lays his head toward the yet unborn imagination of poets, and folklore is relighted. There is blood again in the diastole of myth and symbol.

All things ancestral were perfectly fulfilled—the death of the Abel, who had inherited the blessing of his Founding Fathers; the riderless horse beneath his spirit; the little son saluting in grave mimesis all human descent; women with a cross; his death in Christ. John Fitzgerald Kennedy has become the seed that must flower in reconciliation. America now looks inward on unfolding light.

"He told an entire generation there was room for intelligence and idealism in public life, that politics was not just a way to live but a way to live greatly...."

ADLAI EWING STEVENSON
(1900–1965)

by

RICHARD N. GOODWIN
(1931–)

Adlai Stevenson, the urbane and witty former governor of Illinois, ran twice for the presidency on the Democratic ticket against Dwight D. Eisenhower. In 1960, he declined the party's nomination, and John Kennedy ran successfully against Richard Nixon. Kennedy appointed Stevenson U.S. ambassador to the United Nations, an organization Stevenson had helped to found. He remained in that post until he died.

Richard Goodwin was a speechwriter for both Presidents John Kennedy and Lyndon Johnson. Responsible for developing the domestic Great Society program, he is the author of numerous books, including Triumph or Tragedy: Reflections on Vietnam *and* Promises to Keep.

Twice he had come as close as a man could to leadership of the American nation. Yet no one noticed when, for a moment, Adlai Stevenson looked toward the draped statue of Franklin Roosevelt, walked a few hundred yards, grasped the thin steel columns of a sidewalk railing, and died.

Questions of a man's survival, of war, and of human progress had very nearly rested on the qualities of his personal mind and will. The destiny of every man and woman he passed that afternoon was almost placed in his hand. Yet no one cheered or even waved as he turned to stare.

For he had escaped power. And for a politician, power is the tool that etches out one man's figure from among his companions.

The fact is that no man who has not been president can survive analysis of his capacity for the task. Nor can we predict his qualities until they pass through the purification of power and responsibility. We do know Adlai Stevenson had more promise than most. We do know the impressive qualities of mind and spirit his career permitted him to reveal. We also know he was ambitious. For you do not run for president unless your ambitions are greater than those of other men.

Was that ambition tinged with self-doubt? It is for every man except the very dangerous. Did he have the courage of his decision? His own words . . . cloud judgment. But perhaps they only mask the fact that never in his public life did he fail to decide when it was time to decide—except in 1960, when the shameful prospect of leading his party to a third defeat postponed judgment beyond the reach of action.

Where public issues were concerned, he spoke . . . with a clarity of conviction few had courage to match. And on this question the judgment of those who knew him is disfigured by the tortured musings of a man who had never quite learned the trick of hiding his soul, whose confidence had been twisted and battered by defeat and by the indifference and contempt of lesser men, which finally killed him.

. . . He told an entire generation there was room for intelligence and idealism in public life, that politics was not just a way to live but a way to live greatly, that each of us might share in the passions of the age . . . it was not the first time we had seen this quality, nor the last. But how rare it is in those who find their way to power.

Part of it was in his lesson. It was not a new lesson. It runs like a vein of light through the dark history of the race. It suffuses the religion and beliefs of every people. It says that man is more than the sum of his deeds and fears. It ennobles those who look beyond their own interest to great principle. It acclaims, not wealth and power, but the charity of the spirit and the reach of the heart.

That is what he wanted for the American people. And although we may never be equal to it, many loved him for thinking we could.

The rest was the man himself. You didn't need to know him to feel it, although knowing brought confirmation. There was a gentleness, a spaciousness of sensibility, a love that in unseen ways was felt by millions. He could laugh and be cynical. Were he to read these words, he would joke about them, and he would deride this writing with soft self-deprecation. But all the wonderful humor, the urbanity, the captiousness, was, in large part, a mask to protect himself from a world that so easily confused humility with weakness, sentiment with unreality, amplitude of understanding with failure of will. Many who met him were fooled. Millions who never met him knew the truth. . . .

He has often been compared to Hamlet. And those who make the comparison do so as a metaphor of irresolution. *Hamlet* is the story of a man who tries to understand and reach for certainty before he strikes. But he does strike: and for justice loses kingship and life while the election lights on a young and valiant captain.

Our judgment must echo Shakespeare's own when the new king stands beside Hamlet's body, saying:

> *Let four captains*
> *Bear Hamlet like a soldier to the stage,*
> *For he was likely, had he been put on,*
> *To have proved most royally . . .*

☙

"Hubert liked words and language. In speech, he was something like a jazz trumpet player. He would go along rather quietly, with little inspiration, then inspiration would come. What he would then say sometimes surprised even Hubert."

SEN. HUBERT HORATIO HUMPHREY
(1911–1978)

by

EUGENE J. MCCARTHY
(1916–)

Minnesota senator Hubert Horatio Humphrey become vice president under Lyndon Johnson from 1965 to 1969. A Roosevelt New Dealer who believed government had clear obligations to assist the needy, Humphrey was an early champion of the civil rights movement and is credited with the idea that led to the creation of the Peace Corps.

In 1968, fellow Democratic Minnesota senator Eugene J. McCarthy ran for his party's nomination for president, an act of conscience against Lyndon Johnson's Vietnam War policies. Humphrey won the Democratic Party's nomination, but lost narrowly to Republican Richard Nixon. McCarthy is credited with forcing President Johnson to resign.

Humphrey and others joke about his long speeches. He did give long speeches. I recall having gone to a town in far northwestern Minnesota, near the Canadian border, to give a speech. I spoke for about forty-five minutes, rather a long speech I thought, only to have a number of farmers complain to me for not having spoken longer. Hubert, they said, speaks for at least an hour whenever he comes here. It was not that he liked giving long speeches, and not just that he had a lot to say—although this did figure in determining the length of a speech; it was something more basic. Hubert liked words and language. In speech, he was something like a jazz trumpet player. He would go along rather quietly, with little inspiration, then inspiration would come. What he would then say sometimes surprised even Hubert. For example, during the Eisenhower administration in the early fifties, Senator Humphrey was being very restrained. He was being most considerate of the president and the Republicans. The press began to write about the "new Humphrey." And then, in the midst of a structured and contained speech, he took off. "Ike," he said, "is a bird in a gilded cage—kept by the Republicans in the parlor, where he sings sweet songs to all who pass by the window, while back in the kitchen, the Republican blackbirds are eating up the public pie." The speech went on from there to even greater heights, or depths, with references to the creeping, pale, crawling things that grow in the darkness of the Republican basement. Subsequently, I asked him what had happened to the new Humphrey. He said something like "How about that? I just heard the whistle blow."

In a way his gift for language was a political handicap. In American politics, possibly in democratic politics everywhere, one can say rather extreme, even radical things, if one says them in such a way that people don't remember what one said or who said them. In Humphrey's case what was said was remembered, and it was also remembered that he said them.

Sticking with adjectives or an occasional adverb as a mark on one's language is a much safer way for politicians to speak than going with statements like this one from Humphrey's civil rights speech: "The time has arrived for the Democratic Party to get out of the shadow of states' rights and walk forthrightly into the bright sunshine of human rights." Clear language and metaphor in politics is dangerous.

Hubert always seemed to like what he was doing. His affection for his family was well-known. He always spoke glowingly of his father and of the family drugstore back in Huron, South Dakota, to the point that one sensed that he came close to envying his brother Ralph, who ran the store, dispensing pills and encouragement, talking politics and philosophy. Being a druggist, Hubert thought, was good work, and Huron was a good town.

He loved his home on Lake Waverly in Minnesota. Lake Waverly is a very minor lake named after the town of Waverly. One can get a rough measure of a lake and town by the manner of the naming. If the town is named after the lake, it usually indicates that the lake is a good one. If the lake is named after the town, the quality of the lake is usually questionable. Lake Waverly was less than the town, but by a narrow margin. Nonetheless, Humphrey loved the lake, saw the best in it, and talked only of its positive qualities. It held water, it would float a boat, it froze over in the winter, one could skate on it, it had some fish, and it was blue for a few months before it turned green. What more could one expect from a lake. . . .

Two elements of Humphrey's life are consistently noted as tragic by his biographers: his financial troubles and his failure to be elected president.

Humphrey's financial troubles were not very different from those of many other politicians of his age and time. This is especially true of those who came into politics immediately after World War II, without private fortunes, inherited money, or patrons. His problems were common to most people coming into adulthood in the Depression and post-Depression years. They continued through most of his political life and ended only in the years after his 1968 defeat for the presidency. Running for the presidency even in the time of less costly politics of the 1950s and 1960s was expensive. Humphrey had no personal fortune or wealthy relatives to draw from, and only a few people who might be called large or reliable contributors. Much of his support was sparse and marginal, and often demanding.

He summarized his feelings about his fiscal dependency one day when he was showing me his new house on Lake Waverly. This was before he had become vice president. First he told me that the house was a copy of Lyndon Johnson's guesthouse. I accepted this, never having been in Lyndon's guesthouse myself. Then, as we were moving through the kitchen, he paused suddenly and said, "Do you know what my problem is?" I said that I did not. He continued, "Well, I'll tell you. I've got too damn many friends who can get it for me wholesale." He then went around the kitchen, cataloging appliances, fixtures, linoleum, noting what he had paid for each wholesale, and what he would have paid if he had equipped the room on his own at retail. A refrigerator—this is twenty-five or more years ago—that cost him five hundred dollars wholesale was two hundred dollars more than the one he had planned to buy retail. In each case the wholesale price was higher, obviously for better appliances and installations than he would have paid at retail, which he had thought was adequate. He had spent much more than he would have originally spent, and also incurred obligations.

So, too, in politics. Whenever Hubert got straightaway on his own—retail, so to speak—he handled it well and competently: the office of the mayor of Minneapolis, his seat in the U.S. Senate. What he got, or was led to believe he got, "wholesale," both the vice presidency, or at least the nomination, and the Democratic nomination for the presidency in 1968 from Lyndon Johnson, proved to be bad bargains. He gave too much and got too little.

His not being elected to the presidency was just short of tragedy. But this and other disappointing elements of his career were largely offset by his successes and achievements. The energy and time, the spirit that Humphrey gave to speeches, are treated by some of his biographers almost as though Humphrey had been indulging in a bad habit, when in fact it was through these speeches that he may well have made his greatest contribution to the good of the commonwealth.

During the years from 1948 to 1964, when there was little legislative progress in the field of civil rights, he was on the speaking trail, giving hope to victims of discrimination, encouraging their leaders to action, and challenging politicians in power or seeking power to act. He was a favored and willing speaker not just in the cause of civil rights, but of Israel, labor, agriculture, and the poor. His proficiency and readiness as a speaker may have hurt his chances for presidential office. He who preaches the crusade may not be called to lead it, at least not to Jerusalem.

⟨∞⟩

CHAPTER FOUR

REFORMERS
AND RENEGADES

They often lead hard lives, see the insides of a lot more jails than other people, and experience at least as much vilification as they do honor. We don't necessarily want to follow in their footsteps, but we are fascinated by the length of their stride.

Robert Kennedy, who stood on a flatbed truck in Indianapolis on the night of Martin Luther King's assassination and quoted Aeschylus, was himself assassinated two months later. These are dramatic people who lead dramatic lives, not because they are exhibitionists—although some are—but because they tend to position themselves on the front lines, where the demarcation between good and evil is most clearly and dangerously defined.

All of the men and women assembled here were, to a greater or lesser extent, powerful: governors, labor leaders, founders of institutions, church prelates. One was a senator and the brother of a president, the other a president's wife. Their backgrounds vary widely—from lettuce picker to lawyer—but they were a confederacy of democrats who held one deeply democratic value in common: that the many had a responsibility to the one and—its corollary— that one could make a difference.

Some did not seem particularly well-equipped to be world-savers. Jane Addams was born with a misshapen spine and told she would be an invalid. Eleanor Roosevelt was desperately shy, Bishop Pike an alcoholic. Governor Altgeld had a way of antagonizing his enemies so effectively that they could not forget him. But they all had what T. S. Eliot called an "experiencing nature." They were vulnerable to life, could be affected and altered by it, and had—in larger measures than most—compassion for their fellow human beings. It is this last quality—of compassion—that attracts us to these human beings who, despite their handicaps and failings, moved ahead.

Every eulogy, even for an infant, gives us a glimpse of history. But some glimpses are longer than others. In assembling the tributes below, certain parts of American history were exhumed. At the end of the nineteenth century, Chicago was the center of a rough, raw capitalism where the powerful railroad magnate George Pullman waged war against his own workers, which caused a railroad fireman from Terre Haute, Indiana, to change his mind.

Conservative Eugene Debs became Socialist Eugene Debs when he realized that capitalism was, at its base, indifferent to the laborer—an insight that soon-to-be Illinois governor John Altgeld extended to America's penal system.

"The truth," wrote Altgeld in the book that permanently changed the mind of the great trial lawyer Clarence Darrow, "is that the great multitudes annually arrested . . . are the poor, the unfortunate, the young and the neglected. . . . In short, our penal machinery seems to recruit its victims from among those that are fighting an unequal fight in the struggle for existence."

Jane Addams, a colleague and sympathizer of Altgeld, inveighed against the hypocrisy of those who could not understand the women who became prostitutes in order to pay for a pair of shoes they could not otherwise afford. Debs and Addams both campaigned vigorously against World War I, which eventually earned Addams the Nobel Prize for Peace and Debs a ten-year jail sentence. He ran for president from a jail cell in Atlanta, winning nearly a million votes in the 1926 election.

In the second half of the twentieth century, the focus shifted to the rights of black Americans, women, and the poor, including the migrant workers, and the Vietnam War. The issue of ordaining women ministers will not go away. The railroads have been replaced by the powerful information highway interests; corrupt ties between business and politics are still the order of the day. There is a new, nonunionized underclass. New muckrakers, such as Jessica Mitford, are needed to replace the old.

In Emerson's eulogy for Thoreau, he laments his early death. "It seems an injury that he should leave in the midst his broken task, which none else can finish. . . ." In the obvious sense this is true. But whether one agrees with the statement in the larger sense depends upon how one judges the utility of Thoreau's life now that it is done.

Thoreau, who died at forty-five, was known only to a few people. He did not travel widely and his passion for solitude and independence made his personal life more socially circumscribed than most. But Thoreau is proof that every life, once it is over, is a potential hand-me-down. Whether it can be worn again depends upon who wore it first.

"He had no talent for wealth, and knew how to be poor without the least hint of squalor or inelegance. Perhaps he fell into his way of living, without forecasting it much, but approved it with later wisdom."

HENRY DAVID THOREAU
(1817–1862)

by

RALPH WALDO EMERSON
(1803–1882)

Thoreau, the great naturalist, and Emerson, the great idealist, were neighbors in Concord, Massachusetts, and best friends. Three months after Thoreau died, Emerson's long memorial essay, portions of which are extracted here, appeared in the Atlantic Monthly. *Emerson's is the portrait we have today of Thoreau—a brilliant and eccentric individualist whose life centered on the observation of nature and subtracting from life all that was not necessary for the living of it. The eulogy also gives us a sustained glimpse of Emerson, who is here less the great epigrammatist than a human being who has lost the companion of his soul.*

He was a protestant *à l'outrance* and few lives contain so many renunciations. He was bred to no profession; he never married; he lived alone; he never went to church; he never voted; he refused to pay a tax to the state; he ate no flesh, he drank no wine, he never knew the use of tobacco; and, though a naturalist, he used neither trap nor gun. He chose wisely, no doubt, for himself to be the bachelor of thought and nature. He had no talent for wealth, and knew how to be poor without the least hint of squalor or inelegance. Perhaps he fell into his way of living, without forecasting it much, but approved it with later wisdom. "I am often reminded," he wrote in his journal, "that, if I had bestowed on me the wealth of Croesus, my aims must be still the same, and my means essentially the same." He had no temptations to fight against; no appetites, no passions, no taste for elegant trifles. A fine house, dress, the manners and talk of highly cultivated people were all thrown away on him. He much preferred a good Indian, and considered these refinements as impediments to conversation, wishing to meet his companion on the simplest terms. He declined invitations to dinner parties, because there each was in every one's way, and he could not meet the individuals to any purpose. "They make their pride," he said, "in making their dinner cost much; I make my pride in making my dinner cost little." When asked at a table what dish he preferred, he answered "the nearest." He did not like the taste of wine, and never had a vice in his life. He said, "I have a faint recollection of pleasure derived from smoking dried lily stems before I was a man. I had commonly a supply of these. I have never smoked anything more noxious." . . .

Thoreau was sincerity itself, and might fortify the convictions of prophets in the ethical laws, by his holy living. It was an affirmative experience which refused to be set aside. A truth-speaker he, capable of the most deep and strict conversation; a physician to the wounds of any soul; a friend knowing not only the secret of friendship, but almost worshipped by those few persons who resorted to him as their confessor and prophet, and knew the deep value of his mind and great heart. He thought that without religion or devotion of some kind, nothing great was ever accomplished; and he thought that the bigoted sectarian had better bear this in mind.

His virtues of course sometimes ran into extremes. It was easy to trace to the inexorable demand on all for exact truth that austerity which made this willing hermit more solitary even than he wished. Himself of a perfect probity, he required not less of others. He had a disgust at crime, and no worldly success could cover it. He detected paltering as readily in dignified and prosperous persons as in beggars, and with equal scorn. Such dangerous frankness was in his dealing, that his admirers called him "that terrible Thoreau," as if he spoke, when silent, and was still present when he had departed. I think the severity of his ideal interfered to deprive him of a healthy sufficiency of human society. . . .

Had his genius been only contemplative, he had been fitted to his life, but with his energy and practical ability, he seemed born for great enterprise and for command; and I so much regret the loss of his rare powers of action, that I cannot help counting it a fault in him that he had no ambition. Wanting this, instead of engineering for all America, he was the captain of a huckleberry party. Pounding beans is good to the end of pounding empires one of these days, but if, at the end of years, it is still only beans!

But these foibles, real or apparent, were fast vanishing in the incessant growth of a spirit so robust and wise, and which effaced its defects with new triumphs. . . . He loved nature so well, was so happy in her solitude, that he became very jealous of cities, and the sad work which their refinements and artifices made with man and his dwelling. The axe was always destroying his forest—"Thank God," he said, "they cannot cut down the clouds. All kinds of figures are drawn on the blue ground, with this fibrous white paint."

I subjoin a few sentences taken from his unpublished manuscripts not only as records of his thought and feeling, but for their power of description and literary excellence:

"Some circumstantial evidence is very strong, as when you find a trout in the milk.". . .

"The blue bird carries the sky on his back."

"Nothing is so much to be feared as fear. . . ."

"How did these beautiful rainbow tints get into the shell of the fresh-water clam, buried in the mud at the bottom of our dark river?"

"How can we expect a harvest of thought, who have not had a seed-time of character?"

"Only he can be trusted with gifts, who can present a face of bronze to expectations."

"I asked to be melted. You can only ask of the metals that they be tender to the fire that melts them. To nought else can they be tender."

The country knows not yet, or in the least part, how great a son it has lost. It seems an injury that he should leave in the midst his broken task which none else can finish—a kind of indignity to so noble a soul that he should depart out of Nature before yet he has been really shown to his peers for what he is. But he, at least, is content. His soul was made for the noblest society; he had in a short life exhausted the capabilities of this world; wherever there is knowledge, wherever there is virtue, wherever there is beauty, he will find a home.

ᘒᙏᙙᘉ

"[He] was called John Pardon Altgeld by those who would destroy his powers. We who stand today around his bier . . . are glad to adopt this name."

JOHN PETER ALTGELD
(1847–1902)

by

CLARENCE S. DARROW
(1857–1938)

After being elected governor of Illinois in 1896, Altgeld decided to pardon three anarchists who had been imprisoned without sufficient evidence after the Haymarket Square bombing in Chicago. As Altgeld himself predicted to Darrow, "If I conclude to pardon those men . . . I will be a dead man." His political career did not survive.

Clarence Darrow, a brilliant courtroom defense lawyer who never lost a client to the gallows, considered Altgeld his closest friend and the reason why he forsook corporate law and undertook to defend the defenseless in court. When Darrow died, the eulogy for Altgeld was read for him.

In the great flood of human life that is spawned upon the earth, it is not often that a man is born. . . . We who knew him, we who loved him, we who rallied to his many hopeless calls, we who dared to praise him while his heart still beat, can not yet feel that we shall never hear his voice again. . . . Liberty, the relentless goddess, had turned her fateful smile on John P. Altgeld's face when he was but a child, and to this first fond love he was faithful unto death.

Liberty is the most jealous and exacting mistress that can beguile the brain and soul of man. She will have nothing from him who will not give her all. She knows that his pretended love serves but to betray. But when once the fierce heat of her quenchless, lustrous eyes has burned into the victim's heart, he will know no other smile but hers. Liberty will have none but the great devoted souls, and by her glorious visions, her lavish promises, her boundless hopes, her infinitely witching charms, she lures these victims over hard and stony ways, by desolate and dangerous paths, through misery, obloquy, and want to a martyr's cruel death. Today we pay our last sad homage to the most devoted lover, the most abject slave, the fondest, wildest, dreamiest victim that ever gave his life to Liberty's immortal cause.

In the history of the country where he lived, the life and works of our devoted dead will one day shine in words of everlasting light. When the bitter feelings of the hour have passed away, when the mad and poisonous fever of commercialism shall have run its course, when conscience and honor and justice and liberty shall once more ascend the throne from which the shameless, brazen goddess of power and wealth have driven her away; then this man we knew and loved will find his rightful place in the minds and hearts of the cruel, unwilling world he served. No purer patriot ever lived than the friend we lay at rest today. His love of country was not paraded in the public marts, or bartered in the stalls for gold; his patriotism was of that pure ideal mold that placed the love of man above the love of self.

In the days now past, John P. Altgeld, our loving, peerless chief, in scorn and derision was called John Pardon Altgeld by those who would destroy his powers. We who stand today around his bier and mourn the brave and loving friend are glad to adopt this name. If, in the infinite economy of nature, there shall be another hand where crooked paths shall be made straight, where heaven's justice shall review the judgments of the earth—if there shall be a great, wise, humane judge, before whom the sons of man shall come, we can hope for nothing better for ourselves than to pass into that infinite presence as the comrades and friends of John Pardon Altgeld, who opened the prison doors and set the captive free.

Even admirers have seldom understood the real character of this great human man. These were sometimes wont to feel that the fierce bitterness of the world that assailed him fell on deaf ears and an unresponsive soul. They did not know the man, and they did not feel the subtleties of human life. It was not a callous heart that so often led him to brave the most violent and malicious hate; it was not a callous heart, it was a devoted soul. He so loved justice and truth and liberty and righteousness that all the terrors that the earth could hold were less than the condemnation of his own conscience for an act that was cowardly or mean.

John P. Altgeld, like many of the earth's great souls, was a solitary man. Life to him was serious and earnest—an endless tragedy. The earth was a great hospital of sick, wounded, and suffering, and he a devoted surgeon, who had no right to waste one moment's time and whose duty was to cure them all. While he loved his friends, he yet could work without them, he could live without them, he could bid them one by one good-bye, when their courage failed to follow where he led; and he could go alone, out into the silent night, and, looking upward at the changeless stars, could find communion there.

My dear, dear friend, long and well have we known you, devotedly have we followed you, implicitly have we trusted you, fondly have we loved you. Beside your bier we now must say farewell. The heartless call has come, and we must stagger on the best we can alone. In the darkest hours we will look in vain for your loved form, we will listen hopelessly for your devoted, fearless voice. But, though we lay you in the grave and hide you from the sight of man, your brave words will speak for the poor, the oppressed, the captive, and the weak; and your devoted life inspire countless souls to do and dare in the holy cause for which you lived and died.

☙

"He was never the brains of his party. . . . But when his great moment came, a miracle occurred. . . . If anybody told me that tongues of fire danced upon his shoulders as he spoke, I would believe it."

EUGENE VICTOR DEBS
(1855–1926)

by

HEYWOOD CAMPBELL BROUN
(1888–1939)

Indiana-born Eugene Debs, a Socialist labor leader, led the famous Pullman strike that immobilized the railroads in 1894. Several times he ran for president on the Socialist ticket, and in 1918 he was sent to prison after being convicted of trying to obstruct the draft for World War I. When he was sentenced, he delivered a speech that began, "Your Honor, years ago I recognized my kinship with all living beings, and I made up my mind that I was not one bit better than the meanest on earth. I said then, and I say now, that while there is a lower class, I am in it; while there is a criminal element, I am of it; while there is a soul in prison, I am not free."

Heywood Broun was a newspaper columnist and critic, whose strong interest in social justice was a constant theme in his work. The founder of the American Newspaper Guild, he ran, unsuccessfully as a Socialist, for Congress in 1930.

Eugene V. Debs is dead, and everybody says that he was a good man. He was no better and no worse when he served a sentence at Atlanta.

I imagine that now it would be difficult to find many to defend the jailing of Debs. But at the time of the trial he received little support outside the radical ranks.

The problem involved was not simple. I hated the thing they did to Debs even at the time, and I was not then a pacifist. Yet I realize that almost nobody means precisely what he says when he makes the declaration "I'm in favor of free speech." I think I mean it, but it is not difficult for me to imagine situations in which I would be gravely tempted to enforce silence on anyone who seemed to be dangerous to the cause I favored.

Free speech is about as good a cause as the world has ever known. But, like the poor, it is always with us and gets shoved aside in favor of things which seem at some given moment more vital. They never are more vital. Not when you look back at them from a distance. When the necessity of free speech is most important, we shut it off. Everybody favors free speech in the slack moments when no axes are being ground.

It would have been better for America to have lost the war than to lose free speech. I think so, but I imagine it is a minority opinion. However, a majority right now can be drummed up to support the contention that it was wrong to put Debs in prison. That won't keep the country from sending some other Debs to jail in some other day when panic psychology prevails.

You see, there was another aspect to the Debs case, a point of view which really begs the question. It was foolish to send him to jail. His opposition to the war was not effective. A wise dictator, someone like Shaw's Julius Caesar, for instance, would have given Debs better treatment than he got from our democracy.

Eugene Debs was a beloved figure and a tragic one. All his life he led lost causes. He captured the intense loyalty of a small section of our people, but I think that he affected the general thought of his time to a slight degree. Very few recognized him for what he was. It became the habit to speak of him as a man molded after the manner of Lenin or Trotsky. And that was a gross misconception. People were constantly overlooking the fact that Debs was a Hoosier, a native product in every strand of him. He was a sort of Whitcomb Riley turned politically minded.

It does not seem to be that he was a great man. At least he was not a great intellect. But Woodward has argued persuasively that neither was George Washington. In summing up the Father of His Country, this most recent biographer says in effect that all Washington had was character. By any test such as that, Debs was great. Certainly he had character. There was more of goodness in him than bubbled up in any other American of his day. He had some humor, or otherwise a religion might have been built up around him, for he was thoroughly messianic. And it was a strange quirk which set this gentle, sentimental Middle Westerner in the leadership of a party often fierce and militant.

Though not a Christian by any precise standard, Debs was the Christian-Socialist type. That, I'm afraid, is outmoded. He did feel that wrongs could be righted by touching the compassion of the world. Perhaps they can. It has not happened yet. Of cold, logical Marxianism, Debs possessed very little. He was never the brains of his party. I never met him, but I read many of his speeches, and most of them seemed to be second-rate utterances. But when his great moment came, a miracle occurred. Debs made a speech to the judge and jury at Columbus after his conviction, and to me it seemed one of the most beautiful and moving passages in the English language. He was for that one afternoon touched with inspiration. If anybody told me that tongues of fire danced upon his shoulders as he spoke, I would believe it.

Whenever I write anything about churches, ministers write in and say, "But of course you have no faith in miracles and the supernatural." And that is a long way off the target. For better or worse, I can't stand out for a minute against mysticism. I think there are very few ministers ready to believe in as many miracles as I accept, because I cannot help myself. The speech which Debs made is to me a thing miraculous, because in it he displayed a gift for singing prose which was never with him on any other day of his life. And if you ask me, I'll also have to admit that I don't see how Lincoln came to the Gettysburg Address by any pathway which can be charted. . . .

Something was in Debs, seemingly, that did not come out unless you saw him. . . . A hard-bitten Socialist told me once, "Gene Debs is the only one who can get away with the sentimental flummery that's been tied onto Socialism in this country. Pretty nearly always it gives me a swift pain to go around to meetings and have people call me 'comrade.' That's a lot of bunk. But the funny part of it is that when Debs says 'comrade,' it's all right. He means it. That old man with the burning eyes actually believes that there can be such a thing as the brotherhood of man. And that's not the funniest part of it. As long as he's around, I believe it myself." . . .

I've said that it did not seem to me that Debs was a great man in life, but he will come to greatness by and by. There are in him the seeds of symbolism. . . . He carried on an older tradition. It will come to pass. There can be a brotherhood of man.

⌒∞⌒

"Much nonsense has been written about Miss Addams as 'the angel of Hull House' . . . who surrendered comfort, ease, all the amenities of life, to lose herself in the poverty of Chicago's needy, and to share her crusts as she passed from tenement door to tenement door. The very idea requires a complete misconception of Miss Addams's outlook on life."

JANE ADDAMS
(1860–1935)

by

CHRISTIAN CENTURY EDITORIAL

Jane Addams, the daughter of a wealthy Illinois flour mill owner, was born with a severely misshapen spine, and at the age of twenty-seven, she became an invalid. Sent on a grand tour of Europe to restore her health, she became aware of the plight of the poor, whom she had always had a strong but undefined desire to serve. She returned home with a clear vision of what she wanted to do—open a neighborhood center in the tenement section of Chicago where the poor and newly arrived immigrants could receive training and support. The opening of Hull House in 1889 marked the first attempt in the United States to provide in-depth social services. Convinced that war was not only antithetical to reform but only served the interests of munitions makers and political oppressors, she campaigned against World War I and helped found the Women's International League for Peace and Freedom. In 1931 she was the first woman awarded the Nobel Prize for Peace.

Much nonsense has been written about Miss Addams as "the angel of Hull House," and an unfortunate amount of it has been repeated in the days immediately following her death. The mistaken purpose has been to establish a traditional figure of the St. Francis sort—the figure of a woman who surrendered comfort, ease, all the amenities of life, to lose herself in the poverty of Chicago's needy, and to share her crusts as she passed from tenement door to tenement door. The very idea requires a complete misconception of Miss Addams's outlook on life. She had no interest in descending to the poverty level. Her interest was in lifting the level all about her to new heights. For that reason, Hull House under her hand was always a place in which beauty was served, and the emphasis was on the maximum of enjoyment to be extracted from the widest possible spread of human interests and activities.

If Miss Addams visited the tenements of Chicago's slum areas—as she did—it was not as a romantic sharer of crusts. She went there as the duly commissioned inspector of streets and alleys, determined to make the agencies of government operate in such a way as to protect the dwellers in underprivileged areas. Her "theory" of social work, if she had a theory, was always to insist that the fullest possible good be required from the working of existing public and social agencies, to demand new agencies when the old had proved inadequate, and to deal with people on the level of their highest potentialities.

꩜

"It was said of her contemptuously at times that she was a do-gooder, a charge leveled with similar derision against another public figure 1,962 years ago."

ELEANOR ROOSEVELT
(1884–1962)

by

ADLAI EWING STEVENSON
(1900–1965)

*Eleanor Roosevelt was the first First Lady to hold a press conference, write
a newspaper column, and move beyond the confines of the White House to
find out what ordinary Americans were experiencing and thinking. After
her husband Franklin's death she continued to write, speak, and work for
the interests of the poor and minorities and for civil and women's rights.*

*Adlai Stevenson, the Illinois governor who twice ran for president, was a
close friend of Mrs. Roosevelt's. He delivered a eulogy, from which this is
excerpted, at her funeral at the Cathedral of St. John the Divine in New York.*

One week ago this afternoon, in the Rose Garden at Hyde Park,
Eleanor Roosevelt came home for the last time. Her journeys are
over. The remembrance now begins. . . .

She lived seventy-eight years, most of the time in tireless activity
as if she knew that only a frail fragment of the things that cry out to
be done could be done in the lifetime of even the most fortunate. One
has the melancholy sense that when she knew death was at hand,
she was contemplating not what she achieved, but what she had not
quite managed to do. And I know she wanted to go when there was
no more strength to do. . . .

It was said of her contemptuously at times that she was a do-
gooder, a charge leveled with similar derision against another public figure 1,962 years ago.

We who are assembled here are of various religious and political
faiths, and perhaps different conceptions of man's destiny in the universe. It is not an irreverence, I trust, to say that the immortality Mrs.
Roosevelt would have valued most would be found in the deeds and
visions her life inspired in others, and in the proof that they would
be faithful to the spirit of any tribute conducted in her name.

And now one can almost hear Mrs. Roosevelt saying that the
speaker has already talked too long. So we must say farewell. We are
always saying farewell in this world, always standing at the edge of

loss attempting to retrieve some memory, some human meaning, from the silence, something which was precious and is gone.

Often, although we know the absence well enough, we cannot name it or describe it even. What left the world when Lincoln died? Speaker after speaker in those aching days tried to tell his family or his neighbors or his congregation. But no one found the words, not even Whitman. "When Lilacs Last in the Dooryard Bloomed" can break the heart, but not with Lincoln's greatness, only with his loss. What the words could never capture was the man himself. His deeds were known; every schoolchild knew them. But it was not his deeds the country mourned; it was the man—the mastery of life which made the greatness of the man.

It is always so. On that April day when Franklin Roosevelt died, it was not a president we wept for. It was a man. . . .

It is so now. What we have lost in Eleanor Roosevelt is not her life. She lived that out to the full. What we have lost, what we wish to recall for ourselves, to remember, is what she was herself. And who can name it? But she left "a name to shine on the entablatures of truth, forever."

We pray that she has found peace, and a glimpse of sunset. But today we weep for ourselves. We are lonelier; someone has gone from one's own life who was like the certainty of refuge; and someone has gone from the world who was like a certainty of honor.

ᏬᎿᎯᎾ

" 'He lived with the presence of God, with the simplicity of one who takes a walk through the streets of his native town.' "

POPE JOHN XXIII
(1881–1963)

by

LEON JOSEPH CARDINAL SUENENS
(1905–1996)

John XXIII (Angelo Roncalli), the peasant-born successor to the aristo-cratic Pius XII, was already an old man when he was elevated to the papacy

104

in 1958. It was assumed, wrongly, that he would be only an interim pope. Instead, he went on a massive housecleaning of the Church, doubled the size and diversity of the College of Cardinals, and urged the bishops to have greater pastoral involvement in the lives of the poor. His most lasting act, which continues to have reverberations throughout the Church and its communities everywhere, was his convening of a Vatican council (called Vatican II) to reform the Church and examine its relevance to the modern world. In a dramatic departure from tradition, he invited members of Protestant and Eastern Orthodox churches to send representatives. Known for his humor and humility, in a letter he once advised a young boy to be a policeman "because that cannot be improvised. As regards being pope . . . anybody can be pope; the proof of this is that I have become one."

Belgian cardinal Leon Joseph Suenens was a leading progressive voice in the hierarchy. This tribute is excerpted from a homily delivered in memory of John XXIII at the opening of the second session of Vatican II.

John XXIII was a man surprisingly natural and at the same time supernatural. Nature and grace produced in him a living unity, filled with charm and surprises.

Everything about him sprang from a single source. In a completely natural way he was supernatural. He was natural with such supernatural spirit that no one detected a distinction between the two.

Filling his lungs, as it were, he breathed the faith just as he breathed physical and moral health.

"He lived with the presence of God," one wrote, "with the simplicity of one who takes a walk through the streets of his native town."

He lived with both feet on the ground, and with vibrant sympathy he was interested in the everyday concerns of people. He knew how to stop at the side of a road to talk with ordinary people, to listen to a child, to console an invalid. He was concerned with the construction of an airport and he prayed for the astronauts.

But he also lived completely in the world of the supernatural, in the familiar company of the angels and the saints . . . in him there was no dualism. John's spontaneous, forthright, ever-alert goodness was like a ray of sunshine which dispels fog, which melts the ice, which filters its way through, as of a right, without even being noticed. Such a ray of sunshine creates optimism along its path, spreads happiness with its unexpected appearance, and makes light of all obstacles.

It is thus that John XXIII appeared to the world, not as the sun of the tropics, which blinds one with the intensity of its brilliance, but the humble, familiar, everyday sun, which is simply there in its place, always true to itself even when veiled by cloud—a sun which one hardly notices, so certain of its presence.

John XXIII was not so naive as to believe that goodness will solve all problems, but he knew that it would open hearts to dialogue, to understanding, and to mutual respect. He had confidence in the power of the charity of Christ burning in a human heart.

He knew also that truth penetrates more easily into the hearts of men when it appears to them as a revelation of love. . . . But there is a secret to loving others to this extent: a man must forget himself. Charity, it has been said, is "pure concentration on the existence of others."

To be completely dedicated to others, one must banish all self-interest. Forgetfulness of oneself conditions the gift of oneself.

John XXIII leaves us the memory of someone who in his own eyes did not exist. He put himself beyond all earthly vanity: self-denial was a constant value for his soul. This fundamental humility allowed him to speak of himself with detachment and with humor, as if he were speaking of somebody else.

Let us listen to him as he introduces himself to his newly acquired subjects, the faithful of the patriarchate of Venice:

"I wish," he told them, "to speak to you with the utmost frankness. You have waited impatiently for me; people have told you about me and written you accounts that far surpass my merits. I introduce myself as I really am. Like ever other person who lives here on earth I come from a definite family and place. Thank God, I enjoy bodily health and a little good sense, which allows me to see matters quickly and clearly. . . .

"I come of humble stock. I was raised in the kind of poverty which is confining but beneficial, which demands little, but which guarantees the development of the noblest and greatest virtues and which prepares one for the steep ascent of the mountain of life. Providence drew me out of my native village and made me traverse the roads of the world in the East and in the West. The same Providence made me embrace men who were different both by religion and by ideology."

The same authentic accents are heard again a few weeks before his death on the occasion of the bestowal of the Balzan Peace Prize: "The humble pope who speaks to you," he said, "is fully conscious of being personally a very small thing in the sight of God."

No one was surprised to read in his personal diary reflections such as the following:

"This year's celebrations for my priestly jubilee have come to an end. . . . What an embarrassment for me! Countless priests already dead or still living after twenty-five years of priesthood have accomplished wonders. . . . And I, what have I done? My Jesus mercy! But while I humble myself for the little or nothing that I have achieved up to now, I raise my eyes toward the fuure. There still remains light in front of me; there still remains the hope of doing some good. Therefore, I take up again my staff, which from now on will be the staff of old age, and I go forward to meet whatever the Lord wishes for me. (Sofia, October 30, 1929) . . .

"The Vicar of Christ? Ah! I am not worthy of this title, I, the poor son of Baptist and Mary Ann Roncalli, two good Christians, to be sure, but so modest and so humble." (August 15, 1961)

And this is why they wept for him as children for their father, pressing around him to receive his blessing.

And the poor wept for him; they knew he was one of them and that he was dying poor like them, thanking God for the poverty that for him had been such a grace.

And the prisoners wept for him; he had visited them and encouraged them with his presence. Who does not remember that visit to the prison of Rome? Among the prisoners were two murderers. After having heard the Holy Father, one of them approached and said, "These words of hope that you have just spoken, do they also apply to me, such a great sinner?" The pope's only answer was to open his arms and clasp him to his heart. . . .

He will be for history the pope of welcome and hope. This is the reason his gentle and holy memory will remain in benediction in the centuries to come. At his departure, he left men closer to God, and the world a better place for men to live.

⚬⚬⚬⚬

"Men find God by discovering each other. There is no other way. Yet, he was careful to distinguish between God and man—the difference between them, he said, is the difference between finitude and infinity."

MARTIN BUBER
(1878–1965)

by

NEW YORK TIMES EDITORIAL

Philosopher Martin Buber was born in Vienna and educated in Germany. Fleeing the Nazis in 1938, he lived until his death in Israel, where he taught at the Hebrew University in Jerusalem. Buber was greatly influenced by the eighteenth-century Hasidim movement, which encouraged joyful worship through dance and singing and stressed the mercy of God, who was more pleased with a pure heart than an educated mind. These ideas, particularly as conveyed by Buber in his writings, including his most influential book, I and Thou, *have had a significant impact upon modern Jewish and Christian thought. Buber was a Zionist, but he was an active supporter of greater Arab-Israeli understanding. At his funeral a delegation of Arab students laid a wreath of flowers upon his tomb.*

Martin Buber was the foremost Jewish religious thinker of our time and one of the world's most influential philosophers. He was a theological bridge-builder long before ecumenism achieved its present popularity. He served as a kind of patron saint for such towering Christian intellectuals as Paul Tillich, Reinhold Niebuhr, Jacques Maritain, and Gabriel Marcel. For many in the Jewish community, the bearded old man in Jerusalem was the quintessential scholar, the teacher and exponent of a tradition that reaches back to the biblical ages.

If today the ancient cold war between the faiths is being replaced by dialogue and friendly personal confrontation, much of the credit must be given to Martin Buber. It was he, with his doctrine of "I-Thou" personalism, who showed the way. For Buber, the God of Abraham was no icy abstraction or loveless Prime Mover but a Person, infinitely lovable and loving.

Love, he said again and again, is the key to the mystery of existence and points the way to divinity. "Every particular Thou is a glimpse through to the eternal Thou." Men find God by discovering each other. There is no other way. Yet, he was careful to distinguish between God and man—the difference between them, he said, is the difference between finitude and infinity.

Sometimes, Buber taught, men find God even when they believe they are escaping from Him or denying Him. "When he who abhors the name and believes himself to be godless, gives his whole being to addressing the Thou of his life, as a Thou that cannot be limited by another, he addresses God."

Because Martin Buber lived, there is more love in the world than there would have been without him. And for him that was the reason above all others for the gift of life.

ତ୍ରୟୋ

"When he started talking to them, you could hardly hear what he said, it was so soft, and his eyes changed from those of a presidential candidate to something else. And he kept talking and stroking their fingers with his, and then one little boy said, 'Hey, you're on television, aren't you?' and Kennedy nodded and said yes, he was."

ROBERT F. KENNEDY
(1926–1968)

by

DAVID MURRAY
(1925–)

In 1968, Robert Kennedy was campaigning in Indiana for the presidency when a reporter for the Chicago Sun-Times *wrote the following column that became a posthumous tribute when Kennedy was assassinated the following month in Los Angeles.*

At first there was no joy at all on the faces of the dozen or so five-year-olds in the tiny, dirty playground at the day nursery.

They stared with wide, solemn eyes through the old Cyclone

fence topped with drooping barbed wire at Robert F. Kennedy, who had walked a hundred feet down the street Tuesday to see them as they stood in their cage.

Tentatively, they poked their fingers at him through the fence, and he pushed his fingers back at them and there was a smile or two, on both sides. But the children still didn't quite know what to make of this man who was surrounded by all the other people with the cameras and microphones and tape recorders and notebooks.

When he started talking to them, you could hardly hear what he said, it was so soft, and his eyes changed from those of a presidential candidate to something else. And he kept talking and stroking their fingers with his, and then one little boy said, "Hey, you're on television, aren't you?" and Kennedy nodded and said yes, he was.

The place was the Day Nursery Association of Indianapolis, and it lies in a grubby section only a few steps away from James Whitcomb Riley's house. Kennedy had gone to the Riley house as part of his campaign for the presidency.

Outside the Riley house, there had been a bunch of screaming teenage girls from a nearby parochial school. When reporters asked some of them why Kennedy turned them on, they couldn't explain except to say he was "so neat," or that he was "just great."

Kennedy turned away from his blue-uniformed idolaters, then walked in the bright sunlight to the day nursery and talked for a minute with the women who run it. They said it was mostly for children of broken homes and that the ones here were all five-year-olds from different parts of the city.

So Kennedy stopped with the children for a minute, and after they got to know him a bit better, the man who wants to be president pushed open a gate and went inside and hunkered down and talked to them some more. The television cameras and microphones were there, but that didn't make any difference to the children.

Some of them continued to slide down the sliding board or climb on the jungle gym, but the others clustered around Kennedy, not saying much, some of them, but just trying to hold on to him.

Two little girls came up and put their heads against his waist and he put his hands on their heads. And suddenly it was hard to watch, because he had become in that moment the father they did not know or the elder brother who couldn't talk to them or, more important, listen to them, because most elder brothers and most fathers don't know how to listen to five-year-olds without thinking of other things.

He had gone to the Riley house because when you are fighting a campaign in Indiana, you have to pay homage to the Hoosier Keats. Before that, there had been a day of talking to union officials and a big walking tour, getting mobbed in this city's Monument Circle. And after that there was going to be another visit to a factory and a reception and all the usual paraphernalia of a big, snazzy, first-cabin presidential primary campaign.

But this hiatus, in front of a gray, American Gothic house with the paint peeling off it, was something else. Gone, for just a moment, was the rhetoric and the playing with audiences and the motorcades and the adulation and the criticism.

The word that came on strongest, as he sat and listened to the children and made a quiet remark now and then, was the word *compassion*. This is because—and anyone who has ever dealt with five-year-olds knows this—you can fool a lot of people in a campaign, and you can create phony issues if you want to, and you can build an image with a lot of sharpsters around you with their computers and their press releases. But lonely little children don't come up and put their heads on your lap unless you mean it.

⚬≈≈≈⚬

"After Bishop Pike was censured in 1966 by the Episcopal House of Bishops, he received a letter from an elderly woman, who wrote: 'This is about the way I prayed for you—"Now look, Jesus and Moses, you have to help Bishop Pike. The wolves are after him."'"

BISHOP JAMES ALBERT PIKE

(1913–1969)

by

WILLIAM STRINGFELLOW

(1908–1976)

Bishop James Pike was a controversial Episcopal clergyman, a former lawyer who rose rapidly within the Church to become bishop of Grace

Cathedral in San Francisco and the Cathedral of St. John the Divine in New York. A critic of McCarthyism and an outspoken advocate of civil rights and Planned Parenthood, Pike was candid about his theological doubts and the conviction that women should be allowed to be priests. His death was as dramatic as his life. While driving across the Judean desert with his wife, their car ran out of gas and his wife, alone, went for help. He was found dead upon her return several days later.

William Stringfellow, a human rights lawyer, Episcopal lay theologian, and author, was involved in the anti–Vietnam War movement, church reform, and legal advocacy for the poor.

Three days before James Pike was found dead in Judea, the vicar of St. Clement's told me that this congregation desired the service this morning to be a thanksgiving for the life and for the witness of Bishop Pike. The intention, he said, was that this Eucharist happen whatever the outcome of the search in the desert: whether by this morning Pike remained missing or, if discovered, he be dead or living.

The subsequent events make this a requiem: Jim Pike is buried in the ground and we pray for his repose. Yet the original intent for this service was different from a dirge, and that intent—which is the only thing which persuaded me to participate—remains sound. Whatever the particulars of his fate, there is good reason in the church today, as there was ten years ago and as there was a year ago and, for that matter, as there will be ten years from now, to pause in gratitude to God for Bishop Pike. . . .

None of us here can overlook the fact of Bishop Pike's death, or the way he died or where he died.

We can say nothing of his private death save to affirm God's mercy, though there are many who knew him or who knew of him who have spent a week titillating themselves with gruesome guesses and cruel speculation about that.

Yet beyond his solitary crisis, there has been the public death of Bishop Pike, which the whole world, more or less, has beheld and by which, it cannot be gainsaid, many have been fearfully edified. Discontent with the fables and fairy tales about Jesus which churchly tradition has hallowed, and unsatisfied, if nonetheless respectful, about mere scholarship, Pike wanted to know the truth about Jesus—or, at the least, he had to have all of the truth that he could know of Jesus. He had, in the last years, become excited by glimpses of the splendid humanity of Jesus, and he had to see more. How unusual—how threatening to some of his peers; how efficacious for other folk to have a bishop with such a passion for Jesus that he forsook ecclesiology! . . .

One of the incidental indignities which the dead must suffer is the condescension of their survivors. . . . In this condescending vein, many who survive Bishop Pike remark how marred by tragedy his life was. One marriage ended in annulment, another in divorce, a third was criticized ecclesiastically as a scandal. A son committed suicide. A close working associate died in a bizarre incident. He was an alcoholic and even joined AA. You know as well as I do how this conversation goes.

I refute none of these facts, but I deny that Jim Pike's life was a chronicle of tragedy. I see it as triumphant.

There is, as the dead know, no immortality, but there is resurrection. These are different things, though they be carelessly confused, especially in church. . . . The credibility of the resurrection as an ultimate promise for humanity rests upon specific triumphs over the power of death which occur in common life.

Death, in many guises, pursued Bishop Pike relentlessly, and in many instances did Pike live in the resurrection, transcending death's power. The most obvious example is Pike's witness against racism, symbolized early in his public career by his refusal of the Sewanee honorary doctorate in "white divinity." Racism is a work of death in this world, and the effectual undoing of racism is an instance of resurrection.

This is how I think of Bishop Pike's concern in situations like his son's suicide, which others call tragedies. I see them as among death's assaults, not to be borne as devastation or defeat, but to be transcended in the power of the resurrection to which human beings have access now. . . .

After Bishop Pike was censured in 1966 by the Episcopal House of Bishops, he received a letter from an elderly woman, who wrote: "This is about the way I prayed for you—'Now look, Jesus and Moses, you have to help Bishop Pike. The wolves are after him.' " . . .

The wolves seemed always to be after him. . . . Most poignant, perhaps, was the lust of that pursuit of him within the church. The plain truth is that some bishops, and some others of the church, were determined to kill Bishop Pike. He, somehow, in his existence incarnated so much that threatened and frightened them as men that they conspired to murder him. I am speaking now theologically, their malice amounted to murder, as the Sermon on the Mount puts it—but I am equally speaking empirically—murder took possession of them. Some bishops, not all bishops; there were others: there were a few whose side was the same as Pike's on the issues, personalities aside; there were a lot of temporizers in between. What do you say of men who temporize when life is at stake? The Book of Common Prayer counts temporizers as accomplices. So does St. Paul. So did Bishop Daniel Corrigan, during the censure debate, when he described what he saw happening:

"I speak here against this statement, not as a bishop, not even as a Christian, just as—just as a man. The substance I would not wish to argue. The whole process by which a man is publicly tried, excoriated really, and condemned, condemned in some deep sense to death by God!—heresy is nothing . . . to what we say about this man!"

Only Bishop Pike's death will satisfy them. Now he is dead but they are confounded and in shame because their malice is not what killed him. He died in the wilderness in Judea, but the wolves had not hurt him. . . .

The days when Bishop Pike was missing in the Holy Land coincided with a general convention of the Episcopal Church held at Notre Dame University. A newspaperman tells me that he noted no prayer was said at the convention when the report of Pike being lost first reached South Bend. The journalist asked a dignitary—"Can't you guys even pray for Pike?" "We haven't had a chance to consult about it," was the reply. At the next session, my informant reports, there was a prayer—a "composite" prayer, he called it, mentioning in the same breath Bishop Pike and Ho Chi Minh. As the reporter concluded, "They prayed for all their enemies, all together." . . .

In the Book of Common Prayer, the heading for the Fortieth Psalm is *"Expectans expectavi,"* which is translated, variously, "I wanted and waited," "I waited patiently," "I waited eagerly." I take that as a rubric for these remarks.

I commend to you James Albert Pike: he waited and waited patiently, eagerly, for the Lord. The Lord did not tarry long.

৩৩৩৩

"She was able to tell a bawdy joke, much to the dismay of some of those who happened to encounter this side of Dorothy. She was also, at times, surprisingly shy, almost girlish, long after she had acquired gray hair. Then again she could be as fierce and determined as one of those Russian women who repaired the streets and kept going to church even in the years of Stalin."

DOROTHY DAY
(1897–1980)

by

Jim Forest
(1941–)

Dorothy Day was an unusual combination of a conservative Catholic wedded to radical ideas—a loyal member of a church that she frequently called, with sarcasm, "the cross upon which Christ was crucified." An antiwar activist who had a profound effect upon Thomas Merton and anti–Vietnam War protesters Fathers Daniel and Philip Berrigan, Day founded the Catholic Worker *newspaper (a penny a copy) in 1933. She built a network of "houses of hospitality" to feed the poor, shelter the homeless, and promote the cause of social justice. She is credited with reestablishing the value of nonviolent social action—as practiced by Gandhi and others—within the Catholic Church.*

In this excerpt from his biography of Day, Love Is the Measure, *Jim Forest recounts his impressions of her.*

I first met Dorothy a few days before Christmas in 1960. . . . I went to the Catholic Worker's rural outpost on the southern tip of Staten Island. In the large, faded dining room of an old farmhouse, I found half a dozen people gathered around a pot of tea and a pile of mail at one end of a large table. Dorothy Day was reading letters aloud.

What a handsome woman! Her face was long, with high, prominent cheekbones underlining large, quick eyes that could be teasing one moment and laughing the next. Her hair was braided and circled the top of her head like a garland of silver flowers. The suit she wore was plain and well-tailored, good quality and yet, almost certainly, from the Catholic Worker clothing room on Spring Street, a distribution center for discarded garments open daily, except Sundays, to street people.

The only letter I still recall from that day's reading was one from Thomas Merton, the famous monk whose autobiography, *The Seven Storey Mountain*, had held many people in its grip, including me. Nineteen years earlier, Merton had withdrawn from "the world" to a Trappist monastery with a slam of the door that eventually was heard around the world. I had assumed he wrote to no one outside his family. Yet here he was in correspondence with someone who was not only in the thick of the world, but one of its more controversial figures.

In his letter, Merton told Dorothy that he was deeply touched by her witness for peace, which had several times resulted in arrest and imprisonment. "You are right in going along the lines of *satyagrapha* [Gandhi's term for nonviolent action; literally, "the power of truth"]. I see no other way. . . . Nowadays it is no longer a question of who is right but who is at least not criminal. . . . It has never been more true than now that the world is lost in its own falsity and cannot see true values. . . . God bless you." This was one of Merton's first letters to Dorothy. Before long he was publishing in the *Catholic Worker,* and getting into trouble with his religious order for doing so.

Merton was one of countless people drawn to Dorothy and influenced by her. She had a great gift for making those who met her, even if only through letters or her published writings, look at themselves in a new light and question their ideas, allegiances, and choices.

I met her when I was nineteen and she was sixty-three. Half a year later, after being discharged from the Navy as a conscientious objector, I joined the Catholic Worker staff in New York. . . .

Being part of the Catholic Worker household in New York City was a mixed blessing. At that time, probably, it was one of the less happy communities in the Catholic Worker movement. In fact we were hardly a community at all. But there was one great blessing about being in that stressful setting; it was getting to know Dorothy, and to be known by her.

As I had discovered that first day at the farm on Staten Island, she was a wonderful and tireless storyteller. She didn't just read the letters she received to herself, but read them aloud to those she worked with, oftentimes telling about the people who sent them.

I recall her reading a letter from the Gauchat family, founders of a

Catholic Worker community in Ohio. Dorothy told us how the Gauchats had taken in a six-month-old child who was expected to die at any time. The child was deaf and blind, with a fluid-filled lump on his head larger than a baseball. "Bill Gauchat made the sign of the cross over that child's face," Dorothy said, "and he saw those dull eyes followed the motion of his hand. The child *could* see! Within a year David—that was his name—was well enough to be taken home by his real parents. His life was saved by the love in the Gauchat home."

Hearing stories like these day after day, we were learning something about life that you don't get in any classroom or even in many churches. At the core of each story there were always just a few people, maybe just one person, for whom following Christ was the most important thing in the world. What astonishing things came from that kind of discipleship!

Another story I recall her telling had to do with a prostitute named Mary Ann with whom Dorothy was briefly in prison in Chicago in the early 1920s. Dorothy hadn't planned to be arrested and was terrified of the guards. "You must hold your head high," Mary Ann told her, "and give them no clue that you're afraid of them or ready to beg for anything, any favors whatsoever. But you must see them for what they are—never forget that they're in jail, too."

. . . In this period of acute nervousness about sexual roles, there is some hesitancy to say anyone is or ever was feminine, but Dorothy certainly was that. As she was usually ill at ease when anyone pointed a camera at her, her femininity rarely shows in her photos. Hers was a hearty femininity, such as you find in Chaucer's Wife of Bath. Like the Wife of Bath, she could be, indeed often was, shocking in her plain-speaking way. She was able to tell a bawdy joke, much to the dismay of some of those who happened to encounter this side of Dorothy. She was also, at times, surprisingly shy, almost girlish, long after she had acquired gray hair. Then again she could be as fierce and determined as one of those Russian women who repaired the streets and kept going to church even in the years of Stalin.

Her direct, at times shocking, way of getting to the heart of things was much in evidence one night when she was speaking to a Catholic student group at New York University, not far from Washington Square Park. The Cold War was at its most frozen in that packed and smoky room. Clearly some of those present considered

Dorothy an acolyte for the Kremlin. One of them demanded to know what Dorothy would do if the Russians invaded the United States. Would she not admit that in this extreme, at least, killing was justified, even a duty? "We are taught by Our Lord to love our enemies," Dorothy responded without batting an eye. "I hope I could open my heart to them with love, the same as anyone else. We are all children of the same Father." There was a brief but profound quiet in the room before Dorothy went on to speak about nonviolent resistance and efforts to convert opponents.

☙

"For most of his life, Cesar Estrada Chavez chose to live penniless and without property. . . . Five feet six, and a sufferer from recurrent back pain, [he] seemed an unlikely David to go up against the $4 billion Goliath of California agribusiness."

CESAR ESTRADA CHAVEZ
(1927–1993)

by

PETER MATTHIESSEN
(1927–)

Cesar Chavez, an American-born migrant worker, organized the first successful boycott against table-grape growers in California in 1962. He went on to found the United Farm Workers, widening his efforts to secure living wages and better benefits for workers in lettuce and citrus fields in California and Florida. Chavez's successes led to clashes with the International Brotherhood of Teamsters over jurisdiction and organization of field-workers, and while the power of the UFW was diminished, Chavez's commitment to the cause of the migrant workers never dimmed.

Peter Matthiessen, a writer and friend of Chavez's, wrote this appreciation for the New Yorker *magazine when Chavez died.*

Cesar Chavez was on union business when his life ended quietly in his sleep, at 10:30 or 11 P.M. on April 22, in the small border town of San Luis, Arizona, thirty-five miles and sixty-six years distant from

118

the childhood farm in the Gila River Valley which his parents lost at the end of the Depression. On April 29, in ninety-degree heat, an estimated thirty-five thousand people, in a line three miles long, formed a funeral procession from Memorial Park in Delano, California, to the burial Mass, at the United Farm Workers field office north of town.

With the former scourge of California safely in his coffin, state flags were lowered to half-mast by order of the governor, and messages poured forth from the heads of church and state, including the Pope and the President of the United States . . . "We have lost perhaps the greatest Californian of the twentieth century," the president of the California State Senate said, in public demotion of Cesar Chavez's sworn enemies Nixon and Reagan.

For most of his life, Cesar Estrada Chavez chose to live penniless and without property, devoting everything he had, including his frail health, to the UFW, the first effective farmworkers' union ever created in the United States. "Without a union, the people are always cheated, and they are so innocent," Chavez told me when we first met, in July 1968, in Delano, where he lived with his wife, Helen, and a growing family. Chavez, five feet six, and a sufferer from recurrent back pain, seemed an unlikely David to go up against the $4 billion Goliath of California agribusiness. Not until January 1963, after many hard years of door-to-door organizing of uneducated and intimidated migrant workers, had his new independent union felt strong enough to attempt a nationwide boycott of table grapes, publicized by the first of many prolonged religious fasts. On July 29, 1970, the main Delano growers all but ended the boycott by signing union contracts with the UFW.

This historic victory was no sooner won when the UFW was challenged by the Teamsters Union, which rushed in to sign up lettuce workers in the Salinas Valley. Chavez was angered by the perfidy of the growers, who were bent on conspiring with the Teamsters to steal from behind the UFW's back what it had won in a fair, hard fight. He also resented the hostility of almost all municipal and state officials, from the ubiquitous police to Governor Reagan, which exposed his farmworkers to an unrestrained climate of violence and took the lives of five UFW members in the course of strikes and organizing campaigns. For Chavez, that hostility led to a resurfacing of emotional injuries he had suffered as a child, all the way back to the bank foreclosure on the small family farm and the brutal racism in such signs as "No Dogs or Mexicans Allowed." "Getting rejected hurts very deep," he told me once, recalling a time in Indio, California, during his migrant days when he followed his father into a decrepit diner to buy morning coffee, only to be contemptuously ordered out. To this day, he said, he could remember the expression on his father's face, and though it has been twenty years or more since Cesar told me that story, I can still recall his expression when he told it—that seraphic Indian face with the dark, sad, soft eyes and delighted smile turned crude and ugly.

In recent years, beset by the unremitting prejudice of California's Republican administrations, which were elected with the strong support of agribusiness, the embittered Chavez embarked upon a table-grape and lettuce boycott against nonunion growers, protesting the use of dangerous pesticides, which threaten the public. The new boycott never took hold. What was lacking seemed to be the fervor of those exhilarating marches under union flags, the facts, damaging, and the chanting—"*Viva la huelga!*"— that put the fear of God in the rich farm owners of California. These brilliant tactics remained tied in the public perception to La Causa, a labor and civil-rights movement with religious overtones which rose to prominence in the feverish tumult of the sixties; as a mature AFL-CIO union, the UFW lost much of its symbolic power. Membership has now declined to about one-fifth of its peak of a hundred thousand.

With the funeral march over, the highway empty, and all the banners put away, Cesar Chavez's friends and perhaps his foes are wondering what will become of the UFW. A well-trained new leadership (his son-in-law has been named to succeed him, and four of his eight children work for the union) may bring fresh energy and insight. But what the union will miss is Chavez's spiritual fire. A man so unswayed by money, a man who (despite many death threats) refused to let his bodyguards go armed, and who offered his entire life to the service of others, was not to be judged by the same standards of some self-serving labor leader or politician. Self-sacrifice lay at the very heart of the devotion he inspired and gave dignity and hope not only to the farmworkers but to every one of the Chicano people, who saw for themselves what one brave man, indifferent to his own health and welfare, could accomplish.

Anger was a part of Chavez, but so was a transparent love of humankind. The gentle mystic that his disciples wished to see inhabited the same small body as the relentless labor leader who concerned himself with the most minute operation of his union. Astonishingly—this seems to me his genius—the two Cesars were so complementary that, without either, La Causa could not have survived.

During the vigil at the open casket on the day before the funeral, an old man lifted a child up to show him the small, gray-haired man who lay inside. "I'm going to tell you about this man someday," he said.

⁂

"Decca Mitford was not fearless; she was brave. Much as she ridiculed those English public-school virtues, like spunk and pluck, she was herself guilty of one of them: she was gallant.... It sometimes takes courage to see injustice and then stand up and denounce it. Gallantry requires doing so without ever becoming bitter...."

JESSICA MITFORD
(1918–1996)

by

MOLLY IVINS
(1944–)

British-born aristocrat and author Jessica Mitford exemplified the best in the muckraking tradition, writing books that exposed the American funeral industry, medical establishment, and prison system to public scrutiny. In addition, she published magazine articles that targeted everything from overpriced spas and restaurants to the Famous Writers School in Connecticut, which did not survive her exposé. She was quoted as saying, "You may not be able to change the world, but at least you can embarrass the guilty." The year before she died, she decided to fulfill an old dream of becoming a torch singer and formed a rock band called Decca and the Dectones, which produced a rap music CD.

Molly Ivins is the syndicated Texas columnist and author of Molly Ivins Can't Say That, Can She?

Jessica Mitford Romilly Treuhaft, known as Decca, who died last month, was among the handful of great muckraking journalists of our time. Peter Sussman of the Society of Professional Journalists puts her in a class with Upton Sinclair, Rachel Carson, and Ralph Nader. "Only funny."

Always funny . . . Toward the end of her life she was working on an update of *The American Way of Death,* for which reason she arrived in Houston last summer to visit the American Funeral Museum, of which it must be said, it's there. In fact, it's a multimedia museum. We toddled through the exhibits until we reached Embalming, where we perched on a bench to view a short documentary. Pyramids appeared on-screen and the narrator announced portentously, "The art of embalming was first discovered by the ancient Egyptians."

Decca said quietly, "Now *there* was a culture where the funeral directors got *completely* out of control." . . .

The newsmagazines invariably used to start profiles of Decca, "Born the daughter of an eccentric British peer . . . ," as though she had done nothing else in her life. But it was a lulu of a life. To take it at a gallop, her eldest sister was the splendid comic novelist Nancy Mitford; her sister Diana married Sir Oswald Mosley, a leading British Fascist, and spent World War II in prison; her sister Unity fell in love with Hitler and shot herself at the outbreak of the war; her brother, Tom, was killed in Burma; her sister Pamela raised horses; and her sister Debo became the duchess of Devonshire.

Decca Mitford sensibly decided to get out of the nest at an early age; she eloped with her cousin Esmond Romilly when she was nineteen and went off to fight for the Communists in the Spanish Civil War. Since both were scions of great families, a British destroyer was dispatched to bring them back. They married in France, but not until later: *quel scandale.*

The Romillys immigrated to America in 1939, tended bar, sold stockings, what have you. All fodder for great stories later told by Decca. Romilly enlisted in the Royal Canadian Air Force ("I'll probably find myself being commanded by one of your ghastly relations," he observed) and was killed in action in 1941, leaving Decca with their baby daughter, Dinky. . . .

In 1943, Decca married Robert Treuhaft, a calm, witty, radical, Harvard-trained lawyer. They were married for fifty-three years and for fifty-three years she was in love with him. . . . Her dear friend Maya Angelou recalled, "My God, they had been married for two hundred years and every time she heard his car pull up in the driveway she'd say, 'Bob's here; it's Bob.' "

Decca once said she felt she had never really known her sister Nancy because she lived within an "armor of drollery." Decca herself would make almost anything into a joke: when summoned to appear before the House Un-American Activities Committee in San Francisco, she took the per diem expense check she got from the government and donated it to the Communist Party. She and her husband remained Party members in Oakland, California, until 1958. . . .

She had long since realized that fund-raisers and parties were part of "the stuggle." Some humorless party apparatchik had entrusted her with organizing a chicken dinner for the faithful and was giving her instructions. When it came to procuring the main course, he wanted to direct Decca to politically correct poultry farmers. He looked left and looked right, apparently suspicious of FBI wiretaps. "There are certain comrades in—" He broke off. He scribbled a note and pushed it across his desk. "Petaluma," it read. After further instruction, Decca said she had just one question. "Do you think the chickens should be—" she began. She looked left, looked right, checking for bugs, and scribbled, "Broiled or fried?"

A not-so-funny Decca story. At the height of the McCarthy era, that great liberal Hubert H. Humphrey proposed that membership in the Communist Party be made a crime. Decca was trying to explain to Dinky, then eight, that all of them might be sent away to detention camp. "Camp?!" cried Dinky in delight, envisioning tennis and canoeing. Decca told it as a good story. Armored with drollery.

Decca Mitford was not fearless: she was brave. Much as she ridiculed those English public-school virtues, like spunk and pluck, she was herself guilty of one of them: she was gallant. Her gallantry was beyond simple courage. It sometimes takes courage to see injustice and then stand up and denounce it. Gallantry requires doing so without ever becoming bitter; gallantry requires humor and honor. . . .

She was not much given to regrets—I don't think anyone ever heard her whine about anything, even though she lost two children and her first love—but she remained deeply aggrieved that she had never been allowed to have a formal education. Her mother, Lady

Redesdale, reactionary even for her day, believed girls did not need school. . . .

One of the best stories is about the time Decca was invited to become a distinguished professor at San Jose State University. She was deeply thrilled, but the position required her to take a loyalty oath. She refused to give the school her fingerprints, providing toe prints instead. A great and glorious uproar ensued, and, alas, it ended with her becoming, as she put it, "an extinguished professor." She learned recently that plans were afoot at the University of California, Berkeley, to raise money for a chair in her name in investigative journalism. "I'm to be a chair, Bobby," she marveled. "A chair."

In her long life as a journalist-activist—interviewing prisoners, scouring the fringes of Oakland for her husband's labor and civil rights cases, going to Mississippi, confronting police chiefs, taking on the medical profession—she never lost the sense that it was all a grand adventure. Shortly before her death, she said, "Well, I had a good run, didn't I?"

⊙▥▥⦿

CHAPTER FIVE

WARRIORS IN THE AFRICAN-AMERICAN STORY

ᎶᏍᏍᎧ

In 1965, I went to work as a research assistant in the Civil Rights Division of the Justice Department. Not long after I arrived, someone showed me an FBI photograph stamped "Secret." Taken just moments after they had been unearthed, it was an eight-by-ten shot of the bodies of the three civil rights workers who had been murdered the previous Freedom Summer in Mississippi. It was the most shocking photograph I had ever seen—the more so because it was so clearly intended not to shock but to document a methodical process, the way one might document stages in an archaeological dig.

It was a black-and-white close-up of the backsides of three pairs of jeans, their wearers still buried facedown in the gravel pit where they had been discovered. That's all you could see. It looked as if someone might have used a broom to brush them off before taking the picture. One of the boys was wearing Levi's jeans. I could see the trademark quite clearly, and I kept staring at it, as if the all-American label could, by its mere presence, change the meaning of the photo.

Later there were other pictures—fire hoses flattening heads against sides of buildings, charred bodies hanging from nooses, burnt churches, walls of cold eyes and distorted mouths yelling at terrified schoolchildren. On one assignment in Texas, to do research on the conditions that led up to the enactment of the poll tax, I sorted through boxes and boxes of microfilm of turn-of-the-century newspapers to determine the temper of the times.

"Black fiend lynched in Hempstead" screamed one headline at the turn of the century, when young W. E. B. Du Bois—destined to become one of the leading black intellectuals in the country—was teaching in Atlanta, Georgia.

In April of 1899, a black farmer outside of Atlanta got into an argument with a white farmer over a debt and killed him. There was mass hysteria among the whites, two thousand of whom assembled to watch him be lynched, after which he was doused with gasoline and burned. Finally, the crowd descended upon him and tore the corpse apart for souvenirs.

Sickened, Du Bois wrote a letter of protest and set out on foot to deliver it to Joel Chandler Harris at the *Atlanta Constitution*. But on his way, he was told that the knuckles of the black farmer were on display in a shopkeeper's window near the newspaper. Du Bois turned around and went home. Two months later Du Bois's two-year-old son, Burghardt, became ill with diphtheria. There being no white doctor who would treat a black baby, his son died.

Du Bois himself died in 1963, one day before the famous civil rights march on Washington, where Martin Luther King delivered his "I have a dream" speech. Four little girls in the basement of a black Birmingham, Alabama, church would not live out the year.

Nineteen sixty-three was the beginning of another string of bombings, burnings, and murders, among them the 1964 Neshoba County, Mississippi, murders; the 1965 slaying of Rev. James Reeb on the march from Selma to Montgomery, Alabama; the 1965 assassination of Malcolm X in New York; and the 1968 assassination of Martin Luther King in Memphis.

The first eulogy in this section is the bitter tribute of Rev. Theodore Parker for Daniel Webster, the mightiest orator of his day, the most brilliant secretary of state, the highest-paid lawyer, and staunchest defender of the Union and the Constitution. He was also the biggest sellout of the abolitionist cause. The last eulogy is for Marian Anderson, the contralto who was denied the right to sing at the Daughters of the American Revolution's Constitution Hall. Between these two tributes lies the story of the struggle for African-American equality.

Initially, I had not anticipated the need for such a category, and by creating it I am aware that all of the black men and women in *The Book of Eulogies* have been, de facto, segregated into one chapter. But in sequence, these tributes tell a story of great power and momentum.

"What a mouth he had! It was a lion's mouth. Yet there was a sweet grandeur in his smile, and a woman's sweetness when he would. What a brow it was! What eyes! like charcoal fire in the bottom of a deep, dark well. His face was rugged with volcanic fires, great passions, and great thoughts. . . ."

DANIEL WEBSTER
(1782–1852)

by

REV. THEODORE PARKER
(1810–1860)

Daniel Webster, senator from Massachusetts, was a Union supporter who backed the Compromise of 1850, which allowed states created after the Mexican War to decide whether they would be slaveholding and, in the accompanying Fugitive Slave Bill, permitted slave owners to track down escapees in any state. Webster's May 7, 1850, speech on the Senate floor supporting the Compromise horrified the abolitionists, who saw Webster as a fatally compromised man, ambitious to be president at the expense of his soul.

Rev. Theodore Parker was a radical New England theologian and social reformer, a member of the Transcendentalists, and one of "the secret six" who financially supported John Brown. In his eulogy, considered a public scandal at the time it was delivered, it is clear that he loved Webster but hated whom he had become. Richard Henry Dana wrote, "Strange that the best commendation that has appeared yet, the most touching, elevated, meaningful eulogy, with all its censure, should have come from Theodore Parker. Were I Daniel Webster, I would not have that sermon destroyed for all that has been said in my favor."

Do men mourn for him, the great man eloquent? I put on sackcloth long ago. I mourned for him when he wrote the Creole letter which surprised Ashburton, Briton that he was. I mourned when he spoke the speech of the seventh of March. I mourned when the Fugitive Slave Bill passed Congress, and the same cannon that have fired "minute guns" for him fired also one hundred rounds of joy for the forging of a new fetter for the fugitive's foot. I mourned for him when the kidnappers first came to Boston—hated then—now respectable men, the companions of princes, enlarging their testimony in the court. . . . I mourned when Ellen Craft fled to my house for shelter and for succor. . . . I mourned then; I shall not cease to mourn. The flags will be removed from the streets, the cannon will sound their other notes of joy; but for me I shall go mourning all my days. I shall refuse to be comforted, and at last I shall lay down my gray hairs with weeping and with sorrow in the grave. Oh, Webster! Webster! Would God that I had died for thee!

He was a great man, a man of the largest mold, a great body, and a great brain; he seemed made to last a hundred years. Since Socrates, there has seldom been a head so massive, so huge—seldom such a face since the stormy features of Michelangelo. . . . A large man, decorous in dress, dignified in deportment, he walked as if he felt himself a king. Men from the country, who knew him not, stared at him as he passed through our streets. The coal-heavers and porters of London looked on him as one of the great forces of the globe; they recognized a native king. In the Senate of the United States he looked an emperor in that council. Even the majestic Calhoun seemed common compared with him. Clay looked vulgar, and Van Buren but a fox. What a mouth he had! It was a lion's mouth. Yet there was a sweet grandeur in his smile, and a woman's sweetness when he would. What a brow it was! What eyes! like charcoal fire in the bottom of a deep, dark well. His face was rugged with volcanic fires, great passions, and great thoughts:

> The front of Jove himself;
> And eyes like Mars, to threaten and command.

Divide the faculties, not bodily, into intellectual, moral, affectional, and religious; and try him on that scale. His late life shows that he had little religion—somewhat of its lower forms—conventional devoutness, formality of prayer, "the ordinances of religion"; but he had not a great man's all-conquering look to God. It is easy to be "devout." The Pharisee was more so than the publican. It is hard to be moral. . . .

Of the affections, he was well provided by nature—though they were little cultivated—very attractable to a few. Those who knew him loved him tenderly; and if he hated like a giant, he also loved like a king. Of unimpassioned and unrelated love, there are two chief forms: friendship and philanthropy. Friendship he surely had; all along the shore men loved him. Men in Boston loved him; even Washington held loving hearts that worshiped him.

Of philanthropy, I cannot claim much for him; I find it not. Of conscience, it seemed to me he had little; in his later life, exceeding little; his moral sense seemed long besotted; almost, though not wholly, gone. Hence, though he was often generous, he was not just. Free to give as to grasp, he was charitable by instinct, not disinterested on principle.

His strength lay not in the religious, nor in the affectional, nor in the moral part of man. His intellect was immense. His power of comprehension was vast. He methodized swiftly. But if you look at the forms of intellectual action, you may distribute them into three great modes of force: the understanding, the imagination, and the reason—the understanding, dealing with details and methods; imagination, with beauty, with power to create; reason, with first principles and universal laws.

We must deny to Mr. Webster the great reason. He does not belong to the great men of that department—the Socrates, Aristotle, Plato, Leibniz, Newton, Descartes, and the other mighties. He seldom grasps a universal law. His measures of expediency for today are seldom bottomed on universal principles of right which last forever.

I cannot assign to him a large imagination. He was not creative of new forms of thought or of beauty; so he lacks the poetic charm which gladdens the loftiest eloquence. But his understanding was exceedingly great. He acquired readily and retained well; arranged with ease and skill; and fluently reproduced. As a scholar he passed for learned in the Senate, where scholars are few; for a universal man with editors of political and commercial prints. But his learning was narrow in its range, and not very nice in its accuracy. His reach in history and literature was very small for a great man seventy years of age, always associating with able men. . . . He was not a scholar, and it is idle to claim great scholarship for him.

As a statesman his lack of what I call the highest reason and imagination continually appears. To the national stock he added no new idea, created out of new thought; no great maxim, created out of human history and old thought. The great ideas of the time were not born in his bosom. He organized nothing. There were great ideas of practical value seeking lodgment in the body; he aided them not. . . .

What a sad life was his! At Portsmouth his house burned down, all uninsured. His wife died—a loving woman, beautiful and tenderly beloved! Of several children, all save one have gone before him to the tomb. Sad man; he lived to build his children's monument! Do you remember the melancholy spectacle in the street when Major Webster, a victim of the Mexican War, was by his father laid down in yonder tomb—a daughter, too, but recently laid low! How poor seemed then the ghastly pageant in the street—empty and hollow as the muffled drum. For years he has seemed to me like one of the tragic heroes of the Grecian tale, pursued by fate, and latterly, the saddest sight in all this Western World—widowed of so much he loved, and grasping at what was not only vanity, but the saddest vexation of the heart. I have long mourned for him as for no living or departed man. He blasted us with scornful lightning. Him, if I could, I would not blast, but only bless continually and ever more.

You remember the last time he spoke in Boston—the procession, last summer. You remember it well. What a sad and careworn countenance was that of the old man, welcomed with their mockery of applause! You remember when the orator, wise-headed and friendly-hearted, came to thank him for his services, he said not a word of saving the Union; of the compromise measures, not a word; but for his own great services he thanked him.

And when Webster replied, he said, "Here in Boston I am not disowned—at least here I am not disowned." No, Daniel Webster! You were not disowned here in Boston. So long as I have a tongue to teach, a heart to feel, you shall never be disowned. It was by our sin, by Boston's sin, that the great man fell! I pity his victims; you pity them, too. But I pity him more; oh, far more! Pity the oppressed, will you? Will you not pity the oppressor in his sin? . . .

The last time he was in Faneuil Hall—it was last June—the sick old man— . . . you remember the feeble look and the sad face. I felt then that it was his last time, and forbore to look upon that saddened countenance. The last time he was in the Senate, it was to hear his successor speak. He stayed an hour, and heard Charles Sumner demonstrate that the Fugitive Slave Bill was not good religion, nor good morality, nor good constitution, nor good law.

He came home to Boston and went down to Marshfield to die. . . .
The kindly doctor thought to sweeten the bitterness of death with
medicated skill, and when that failed, he gave the great man a little
manna that fell down from heaven three thousand years ago, and the
shepherd David gathered it up and kept it in a psalm:

"The Lord is my shepherd. Though I walk through the valley of
the shadow of death, I will fear no evil. Thy rod and thy staff they
comfort me."

And the great man faltered out his last words: "That is what I
want—thy rod, thy rod; thy staff, thy staff." That great heart had
never renounced God. Oh, no! It had scoffed at his "higher law," but
in the heart of hearts there was religion still! . . .

Let the State go out mindful of his noblest services, yet fearful for
his fate, sad that he would fain have filled him with the husks the
swine do eat, and no man gave to him. Sad and tearful let her
remember the force of circumstance and dark temptation's secret
power. Let her remember that while we know what he yielded to,
and what his sin, God knows what also he resisted, and he alone
knows who the sinner is. The dear old mother of us all! Oh, let her
warn her children to fling away ambition, and let her charge them,
every one, that there is a God who must, indeed, be worshiped, and
a higher law of God which must be kept, though gold and Union
fail.

⊙⟁⟁⟁⟁⟁⟁⟁⟁⟁⟁⟁⟁⟁⟁⟁⟁⟁⟁⟁⟁⟁⟁⟁⟁

"The coming centuries will know but two characters as representatives of this period—Lincoln, the Emancipator, and Grant,
the Soldier. Yet there is another, who from his peculiar part in the
struggle, cannot be soon forgotten—the grim, gray herald of the
conflict."

JOHN BROWN
(1800–1859)

by

JOHN H. FINLEY
(1863–1940)

Abolitionist John Brown inspired many prominent white Northerners such as Wendell Phillips, Ralph Waldo Emerson, and Henry David Thoreau to support his cause, although whether they knew the full extent of his plans is unclear. In 1855, Brown and four of his sons murdered five proslavery settlers on the banks of the Pottawatomie creek, in revenge for the recent sacking of Lawrence, Kansas. In 1859, hoping to seize weapons to supply a fortress where escaped slaves might take refuge, Brown and his followers took over a government armory in the town of Harpers Ferry, West Virginia. Brown was captured by a company of U.S. Marines commanded by Col. Robert E. Lee, convicted of murder, and hanged—but not before he had become a martyr for the abolitionists' cause.

When he was a student, John Huston Finley, who later became president of the University of the State of New York, won first prize in an oratory contest with this essay on Brown.

Far up the wooded slope of one of the Adirondacks there is a lone grave. An old, mossy tombstone resting against a huge rock marks it. There are several inscriptions upon the stone. One faintly records the death of a Revolutionary patriot. Beneath it another reads: "John Brown, executed at Charlestown, Va., December 2d, 1859."

One generation makes history, the next records it. It is ours to collect the memorials of our Civil War. The coming centuries will know but two characters as representatives of this period—Lincoln, the Emancipator, and Grant, the Soldier. Yet there is another, who from his peculiar part in the struggle, cannot be soon forgotten—the grim, gray herald of the conflict. His only monument is a gibbet, his epitaph, "traitor"; yet we seem to hear the war-cry of the Union armies marching to victory, led by that soul whose body lay moldering on the distant mountain.

An old man, Brown left his wild home on the Adirondacks to take part in the slavery struggle in Kansas. With a small band of men, among them his sons, he committed that deed known as the Pottawatomie murders, dragging from their homes at midnight five unarmed proslavery men and killing them in cold blood. In the border warfare thus begun he took so prominent a part that the very name of "Old John Brown" was a source of terror to his enemies. When the struggle ended, he left Kansas and conveyed a number of slaves from Missouri to Canada. A few months later he made his startling appearance at Harpers Ferry; seized the national arsenal, held it for two days. Finally captured, he was tried, convicted, and hanged.

Many judge him wholly by these facts. To them his deeds are the plottings of a heart burning for revenge. He entered Kansas to avenge the wrongs of his sons, to fight Missouri, to incite war between the North and South. Urged by his blind insanity and frenzied hate, he made the foolish and criminal attack upon Harpers Ferry, and was rightly adjudged murderer, insurrectionist, traitor.

The life of John Brown would long since have gone out in darkness did it not shine with the light of eternal right and moral heroism. The purpose which inspired his life was the emancipation of the slave, and behind that purpose was compassion for the oppressed. See him as he sits watching through the long winter night by the bedside of a sick child. Note the kindliness with which he always treated his prisoners; the gentleness with which, when on trial, he met the curses of his foes, the rebukes of his friends; or see him, as on his way to the gallows, he stoops to kiss that Negro child. Can you believe that revenge could live in that heart? Ah! No. It was the wail of a race in bondage ever ringing in his soul that led him on.

The black night of Pottawatomie is past. Through the trees that border the creek, the morning sun shines upon the mutilated and bloody faces of five stark bodies. Where is the murderer? A short distance up the stream in the cover of the forest a little band of roughly clad men are seated around a rude table. They are silent as one of their number, an old man with long, white beard, in low broken tones asks a morning blessing. There are bloodstains on his folded hands. Here is the true man consistent with himself. He saw that dark deed necessary, and he did it. Without the shedding of blood there was no remission of this sin. Slavery was not to be talked, preached, or educated out of existence. Men had talked, but the slave ships only increased their loads. The slave territory was widening. With Kansas, more would be seized. What other means would answer? "Providence," said he, "has made me an actor, and slavery an outlaw." He took the law into his own hands, but for no personal interest. He struck, during a national crisis, upon the solid ground of real principle, in a cause not personal, not local, not even national, but human.

Frantic, madman, fool, if you please; such have been the world's great reformers—men who staked their lives on a principle. With the foresight of a statesman, Brown saw, and said that slavery and the Union could not exist together; but wiser and more truly patriotic than the statesman cried, "The Union, slavery, or no slavery," he said, "Down with slavery!"

His death made all men either friends or foes of slavery. Between the North and South stood John Brown's gibbet. Henceforth it was slavery or Union. Compromise was no longer possible. He had succeeded, he must have failed. His failure was his success. . . .

Fearlessly, heroically, he met his fate. Traitor? Then were the brave who fell at Lexington traitors. They taught us this: "That we may resist with arms a law which violates the principles of natural justice." Emmet did it in Ireland: Wallace, in Scotland; Garibaldi, in Italy, and we honor them; John Brown did it in America, the land of the free, and we hanged him.

Is this his fitting and final reward? The soaring shaft that stands by Potomac's stream answers, "No." The monuments, which a grateful people have erected to the memory of that who died for the slave, say, "No." The gratitude of millions freed from bondage says, "No." And the day will come when even the mountains of Virginia will echo back the answer, "No."

ᕮᘏᘏᕬ

"Viewed from the genuine abolition ground, Mr. Lincoln seemed tardy, cold, dull, and indifferent, but measuring him by the sentiment of his country, a sentiment he was bound as a statesman to consult, he was swift, zealous, radical, and determined."

ABRAHAM LINCOLN
(1809–1865)

by

FREDERICK DOUGLASS
(1817–1895)

Abolitionist, orator, and newspaper editor, Frederick Douglass was born on the Eastern Shore of Maryland, the son of a slave mother and an unknown white father. Taught to read by the wife of his owner in Baltimore, he escaped from slavery in 1838, moved to Massachusetts, and became a leader in the movement to free the slaves. In 1876, Douglass was asked to deliver a speech at the unveiling of the Freedman's Monument in Washington, D.C., which shows Lincoln looking down upon a kneeling black man who is looking up at him in gratitude. Douglass was a friend of Lincoln's, but he did not consider him the black man's president, as his measured remarks make clear.

Fellow citizens, in what we have said and done today, and in what we may say and do hereafter, we disclaim everything like arrogance and assumption. We claim for ourselves no superior devotion to the character, history, and memory of the illustrious name whose monument we have here dedicated today. We fully comprehend the relation of Abraham Lincoln both to ourselves and to the white people of the United States. Truth is proper and beautiful at all times and in all places, and it is never more proper and beautiful in any case than when speaking of a great public man whose example is likely to be commended for honor and imitation long after his departure to the solemn shades, the silent continents of eternity. It must be admitted . . . truth compels me to admit, even here in the presence of the monument we have erected to his memory . . . Abraham Lincoln was not, in the fullest sense of the word, either our man or our model. In his interests, in his associations, in his habits of thought, and in his prejudices, he was a white man.

He was preeminently the white man's president, entirely devoted to the welfare of white men. He was ready and willing at any time during the first years of his administration to deny, postpone, and sacrifice the rights of humanity in the colored people to promote the welfare of the white people of this country. In all his education and feeling he was an American of the Americans. He came into the presidential chair upon one principle alone, namely, opposition to the extension of slavery. His arguments in furtherance of this policy had their motive and mainspring in his patriotic devotion to the interests of his own race. To protect, defend, and perpetuate slavery in the states where it existed, Abraham Lincoln was not less ready than any other president to draw the sword of the nation. He was ready to execute all the supposed constitutional guarantees of the United States Constitution in favor of the slave system anywhere inside the slave states. He was willing to pursue, recapture, and send back the fugitive slave to his master, and to suppress a slave rising for liberty, though his guilty master were already in arms against the government. The race to which we belong were not the special objects of his consideration. Knowing this, I concede to you, my white fellow citizens, a preeminence in this worship at once full and supreme. First, midst, and last, you and yours were the objects of his deepest affection and his most earnest solicitude. You are the children of Abraham Lincoln. We are at best only his stepchildren—children by adoption, children by force of circumstances and necessity. To you it especially belongs to sound his praises, to preserve and perpetuate his memory, to multiply his statues, to hang his pictures high upon your walls, and commend his example, for to you he was a great and glorious friend and benefactor. Instead of supplanting you at this altar, we would exhort you to build high his monuments; let them be of the most costly material, of the most cunning workmanship; let their forms be symmetrical, beautiful, and perfect; let their bases be upon solid rocks, and their summits lean against the unchanging blue, overhanging sky, and let them endure forever! But while in the abundance of your wealth, and in the fullness of your just and patriotic devotion, you do all this, we entreat you to despise not the humble offering we this day unveil to view; for while Abraham Lincoln saved for you a country, he delivered us from a bondage, according to Jefferson, one hour of which was worse than ages of the oppression our fathers rose in rebellion to oppose.

Fellow citizens, ours is no newborn zeal and devotion—merely a thing of this moment. The name of Abraham Lincoln was near and dear to our hearts in the darkest and most perilous hours of the Republic. We were no more ashamed of him when shrouded in clouds of darkness, of doubt, and defeat than when we saw him crowned with victory, honor, and glory. Our faith in him was often taxed and strained to the uttermost, but it never failed. When he tarried long in the mountain; when he strangely told us that we were the cause of the war; when he still more strangely told us to leave the land in which we were born; when he refused to employ our arms in defense of the Union; when, after accepting our services as colored soldiers, he refused to retaliate our murder and torture as colored prisoners; when he told us he would save the Union if he could with slavery; when he revoked the Proclamation of Emancipation of General Frémont; when he refused to remove the popular commander of the Army of the Potomac, in the days of its inaction and defeat, who was more zealous in his efforts to protect slavery than to suppress rebellion; when we saw all this, and more, we were at times grieved, stunned, and greatly bewildered; but our hearts believed while they ached and bled. Nor was this, even at that time, a blind and unreasoning superstition. Despite the mist and haze that surrounded him; despite the tumult, the hurry, and confusion of the hour, we were able to take a comprehensive view of Abraham Lincoln, and to make reasonable allowance for the circumstances of his position. . . .

Though he loved Caesar less than Rome, though the Union was more to him than our freedom or our future, under his wise and beneficent rule we saw ourselves gradually lifted from the depths of slavery to the heights of liberty and manhood; under his wise and beneficent rule, and by measures approved and vigorously pressed by him, we saw that the handwriting of ages, in the form of prejudice and proscription, was rapidly fading away from the face of our whole country; under his rule, and in due time, about as soon after all as the country could tolerate the strange spectacle, we saw our brave sons and brothers laying off the rags of bondage, and being clothed all over in the blue uniforms of the soldiers of the United States; under his rule we saw two hundred thousand of our dark and dusky people responding to the call of Abraham Lincoln, and with muskets on their shoulders, and eagles on their buttons, timing their high footsteps to liberty and union under the national flag; under his rule we saw the independence of the black republic of Haiti, the special object of slaveholding aversion and horror, fully recognized, and her minister, a colored gentleman, duly received here in the city of Washington; under his rule we saw the internal slave trade, which so long disgraced the nation, abolished, and slavery abolished in the District of Columbia; under his rule we saw for the first time the law enforced against the foreign slave trade, and the first slave trader hanged like any other pirate or murderer; under his rule, assisted by the greatest captain of our age, and his inspiration, we saw the Confederate States, based upon the idea that our race must be slaves, and slaves forever, battered to pieces and scattered to the four winds; under his rule, and in the fullness of time, we saw Abraham Lincoln, after giving the slaveholders three months' grace in which to save their hateful slave system, penning the immortal paper, which, though special in its language, was general in its principles and effect, making slavery forever impossible in the United States. Though we waited long, we saw all this and more. . . .

I have said that President Lincoln was a white man, and shared the prejudices common to his countrymen towards the colored race. Looking back to his times and to the condition of his country, we are compelled to admit that this unfriendly feeling on his part may be safely set down as one element of his wonderful success in organizing the loyal American people for the tremendous conflict before them, and bringing them safely through that conflict. His great mission was to accomplish two things: first, to save his country from dismemberment and ruin; and second, to free his country from the great crime of slavery. To do one or the other, or both, he must have the earnest sympathy and the powerful cooperation of his loyal fellow countrymen. Without this primary and essential condition to success his efforts must have been vain and utterly fruitless. Had he put the abolition of slavery before the salvation of the Union, he would have inevitably driven from him a powerful class of the American people and rendered resistance to rebellion impossible. Viewed from the genuine abolition ground, Mr. Lincoln seemed tardy, cold, dull, and indifferent, but measuring him by the sentiment of his country, a sentiment he was bound as a statesman to consult, he was swift, zealous, radical, and determined.

Though Mr. Lincoln shared the prejudices of his white fellow countrymen against the Negro, it is hardly necessary to say that in his heart of hearts he loathed and hated slavery. The man who could say, "Fondly do we hope, fervently do we pray, that this mighty scourge of war shall soon pass away, yet if God wills it continue till all the wealth piled by two hundred years of bondage shall have been wasted, and each drop of blood drawn by the lash shall have been paid for by one drawn by the sword, the judgments of the Lord are true and righteous altogether," gives all needed proof of his feeling on the subject of slavery. He was willing, while the South was loyal, that it should have its pound of flesh, because he thought that it was so nominated in the bond; but farther than this no earthly power could make him go.

Fellow citizens, whatever else in this world may be partial, unjust, and uncertain, time, time! is impartial, just, and certain in its action. In the realm of mind, as well as in the realm of matter, it is a great worker, and often works wonders. The honest and comprehensive statesman, clearly discerning the needs of his country, and earnestly endeavoring to do his whole duty, though covered and blistered with reproaches, may safely leave his course to the silent judgment of time. Few great public men have ever been the victims of fiercer denunciation than Abraham Lincoln was during his administration. He was often wounded in the house of his friends. Reproaches came thick and fast upon him from within and from without, and from opposite quarters. He was assailed by abolitionists; he was assailed by slaveholders; he was assailed by the men who were for peace at any price; he was assailed by those who were for a more vigorous prosecution of the war; he was assailed for not making the war an abolition war; and he was most bitterly assailed for making the war an abolition war.

But now behold the change: the judgment of the present hour, that taking him for all in all, measuring the tremendous magnitude of the work before him, considering the necessary means to ends, and surveying the end from the beginning, infinite wisdom has seldom sent any man into the world better fitted for his mission than Abraham Lincoln. . . .

Upon his inauguration as president of the United States, an office, even where assumed under the most favorable conditions, fitted to tax and strain the largest abilities, Abraham Lincoln was met by a tremendous crisis. He was called upon not merely to administer the government but to decide, in the face of terrible odds, the fate of the Republic.

A formidable rebellion rose in his path before him; the Union was already practically dissolved; his country was torn and rent asunder at the center. Hostile armies were already organized against the Republic, armed with the munitions of war which the Republic had provided for its own defense. The tremendous question for him to decide was whether his country should survive the crisis and flourish, or be dismembered and perish. His predecessor in office had already decided the question in favor of national dismemberment, by denying to it the right of self-defense and self-preservation—a right which belongs to the meanest insect.

Happily for the country, happily for you and for me, the judgment of James Buchanan, the patrician, was not the judgment of Abraham Lincoln, the plebeian. He brought his strong common sense, sharpened in the school of adversity, to bear upon the question. He did not hesitate, he did not doubt, he did not falter; but at once resolved that at whatever peril at whatever cost, the union of the states should be preserved. A patriot himself, his faith was strong and unwavering in the patriotism of his countrymen. Timid men said before Mr. Lincoln's inauguration that we had seen the last president of the United States. A voice in influential quarters said, "Let the Union slide." Some said that a Union maintained by the sword was worthless. Others said a rebellion of 8 million cannot be suppressed; but in the midst of all this tumult and timidity, and against all this, Abraham Lincoln was clear in his duty, and had an oath in heaven. He calmly and bravely heard the voice of doubt and fear all around him; but he had an oath in heaven, and there was not power enough on the earth to make this honest boatman, backwoodsman, and broad-handed splitter of rails evade or violate that sacred oath. He had not been schooled in the ethics of slavery; his plain life had favored his love of truth. He had not been taught that treason and perjury were the proof of honor and honesty. His moral training was against his saying one thing when he meant another. The trust which Abraham Lincoln had in himself and in the people was surprising and grand, but it was also enlightened and well founded. He knew the American people better than they knew themselves, and his truth was based upon this knowledge. . . .

Fellow citizens, I end, as I began, with congratulations. We have done a good work for our race today. In doing honor to the memory of our friend and liberator, we have been doing highest honors to ourselves and those who come after us; we have been fastening ourselves to a name and fame imperishable and immortal; we have also been defending ourselves from a blighting scandal. When now it shall be said that the colored man is soul-less, that he has no appreciation of benefits of benefactors; when the foul reproach of ingratitude is hurled at us, and it is attempted to scourge us beyond the range of human brotherhood, we may calmly point to the monument we have this day erected to the memory of Abraham Lincoln.

"I think it may be said that the blood of Charles Sumner, spilled upon the floor of the Senate because he dared to oppose the slave power of the South . . . spoke silently, but effectively, of the cruelty and inequities of that abominable institution."

CHARLES SUMNER
(1811–1874)

by

JOSEPH H. RAINEY
(1832–1887)

Charles Sumner, a radical Republican senator from Massachusetts, was, early and late, a vehement enemy of slavery. In a speech on the Senate floor in 1856, he verbally attacked Sen. Andrew P. Butler of South Carolina for serving "the mistress to whom he has made his vows . . . the harlot, Slavery." Several days later, a nephew of Butler's attacked Sumner in the Senate, beating him so badly that Sumner fell unconscious to the floor. It was three years before he was able to return to Congress and he never fully recovered from the attack.

Joseph Rainey was the first African-American to serve in the House of Representatives. Elected in 1870 to the Forty-first Congress, and from Butler's state of South Carolina, he was a barber by trade, with a limited education.

Early in life Mr. Sumner espoused the cause of those who were not able to speak for themselves, and whose bondage made it hazardous for anyone else to venture a word in their behalf. No one knew the danger and magnitude of such an undertaking better than the deceased. Public sentiment at that time was opposed to his course; ostracism confronted him; friends forsook him; but undaunted and full of courage he pursued the right, sustained his convictions, and lived long enough to see the fruition of his earnest labors. He was among the first to arouse the Commonwealth of his beloved Massachusetts to consider the justice and equity of mixed schools. The blows he gave were effectual; the separating walls could not withstand them; they consequently tottered and fell. The doors of the schoolhouses flew open to all; prejudice was well nigh consumed by the blaze of his ardent eloquence, and proscription gave way to more liberal views. It was upon his motion that the first colored man was admitted to practice before the Supreme Court of the United States.

These remarks are made to show that the cause of my race was always foremost in his mind; indeed, he was a friend who in many instances stuck closer than a brother. He was one of those who never slumbered upon his lance, but stood ever watchful for the opportunity to hurl the shaft of his forensic powers against the institution of slavery. . . .

During his senatorial career, embracing a period of twenty-three years, he has contended for a moral principle against enemies more daring and intrepid, perhaps, than any other man has encountered in life itself. His conscientious conviction that slavery was a national crime and moral sin could not endure tamely assertions to the contrary. He heeded not the menacing denunciations of those "who eat the bread of wickedness, and drink the wine of violence." Their execrations could not move nor intimidate him. Finding these instruments of wickedness could not deter him or turn the keen edge of his argument, he was brutally and cowardly assaulted in the Senate chamber, in 1856, by Preston S. Brooks, a representative from South Carolina. This occurred a few days after his masterly effort setting forth the "Crime Against Kansas."

Mr. Speaker, that unprovoked assault declared to the country the threatening attitude of the two sections, one against the other, and awakened a determination on the part of the North to resist the encroachments of slavery. The unexpressed sympathy that was felt for him among the slaves of the South, when they heard of this unwarranted attack, was only known to those whose situations at the time made them confidants. Their prayers and secret importunities were ever uttered in the interest of him who was their constant friend and untiring advocate and defender before the high court of the nation.

Mr. Speaker, it is said that "the blood of the martyrs is the seed of the Church." With equal truthfulness and force, I think it may be said that the blood of Charles Sumner, spilled upon the floor of the Senate because he dared to oppose the slave power of the South and to interpose in the path of its progress, was the seed that produced general emancipation; the result of which is too well known to need comment. It spoke silently, but effectively, of the cruelty and inequities of that abominable institution. . . .

Mr. Speaker, the intentness of his thought on the subject of his mission, for which apparently he was born, clung to him to the closing moments of his life. When weary and longing for rest, having his eyes fixed upon that "mansion not made with hands, eternal in the heavens," and just preceding his final step over the threshold of time into the boundless space of eternity, he uttered in dying accents, yet with an eloquence more persuasive and impressive than ever, these words: "Do not let the civil-rights bill fail!" . . .

This sentence, we trust, will prove more potent and availing in securing equality before the law for all men than any of his former efforts. This is not the proper time—neither is the occasion propitious—for further comment on that dying appeal. I therefore with trembling hands and a grateful heart lay it gently in the lap of the Muses, and it may be wrought into imperishable history as an additional evidence of his sincerity in life and his devotion to the grand principle of equal rights even in the embrace of death. He can never be repaid for the services he has rendered the Republic. . . .

Now, sir, my grateful task is done. This humble but heartfelt tribute I lay at the base of the broken column in token of him who was an eminent statesman, renowned philanthropist, and devoted friend to the friendless. "May he rest in peace."

◌◌◌◌◌

"In the poise of his little curl-crowned head did there not sit all that wild pride of being which his father had hardly crushed in his own heart? For what, forsooth, shall a Negro want with pride. . . . Well sped, my boy, before the world had dubbed your ambition insolence, had held your ideals unattainable, and taught you to cringe and bow."

BURGHARDT DU BOIS

(1897–1899)

by

W. E. B. DU BOIS

(1868–1963)

143

W. E. B. Du Bois was one of the leading black intellectuals in America—a
scholar, social historian, prolific writer, and civil rights activist, whose more
radical and less accommodating views clashed with those of the other great
African-American of his era, Booker T. Washington. When Du Bois was
teaching in Atlanta, Georgia, his infant son, Burghardt, developed diph-
theria. No white doctor would treat a black child, and there were no skilled
black doctors; Du Bois's son died. In his essay "Of the Passing of the First-
Born," Du Bois writes of his son's death, and of his walk, with his wife,
behind the horse-drawn wagon bearing his son's coffin to the train which
took him north to be buried.

He died at eventide, when the sun lay like a brooding sorrow above
the western hills, veiling its face; when the winds spoke not, and the
trees, the great green trees he loved, stood motionless. I saw his
breath beat quicker and quicker, pause, and then his little soul leapt
like a star that travels in the night and left a world of darkness in its
train. The day changed not; the same tall trees peeped in at the windows, the same green grass glinted in the setting sun. Only in the
chamber of death writhed the world's most piteous thing—a child-
less mother. . . .

A perfect life was his, all joy and love, with tears to make it
brighter—sweet as a summer's day beside the Housatonic. The
world loved him; the women kissed his curls, the men looked
gravely into his wonderful eyes, and the children hovered and flut-
tered about him. I can see him now, changing like the sky from
sparkling laughter to darkening frowns, and then to wondering
thoughtfulness as he watched the world. He knew no color-line,
poor dear,—and the Veil, though it shadowed him, had not yet darkened half his sun. He loved the white matron, he loved his black
nurse; and in his little world walked souls alone, uncolored and
unclothed. I—yea, all men—are larger and purer by the infinite
breadth of that one little life. She who in simple clearness of vision
sees beyond the stars said when he had flown—"He will be happy
There; he ever loved beautiful things." And I, far more ignorant, and
blind by the web of my own weaving, sit alone winding words and
muttering, "If still he be, and he be There, and there be a There, let
him be happy, O Fate!"

Blithe was the morning of his burial, with bird and song and sweet-smelling flowers. The trees whispered to the grass, but the children sat with hushed faces. And yet it seemed a ghostly unreal day—the wraith of Life. We seemed to rumble down an unknown street behind a little white bundle of posies, with the shadow of a song in our ears. The busy city dinned about us; they did not say much, those pale-faced hurrying men and women; they did not say much—they only glanced and said, "Niggers."

We could not lay him in the ground there in Georgia, for the earth there is strangely red; so we bore him away to the northward, with his flowers and his little folded hands. . . .

All that day and all that night there sat an awful gladness in my heart—nay, blame me not if I see the world thus darkly through the Veil—and my soul whispers ever to me, saying, "Not dead, not dead, but escaped; not bond, but free." No bitter meanness now shall sicken his baby heart till it die a living death, no taunt shall madden his happy boyhood. Fool that I was to think or wish that this little soul should grow choked and deformed within the Veil! I might have known that yonder deep unworldly look that ever and anon floated past his eyes was peering far beyond this narrow Now. In the poise of his little curl-crowned head did there not sit all that wild pride of being which his father had hardly crushed in his own heart? For what, forsooth, shall a Negro want with pride amid the studied humiliations of 50 million fellows? Well sped, my boy, before the world had dubbed your ambition insolence, had held your ideals unattainable, and taught you to cringe and bow. Better far this nameless void that stops my life than a sea of sorrow for you.

Idle words; he might have borne his burden more bravely than we—aye, and found it lighter, too, someday; for surely, surely this is not the end. Surely there shall yet dawn some mighty morning to lift the Veil and set the prisoned free. Not for me—I shall die in my bonds—but for fresh young souls who have not known the night and waken to the morning; a morning where men ask of the workman, not "Is he white?" but "Can he work?" When men ask artists, not "Are they black?" but "Do they know?" Some morning this may be, long, long years to come. But now there wails, on that dark shore within the Veil, the same deep voice, *Thou shalt forgo!* And all have I forgone at that command, and with small complaint—all save that fair young form that lies so coldly wed with death in the nest I had builded.

If one must have gone, why not I? Why may I not rest me from this restlessness and sleep from this wide waking? Was not the world's alembic, Time, in his young hands, and is not my time waning? Are there so many workers in the vineyard that the fair promise of this little body could lightly be tossed away? The wretched of my race that line the alleys of the nation sit fatherless and unmothered; but Love sat beside his cradle, and in his ear Wisdom waited to speak. Perhaps now he knows the All-love, and needs not to be wise. Sleep, then, child—sleep till I sleep and waken to a baby voice and the ceaseless patter of little feet—above the Veil.

⚭

"Your children did not live long, but they lived well."

THE MARTYRED CHILDREN OF BIRMINGHAM
(D. 1963)

by

REV. DR. MARTIN LUTHER KING
(1929–1968)

The Reverend Dr. King delivered this eulogy at the funeral of three of the four young girls (Addie Mae Collins, Denise McNair, Carole Robertson, and Cynthia Wesley) who were killed on September 15, 1963, by a bomb that exploded in the basement of the 16th Street Baptist Church in Birmingham, Alabama.

This afternoon we gather in the quiet of this sanctuary to pay our last tribute of respect to these beautiful children of God. They entered the stage of history just a few years ago, and in the brief years that they were privileged to act on this mortal stage, they played their parts exceedingly well. Now the curtain falls; they move through the exit; the drama of their earthly life comes to a close. They are now committed back to that eternity from which they came.

These children—unoffending; innocent and beautiful—were the victims of one of the most vicious, heinous crimes ever perpetrated against humanity.

Yet they died nobly. They are the martyred heroines of a holy crusade for freedom and human dignity. So they have something to say to us in their death. They have something to say to every minister of the gospel who has remained silent behind the safe security of stained-glass windows. They have something to say to every politician who has fed his constituents the stale bread of hatred and the spoiled meat of racism. They have something to say to a federal government that has compromised with the undemocratic practices of southern Dixiecrats and the blatant hypocrisy of right-wing northern Republicans. They have something to say to every Negro who passively accepts the evil system of segregation and stands on the sidelines in the midst of a mighty struggle for justice. They say to each of us, black and white alike, that we must substitute courage for caution. They say to us that we must be concerned not merely about *who* murdered them, but about the system, the way of life and the philosophy which *produced* the murderers. Their death says to us that we must work passionately and unrelentingly to make the American dream a reality.

So they did not die in vain. God still has a way of wringing good out of evil. History has proven over and over again that unmerited suffering is redemptive. The innocent blood of these little girls may well serve as the redemptive force that will bring new light to this dark city. The holy Scripture says, "A little child shall lead them." The death of these little children may lead our whole Southland from the low road of man's inhumanity to man to the high road of peace and brotherhood. These tragic deaths may lead our nation to substitute an aristocracy of character for an aristocracy of color. The spilt blood of these innocent girls may cause the whole citizenry of Birmingham to transform the negative extremes of a dark past into the positive extremes of a bright future. Indeed, this tragic event may cause the white South to come to terms with its conscience.

So in spite of the darkness of this hour we must not despair. We must not become bitter; nor must we harbor the desire to retaliate with violence. We must not lose faith in our white brothers. Somehow we must believe that the most misguided among them can learn to respect the dignity and worth of all human personality.

May I now say a word to you, the members of the bereaved families. It is almost impossible to say anything that can console you at this difficult hour and remove the deep clouds of disappointment which are floating in your mental skies. But I hope you can find a little consolation from the universality of this experience. Death comes to every individual. There is an amazing democracy about death. It is not aristocracy for some of the people, but a democracy for all of the people. Kings die and beggars die; rich men die and poor men die; old people die and young people die; death comes to the innocent and it comes to the guilty. Death is the irreducible common denominator of all men.

I hope you can find some consolation from Christianity's affirmation that death is not the end. Death is not a period that ends the great sentence of life, but a comma that punctuates it to more lofty significance. Death is not a blind alley that leads the human race into a state of nothingness, but an open door which leads man into life eternal. Let this daring faith, this great invincible surmise, be your sustaining power during these trying days.

At times, life is hard, as hard as crucible steel. It has its bleak and painful moments. Like the ever-flowing waters of a river, life has its moments of drought and its moments of flood. Like the ever-changing cycle of the seasons, life has the soothing warmth of the summers and the piercing chill of its winters. But through it all, God walks with us. Never forget that God is able to lift you from fatigue of despair to the buoyancy of hope, and transform dark and desolate valleys into sunlit paths of inner peace.

Your children did not live long, but they lived well. The quantity of their lives was disturbingly small, but the quality of their lives was magnificently big. Where they died and what they were doing when death came will remain a marvelous tribute to each of you and an eternal epitaph to each of them. They died not in a den or dive nor were they hearing and telling filthy jokes at the time of their death. They died within the sacred walls of the church after discussing a principle as eternal as love.

Shakespeare had Horatio utter some beautiful words over the dead body of Hamlet. I paraphrase these words today as I stand over the last remains of these lovely girls.

"Good night, sweet princesses; may the flight of angels take thee to the eternal rest."

"The white man is not for the black man—we are just there."

JAMES CHANEY
(1943–1964)

by

FANNIE LEE CHANEY

In what came to be known as the Freedom Summer of 1964, three young men—two Jewish civil rights workers, Andrew Goodman and Michael Schwerner from New York City, and one black civil rights volunteer, James Chaney, from Meridian, Mississippi—were murdered in Philadelphia, Mississippi. They had been arrested and held in a Neshoba County jail. Upon their release, they were ambushed by whites (including two county sheriffs), killed, and thrown into a gravel pit. After the FBI found the bodies, the parents of the three men had a memorial service in New York City, at which Fannie Lee Chaney, the mother of James Chaney, spoke.

I am here to tell you about Meridian, Mississippi. That's my home. I have been there all of my days. I know the white man; I know the black man. The white man is not for the black man—we are just there. Everything to be done, to be said, the white man is going to do it; he is going to say it, right or wrong. We hadn't from the time that I know of been able to vote or register in Meridian. Now, since the civil-rights workers have been down in Mississippi working, they have allowed a lot of them to go to register. A lot of our people are scared, afraid. They are still backward. "I can't do that; I never have," they claimed. "I have been here too long. I will lose my job; I won't have any job." So, that is just the way it is. My son James, when he went out with the civil-rights workers around the first of '64, felt it was something he wanted to do, and he enjoyed working in the civil rights movement. He stayed in Canton, Mississippi, working on voter registration from February through March. When he came home, he told me how he worked and lived those few weeks he was there; he said, "Mother, one-half of the time, I was out behind houses or churches, waiting to get the opportunity to talk to people about what they needed and what they ought to do." He said, "Sometime they shunned me off and some would say, 'I want you all to stay away from here and leave me alone.' " But he would pick his chance and go back again. That is what I say about Mississippi right now. There is one more test I want to do there. I am working with the civil rights movement, my whole family is, and my son Ben here, he is going to take his big brother's place.

He has been working for civil rights. Everything he can do, he does it. For his activities, he had been jailed twice before he was twelve years old. He told me when he was in jail he wasn't excited. He is not afraid; he would go to jail again! I am, too, because we need and we've got to go to jail and we've got to get where the white man is. The white man has got Mississippi and we are just there working for the white man. He is the one getting rich. And when he gets rich, we can be outdoors or in old houses and he is going to knock on the door and get his rent money.

This is not something that has just now started, it has been going on before my time and I imagine before my parents' time. It is not just now the white man is doing this; it was borne from generation to generation. So, as I say, Ben is going to take his big brother's place, and I am with him and the rest of the family also. You all read about Mississippi—all parts of Mississippi—but I just wish it was so you could just come down there and be able to see; just try to live there just for one day, and you will know just how it is there.

ᏬᎥᎥᎩ

"Malcolm was our manhood, our living black manhood!... And, in honoring him, we honor the best in ourselves."

MALCOLM X
(1925–1965)

by

OSSIE DAVIS
(1917–)

Malcolm X, the charismatic ex-convict who rose to the top of the American Black Muslim organization run by the Honorable Elijah Muhammad, was a black separatist whose philosophy was antithetical to the nonviolent phi-

losophy of Martin Luther King. Expelled from the Black Muslims in 1963, Malcolm X formed his own separatist organization, but in 1964, after going on a pilgrimage to Mecca where he saw Muslims of different colors and races working together, he returned to the United States saying that he believed, for the first time, that black and white Americans could work together. In 1965, while giving a speech in New York City, he was assassinated, presumably by disgruntled Black Muslims.

Ossie Davis, a prominent American actor, director, and playwright, delivered the following eulogy at Faith Temple, Church of God, in Harlem on February 27, 1965.

Here, at this final hour, in this quiet place, Harlem has come to bid farewell to one of its brightest hopes—extinguished now and gone from us forever. For Harlem is where he worked and where he struggled and fought—his home of homes, where his heart was, and where his people are—and it is, therefore, most fitting that we meet once again, in Harlem, to share these last moments with him.

For Harlem has been ever gracious to those who have loved her, have fought for her, and have defended her honor even to the death. It is not in the memory of man that this beleaguered, unfortunate, but nonetheless proud, community has found a braver, more gallant young champion than this Afro-American who lies before us— unconquered still. I say the word again, as he would want me to: *Afro-American;* Afro-American Malcolm, who was a master, was most meticulous in his use of words. Nobody knew better than he the power words have over the minds of men. Malcolm had stopped being "Negro" years ago. It had become too small, too puny, too weak a word for him. Malcolm was bigger than that. Malcolm had become an Afro-American, and he wanted—so desperately—that we, that all his people, would become Afro-Americans, too.

There are those who still consider it their duty, as friends of the Negro people, to tell us to revile him, to flee, even from the presence of his memory, to save ourselves by writing him out of the history of our turbulent times.

Many will ask what Harlem finds to honor in this stormy, controversial, and bold young captain. And we will smile. Many will say turn away, away from this man, for he is not a man but a demon, a monster, a subverter and an enemy of the black man. And we will smile.

They will say that he is of hate—a fanatic, a racist who can only bring evil to the cause for which you struggle. And we will answer and say unto them, "Did you ever talk to Brother Malcolm? Did you ever touch him or have him smile at you? Did you ever really listen to him? Did he ever do a mean thing? Was he ever himself associated with violence or any public disturbance?" For if you did, you would know him. And if you knew him, you would know why we must honor him. Malcolm was our manhood, our living black manhood! This was his meaning to his people. And, in honoring him, we honor the best in ourselves.

Last year, from Africa, he wrote these words to a friend: "My journey," he says, "is almost ended, and I have a much broader scope than when I started out, which I believe will add new life and dimension to our struggle for freedom and honor and dignity in the States. I'm writing these things so that you will know for a fact the tremendous sympathy and support we have among the African states for our Human-Rights Struggle. The main thing is that we keep a united front wherein our most valuable time and energy will not be wasted with each other."

However much we may have differed with him—or with each other about him and his value as a man—let his going from us serve only to bring us together now. Consigning these mortal remains to earth, the common mother of all, secure in the knowledge that what we place in the ground is no more now a man but a seed, which, after the winter of discontent, will come forth again to meet us. And we shall know him then for what he was and is—a prince, our own black shining prince, who didn't hesitate to die, because he loved us so.

ᏩᎻᏃ

" 'It costs so much to be a full human being that there are very few who have the enlightenment, or the courage, to pay the price.' "

REV. JAMES J. REEB
(1927–1965)

by

ROBERT A. REED

152

James Reeb, a Presbyterian minister and human rights leader from Wichita, Kansas, traveled to Selma, Alabama, to participate in the civil rights march to Montgomery. He was brutally assaulted there on March 9, 1965, and died two days later in a Birmingham hospital.

The eulogy below was given by his longtime friend Robert Reed in the First Presbyterian Church in Casper, Wyoming, where Reeb had attended church as a boy.

. . . [W]e have not come to this house of worship for another eulogy. We are here as men and women of faith to seek the comfort, the strength, the direction of God. You and I who loved Jim Reeb have a sacred obligation, which must begin in these moments of worship. We must open our hearts at the deepest possible level as we seek to understand the full meaning of Jim's life and death. For it is only in such a search for understanding that we can find the courage to live our lives in obedience to the cross.

Jim loved life more than most people do. He was always ready with a story, a stunt, or a smile. He was quick to laugh or clown. His enthusiasms and exuberance were contagious. He never met a stranger; he never met a human being he did not try to like. His spirit was as big as the mountains and the out-of-doors he loved so well. Emerson said, "Let the measure of time be spiritual, not mechanical. Life is unnecessarily long. Moments of insight, of fine personal relation, a smile, a glance—what ample borrowers of eternity these may be." There are men who live and give and feel more in ten minutes than others do in ten years. Jim was one of these.

Jim not only enjoyed life more than most men; he was also more serious than most. Even in his teens he thought more, cared more, believed more. He found many things about this world which he wanted to change, for they were things he believed God wanted changed. Frequently in those years we talked together about the end of the war and what might be done to justify the awful suffering and sacrifice in human life. We spoke of the dreams of brotherhood and freedom for which so many young men had given their lives. It was during this period, while he was so active in this congregation, that Jim began to consider the ministry as a vocation.

There is a verse from the Indian poet Rabindranath Tagore which defines the difference between the true man of God and the rest of mankind:

> *We cling to our seats and never stir,*
> *We allow our flowers to fade in peace,*
>   *and avoid the trouble of bearing fruit.*
> *Let the starlights blazon their eternal folly,*
>   *We quench our flames.*
> *Let the forest rustle and the ocean roar,*
>   *We sit mute.*
> *Let the call of the flood-tide come from the sea,*
>   *We remain still.*

Jim Reeb did not remain still or silent. He did not quench his flame. He did not turn away from the trouble and the suffering that are the price of bearing fruit in life. Jim met life with open arms and open heart.

Two weeks ago when Jim packed his things for Selma, Alabama, he was a mature man. He was fully responsible, fully conscious of all the possible consequences of his actions. Twenty years had passed since he had been moderator of the youth fellowship at First Presbyterian Church here in Casper. He had been an infantry staff sergeant in Alaska during the closing months of World War II. He had graduated from college and seminary and earned a graduate degree in counseling at Temple University.

Jim never wanted an ordinary parish in the safety of the suburbs. As a chaplain in the charity wards of a huge metropolitan hospital, as Y director and inner-city minister, he spent his life on the front lines of human need. He worked with the sick, the underprivileged, the delinquent, the friendless, and the poor. Going to Selma was simply one expression of a lifelong concern for the suffering and oppressed. Jim was concerned with much more than the right to vote, basic as that is. He cared about the shame and hopelessness of those who must spend their entire lives in grinding poverty. He cared about world peace in this age of nuclear terror. Most of all he was disturbed by the violence and injustice still so common in our day.

What the world needs is not a gigantic leap into space, but a gigantic leap into brotherhood. Those who work for a breakthrough in human relations are required to undertake risks no less great than those who pioneer in outer space. There is a high price to be paid by all who would overcome the insanity of hatred and the folly of indifference to the suffering of other men.

Conventional Christians have missed Bonhoeffer's insight that to be a Christian is first of all to be a man! Jim's lifelong struggle was to be a full, free, and compassionate human being. He died as he lived, seeking to take some meaningful action on behalf of brotherhood and justice. To become a man is the first business of life. These words of Morris West, the Catholic novelist, describe for me the kind of man Jim had become: "It costs so much to be a full human being that there are very few who have the enlightenment, or the courage, to pay the price. One has to abandon altogether the search for security, and reach out to the risk of living with both arms. One has to embrace the world like a lover, and yet demand no easy return of love. One has to accept pain as a condition of existence. One has to count doubt and darkness as the cost of existence. One needs a will stubborn in conflict, but apt always to the total acceptance of every consequence of living and dying."

In a few weeks Christians around the world will celebrate Easter. We need to be reminded that the first nonviolent march calculated to stir the conscience of a nation was the procession of rough peasants and simple Galilean hill people led by Jesus of Nazareth into the city of Jerusalem on Palm Sunday. What a demonstration that was! A multitude of men and women and children—shouting, singing, shattering the silence of the city as they proclaimed allegiance to another King and another Kingdom. Caiaphas and Pilate were more subtle than Governor Wallace and Colonel Lingo. They did not meet the multitude with bullwhips and clubs and tear gas. Yet then as now many objected to any spiritual force that directly challenges the kingdoms of this world. The Pharisees demanded that Jesus rebuke his disciples and command them to keep silent.

The world still resists the knowledge that there is another King and another Kingdom. The response still comes, "If these were silent, the very stones would cry out." As on that Palm Sunday long ago a time of crisis has come to a nation. Jim Reeb was not silent. He lived and died in obedience to the cross.

Dag Hammarskjöld wrote in his personal journal: "He who has

surrendered himself to it knows that the Way ends on the Cross—
even when it is leading him through the jubilation of Gennesaret or
the triumphal entry into Jerusalem. Do not seek death. Death will
find you. But seek the road which makes death a fulfillment."

⌘

"For those of you who are black and are tempted to be filled with
hatred ... against all white people, I can only say that I feel in my
own heart the same kind of feeling. I had a member of my family
killed...."

REV. DR. MARTIN LUTHER KING
(1929–1968)

by

ROBERT F. KENNEDY
(1925–1968)

*Martin Luther King, the American civil rights leader and winner of the
Nobel Prize for Peace, was born in Montgomery, Alabama. He rose to
prominence in the civil rights movement of the 1950s, led the famous March
on Washington in 1963, and the March from Selma to Montgomery,
Alabama, in 1965. A brilliant orator and writer, whose insistence upon
nonviolence in the Gandhian tradition accounted for the success of the
movement, Dr. King was assassinated on April 4, 1968, in Memphis, Tennessee, by a white man.*

*On the day King was assassinated, Sen. Robert Kennedy was cam-
paigning for the presidency in Indianapolis, Indiana. He was on his way to
a campaign rally in a black section of the city when he heard that King had
been killed. His aides strongly urged him not to go to the rally, that he
would be endangering his life. But Kennedy insisted, and he stood upon the
back of a flatbed truck and delivered the following extemporaneous eulogy.
Less than two months later, Kennedy was assassinated in Los Angeles.*

I have bad news for you, for all of our fellow citizens, and people
who love peace all over the world, and that is that Martin Luther
King was shot and killed tonight.

Martin Luther King dedicated his life to love and to justice for his fellow human beings, and he died because of that effort.

In this difficult day, in this difficult time for the United States, it is perhaps well to ask what kind of a nation we are and what direction we want to move in. For those of you who are black—considering the evidence there evidently is that there were white people who were responsible—you can be filled with bitterness, with hatred, and desire for revenge. We can move in that direction as a country, in great polarization—black people amongst black, white people amongst white, filled with hatred toward one another.

Or we can make an effort, as Martin Luther King did, to understand and to comprehend, and to replace that violence, that stain of bloodshed that has spread across our land, with an effort to understand that compassion and love.

For those of you who are black and are tempted to be filled with hatred and distrust at the injustice of such an act, against all white people, I can only say that I feel in my own heart the same kind of feeling. I had a member of my family killed, but he was killed by a white man. But we have to make an effort in the United States, we have to make an effort to understand, to go beyond these rather difficult times.

My favorite poet was Aeschylus. He wrote: "In our sleep pain which cannot forget falls drop by drop upon the heart until, in our own despair, against our will, comes wisdom through the awful grace of God."

What we need in the United States is not division; what we need in the United States is not hatred; what we need in the United States is not violence or lawlessness, but love and wisdom and compassion toward one another, and a feeling of injustice towards those who still suffer within our country, whether they be white or they be black. . . .

We've had difficult times in the past. We will have difficult times in the future. It is not the end of violence; it is not the end of lawlessness; it is not the end of disorder.

But the vast majority of white people and the vast majority of black people in this country want to live together, want to improve the quality of our life, and want justice for all human beings who abide in our land.

Let us dedicate ourselves to what the Greeks wrote so many years ago: to tame the savageness of man and to make gentle the life of this world.

Let us dedicate ourselves to that, and say a prayer for our country and for our people.

ᏀᏙᎴᎴᎧ

"When the family was leaving me at college . . . Daddy looked me in the eye, shook my hand firmly, and said, 'Son, you can't come home.'"

VERNON E. JORDAN SR.
(1908–1987)

by

VERNON E. JORDAN JR.
(1935–)

Vernon E. Jordan Jr., former president of the National Urban League, is a prominent Washington, D.C., lawyer. He delivered this eulogy at his father's funeral on July 14, 1987, at Flipper Temple AME Church in Atlanta, Georgia.

If an official biographer was assigned to script the biography of our father, Vernon Eulion Jordan Sr., the facts would read as follows: Born in Jasper County, Monticello, Georgia, June 5, 1908, to Charlie and Annie Jordan, one of seventeen children. He joined St. James AME Church in Monticello at an early age, moved to Atlanta in his teens, married twice, had two sons, one stepson, nine grandchildren, and two great-grandchildren. He worked as a chauffeur, warehouseman, and for almost forty years was a civil servant in the U.S. government, and he served in the Navy during World War II. He lived, and he died July 11, 1987, at the age of seventy-nine.

If the biographer would ask Windsor, Warren, me, his brothers, sisters, coworkers, friends, and neighbors what was he like, who was he, the consensus would be the same. Simply put—Daddy was a good man, possessing plain, clear, unvarnished, uncomplicated values that made for a rich and rewarding life. . . . He loved God, hard work, his family, his friends.

There are memories too numerous to recall which reflect the values and principles of this good man, our father. Several stand out: (1) The Sunday-morning breakfast in University Homes, followed by the walk to Sunday school, rain or shine. Daddy, Windsor, Vernon Jr., dressed in our best walking proudly, happily, through John Hope Homes across the railroad track to Daddy's T. J. Chambliss Bible Class, where they argued about the Bible while Windsor and I were taught the Bible. Sunday school was followed by a Tru-Ade soda or vanilla wafers at the café before Mama joined us at church. (2) The whipping Windsor got for selling the *Atlanta Journal* early-afternoon edition to people who were eager to get the number for the day, although Windsor was not the real newspaper boy. (3) The whipping I got when Daddy discovered Saturday night before Easter that I didn't know my Easter speech. (4) The proud and pleased look when he saw us in our ROTC uniforms during college or Warren and Windsor in theirs during active duty. (5) His stern, serious, no-nonsense, no-excuse approach when we were wrong, and his joy when we did well. (6) His example of strength, tenacity, perseverance on the one hand, and love, warmth, and compassion on the other.

And finally, there was the Sunday night at DePauw University when the family was leaving me at college and saying good-bye. Windsor, happy that our room would be all his for the first time ever, shook my hand and ran to the car. My mother, with tears in her eyes, hugged and kissed me and said, "God bless you." Daddy looked me in the eye, shook my hand firmly, and said, "Son, you can't come home." And I said, "What do you mean I can't come home?" And Daddy said, "The college counselor said your scores are not as good as your classmates', your high school was inferior to theirs, and you are the only black in your class—but you can't come home." So I said, "What am I to do, Daddy?" And Daddy said, "Read, boy, read." I did what he said and graduated four years later. At graduation Windsor congratulated me, my mother hugged and kissed me, and my father, as serious as he was four years before, said simply, "You can come home now."

Well, there was another conversation last Saturday night between Father and son. A conversation between Daddy and God, the Father of us all. And Daddy said to God as did Timothy:

I have fought a good fight
I have finished my course
I have kept the faith

And God said to Daddy—you can come home now, you can come home now, my good and faithful servant.

ᘒᘒᘒ

"Without being in the slightest comforted as a Southerner, or let off the hook, I understood through him that black people regarded all Americans as irredeemably racist, the most sinful of them being not the Georgia redneck . . . but any citizen whatever whose de jure equality was a facade for de facto enmity and injustice."

JAMES BALDWIN
(1924–1987)

by

WILLIAM STYRON
(1925–)

Born in Harlem, James Baldwin became a preacher at the age of fourteen and, after graduating from high school, decided to become a writer. For nine years he lived in France. His works include the novels Go Tell It on the Mountain, Another Country, *and* Blues for Mister Charlie. *With his book of essays* The Fire Next Time, *Baldwin became a voice for black Americans.*

William Styron's book The Confessions of Nat Turner, *about the 1831 slave rebellion in Virginia, won the Pulitzer Prize but created enormous criticism from black intellectuals, who challenged Styron's right, as a white, to write about black history from a black perspective. William Styron is also the author of* Lie Down in Darkness, Sophie's Choice, *and* Darkness Visible. *The following appreciation was written for the* New York Times Book Review *after Baldwin died.*

James Baldwin was the grandson of a slave. I was the grandson of a slave owner. We were virtually the same age and both bemused by our close link to slavery, since most Americans of our vintage—if connected at all to the Old South—have had to trace that connection back several generations. But Jimmy had vivid images of slave times, passed down from his grandfather to his father, a Harlem preacher of fanatical bent, who left a terrifying imprint on his son's life. Jimmy once told me that he often thought the degradation of his grandfather's life was the animating force behind his father's apocalyptic, often incoherent rage.

By contrast my impression of slavery was quaint and rather benign; in the late 1930s, at the bedside of my grandmother, who was then close to ninety, I heard tales of the two little slave girls she had owned. Not much older than the girls themselves at the outset of the Civil War, she knitted stockings for them, tried to take care of them through the privations of the conflict, and at the war's end, was as wrenched with sorrow as they were by the enforced leave-taking. When I told this classic story to Jimmy, he didn't flinch. . . .

Jimmy moved into my studio in Connecticut in the late fall of 1960 and stayed there more or less continuously until the beginning of the following summer. . . . Baldwin was not very well known then . . . but his fame was gradually gaining momentum, and he divided his time between writing in the cottage and trips out to the nearby lecture circuit, where he made some money for himself and where, with his ferocious oratory, he began to scare his predominantly well-to-do, well-meaning audiences out of their pants.

Without being in the slightest comforted as a Southerner, or let off the hook, I understood through him that black people regarded all Americans as irredeemably racist, the most sinful of them being not the Georgia redneck (who was in part the victim of his heritage) but any citizen whatever whose de jure equality was a facade for de facto enmity and injustice.

Jimmy was writing his novel *Another Country* and making notes for the essay "The Fire Next Time." I was consolidating material, gathered over a decade, for a novel I was planning to write on the slave revolutionary Nat Turner. It was a frightfully cold winter, a good time for the Southern writer, who had never known a black man on intimate terms, and the Harlem-born writer, who had known few Southerners (black or white), to learn something about each other. I was by far the greater beneficiary. Struggling still to loosen myself from the prejudices and suspicions that a Southern upbringing engenders, I still possessed a residual skepticism: could a Negro really own a mind as subtle, as richly informed, as broadly inquired, and embracing as that of a white man?

My God, what appalling arrogance and vanity! Night after night Jimmy and I talked, drinking whiskey through the hours until the chill dawn, and I understood that I was in the company of as marvelous an intelligence as I was ever likely to encounter. His voice, lilting and silky, became husky as he chain-smoked Marlboros. He was spellbinding, and he told me more about the frustrations and anguish of being a black man in America than I had known until then, or perhaps wanted to know. He told me exactly what it was like to be denied service, to be spat at, to be called "nigger" and "boy."

What he explained gained immediacy because it was all so new to me. This chronicle of an urban life, his own life, unself-pityingly but with quiet rage spun out to me like a secret divulged, as if he were disgorging in private all the pent-up fury and gorgeous passion that a few years later, in "The Fire Next Time," would shake the conscience of the nation as few literary documents have ever done. . . .

Sometimes friends would join us. The conversation would turn more abstract and political. I am surprised when I recall how certain of these people—well-intentioned, tolerant, "liberal," all the postures Jimmy so intuitively mistrusted—would listen patiently while Jimmy spoke, visibly fretting, then growing indignant at some pronouncement of his, some scathing aperçu they considered too ludicrous for words, too extreme, and launch a polite counterattack. "You can't mean anything like that!" I can hear the words now. "You mean—*burn* . . ." And in the troubled silence, Jimmy's face would become a mask of imperturbable certitude. "Baby," he would say softly, and glare back with vast glowering eyes, "yes, baby. I mean *burn*. We will *burn your cities down*."

Much has been written about Baldwin's effect on the consciousness of the world. Let me speak for myself. Even if I had not valued much of this work—which was flawed, like all writing, but which at its best had a burnished eloquence and devastating impact—I would have deemed his friendship inestimable. At his peak he had the beautiful fervor of Camus or Kafka. Like them he revealed to me the core of his soul's savage distress and thus helped me shape and define my own work and its moral contours. This would be the most appropriate gift imaginable to the grandson of a slave owner from a slave's grandson.

oimo

"He was a black man in a sport that seemed a metaphor for racism—a sport played by white people in white clothes at white country clubs...."

ARTHUR ROBERT ASHE
(1943–1993)

by

NEW YORK TIMES EDITORIAL

Arthur Ashe, from Richmond, Virginia, was the first male African-American tennis player to reach any degree of prominence in the sport. He received a tennis scholarship to the University of California at Los Angeles in 1962; he was the first black U.S. Open champion; in 1970, he won the Australian Open, but was denied a visa to the South African Open on racial grounds. Ashe went before the United Nations to protest the policy. In 1973, he was admitted to South Africa to play, and in 1975 he won the title at Wimbledon.

After an intravenous blood transfusion, Ashe was found to have become HIV-positive, which resulted in his death. He was the first black Virginian to lie in state in the governor's mansion in Richmond.

The rise of Arthur Ashe in tennis, crowned by his Wimbledon victory in 1975, took on the stature of a fable. He was a black man in a sport that seemed a metaphor for racism—a sport played by white people in white clothes at white country clubs—and for a time he was the best there was. He was also a rare champion who believed that personal success imposes broad responsibilities to humanity.

Mr. Ashe's life was linked to two of the great social scourges of his day: racism and AIDS, the disease that led to his death last weekend. He confronted them head-on—driven, until the end, by the unselfish and unswerving conviction that he was duty-bound to ease the lives of others who were similarly afflicted.

In 1970, Mr. Ashe began a public campaign against apartheid, seeking a visa to play in the South African Open. Three years later he won that fight and became the first black man ever to reach the final of the open. His appearance inspired young South African blacks, among them the writer and former tennis player Mark Mathabane. In his memoir, *Kaffir Boy,* Mr. Mathabane wrote that the more he learned about Mr. Ashe the more he dreamed of freedom:

"What if I, too, were someday to attain the same fame and fortune as Arthur Ashe?" Mr. Mathabane wrote. "Would whites respect me as they did him? Would I be as free as he?" That dream came true when Mr. Mathabane won a tennis scholarship and immigrated to America.

Mr. Ashe took his crusade to America's inner cities as well, where he established tennis clinics and preached tennis discipline and provided hope to the young people who most needed it.

He contracted AIDS through a transfusion of tainted blood during heart-bypass surgery a decade ago. He learned of his infection in 1988, but did not disclose it until last April, after *USA Today* told him it planned to publish an article about his illness. After his public admission, Mr. Ashe campaigned vigorously on behalf of AIDS sufferers and started a foundation to combat the disease.

Mr. Ashe did not waste his fame; he used it to leave a mark on the social canvas of his time. For this he remains a model champion.

↢∽∾⊙

"She . . . held multitudes in her hands."

MARIAN ANDERSON
(1897–1993)

by

NEW YORK TIMES EDITORIAL

Contralto Marian Anderson was the first black American to become a permanent member of the Metropolitan Opera Company and the first black American to perform at the White House. In 1939, the Daughters of the American Revolution, who owned Constitution Hall, forbade her to sing there, which caused Eleanor Roosevelt to resign her membership in the DAR and schedule a concert for Marian Anderson on the steps of the Lincoln Memorial. She was a winner of the President's Medal of Freedom and an alternate delegate to the United Nations.

She had a voice that dazzled Toscanini and a dedication that heartened the whole world. Marian Anderson, who died yesterday at ninety-six, sang compellingly that her Lord held the whole world in His hands. With her gloriously quiet manner she, too, held multitudes in her hands.

When a benighted nation tried to keep her back because of her race, Marian Anderson replied with beautiful song, not loud rage. She converted white bigots' hatred into artistic energy. And she laid claim on the consciences of decent Americans, easing the way for recognition of other black Americans, artists and nonartists.

It was fifty-four Easter Sundays ago that Marian Anderson sang to seventy-five thousand people at the Lincoln Memorial because the Daughters of the American Revolution had denied her their hall. She was civilly obedient, willing to let her deep and delicate contralto answer the libels on her race. Past her prime when she reached the stage of the Metropolitan Opera, she still mustered a haunting Ulrica in Verdi's *Un Ballo in Maschera*.

To hear Marian Anderson sing in person was to marvel not only at her vocal mastery but also at the total focus of the singer on her art, shutting out the world as though she hadn't shaken it with her achievements. What a sound, what a presence, what a moment for American music!

CHAPTER SIX

A NATION'S DEAD

ᏨᏁᎠᎠᎯᎤ

Only four of the countless wars human beings have waged against one another are commemorated here. Whether any of them relieved the countries involved of anything except economic insolvency or the desire to exact vengeance depends upon one's view of things. It cannot be counted as good that, in Greece, the Spartans overwhelmed the Athenians. The Civil War saved the Union but did not destroy racism, and World War I did not prevent World War II, which created the Holocaust.

All wars are acts of bankruptcy; the human beings they do not kill outright they corrupt or maim in spirit. Yet it is considered a cruel, even treasonous, act to speak out against a war in which our own countrymen and -women have been involved. To do so is to dishonor the courage, the self-sacrifice, and the service of the soldiers— and ourselves. The idea that we have lost our children to no good end would be too much to bear. So the war dead are revered, new wars are mounted, and the acres of slain soldiers expand to accommodate new rows. But until very recently the honor attached to the names of those who died in service to their country has always obscured the horror of how the honor was earned.

There is a great distance from the war between the Athenians and the Spartans, after which Pericles urged the survivors not to envy the slain, and the Vietnam War, whose survivors America shunned. But the compassionate face of war is found in the sorrowful elegy by Lincoln, the gentle reassurance of Atatürk to the mothers of the Allies, and James O'Neill's anguished reminder that no soldier is unknown. Finally, Elie Wiesel explains why there must be a Day of Remembrance for the Holocaust: "We are scared of what humankind could do to itself. Therefore, we tell the story."

"The whole earth is the sepulchre of illustrious men. . . ."

PERICLES' FUNERAL ORATION
(495–429 B.C.)

A popular Athenian statesman, Pericles delivered an address to the sur-
vivors of the first year of the Peloponnesian War between Athens and
Sparta. Delivered in 431 B.C., the oration was designed to fire up the patri-
otism of the Athenians and spur them on to renewed courage. Pericles first
extols the virtues of democracy and the city-state of Athens ("the only peo-
ple of the world who are found by experience to be greater than in report")
and then, in the oration's final excerpt, praises the slain soldiers and com-
forts their families.

The fatal period to which these gallant souls are now reduced is the
surest evidence of their merit—an evidence begun in their lives and
completed in their deaths. . . . Their last service effaces all former
demerits—it extends to the public; their private demeanors reached
only to a few. Yet not one of these was at all induced to shrug from
danger, through fondness of those delights which the peaceful afflu-
ent life bestows—not one was the less lavish of his life, through that
flattering hope attendant upon want, that poverty at length might be
exchanged for affluence. One passion there was in their minds much
stronger than these—the desire of vengeance on their enemies.
Regarding this as the most honorable prize of dangers, they boldly
rushed toward the mark to glut revenge and then to satisfy those
secondary passions. The uncertain event they had already secured in
hope; what their eyes showed plainly must be done they trusted
their own valor to accomplish, thinking it more glorious to defend
themselves and die in the attempt than to yield and live. From the
reproach of cowardice, indeed, they fled, but presented their bodies
to the shock of battle; when, insensible of fear, but triumphing in
hope, in the doubtful charge they instantly dropped—and thus discharged the duty which brave men owed their country.

As for you who now survive them, it is your business to pray for
a better fate, but to think it your duty also to preserve the same spirit
and warmth of courage against your enemies; not judging of the
expedience of this from a mere harangue . . . but, rather, making

daily increasing grandeur of this community the object of your thoughts. . . . And when it really appears great to your apprehensions, think again that this grandeur was acquired by brave and valiant men, by men who knew their duty, and in the moments of action were sensible of shame—who, whenever their attempts were unsuccessful, thought it no dishonor for their country to stand in need of anything their valor could do for it, and so made it the most glorious present. Bestowing thus their lives on the public, they have every one received a praise that will never decay. . . .

For the whole earth is the sepulchre of illustrious men; nor is it the inscription of the columns in their native land alone that shows their merit, but the memorial of them, better than all inscriptions in every foreign nation, reposited more durably in universal remembrance than on their own tombs. From this very moment, emulating these noble patterns, placing your happiness in liberty, and liberty in valor, be prepared to encounter all the dangers of war. For to be lavish of life is not so noble in those whom misfortunes have reduced to misery and despair, as in men who hazard the loss of a comfortable subsistence and the enjoyment of all the blessings this world affords by an unsuccessful enterprise. Adversity, after a series of ease and affluence, sinks deeper into the heart of a man of spirit than the stroke of death insensibly received in the vigor of life and public hope.

For this reason, the parents of those who are now gone, whoever of them may be attending here, I do not bewail—I shall rather comfort. . . . I know it in truth a difficult task to fix comfort in those breasts which will have frequent remembrances, in seeing the happiness of others, of what they once themselves enjoyed. And sorrow flows not from the absence of those goods we have never yet experienced but from the loss of those to which we have been accustomed. . . . But you whose age is already far advanced compute the greater share of happiness your longer time hath afforded for so much gain, persuaded in yourself the remainder will be but short, and enlighten that space by the glory gained by these. It is greatness of soul alone that never grows old, nor is it wealth that delights in the latter stage of life, as some give out, so much as honor.

To you, the sons and brothers of the deceased, whatever number of you are here, a field of handy contention is opened. For him who no longer is, everyone is ready to commend, so that to whatever height you push your deserts, you will scarce ever be thought to equal, but to be somewhat inferior to these. Envy will exert itself against a competitor while life remains; but when death stops the competition, affection will applaud without restraint.

If after this it be expected from me to say anything to you who are now reduced to a state of widowhood, about female virtue, I shall express it all in one short admonition: it is your greatest glory not to be deficient in the virtue peculiar to your sex, and to give men as little handle as possible to talk of your behavior, whether well or ill.

I have now discharged the province allotted me by the laws and said what I thought most pertinent to this assembly. Our departed friends have by facts been already honored. Their children from this day till they arrive at manhood shall be educated at the public expense of the state, which hath appointed so beneficial a need for these and all future relics of the public contests. For whatever the greatest rewards are proposed for virtue, there the best of patriots are ever to be found. Now let everyone respectively indulge in becoming grief for his departed friends, and then retire.

✄

"The world will little note, nor long remember, what we say here...."

LINCOLN'S GETTYSBURG ADDRESS
(1809–1865)

When Lincoln dedicated the battlefield at Gettysburg, Pennsylvania, on November 19, 1863, the Civil War was still raging. Lincoln chose not to identify the soldiers as Union or Confederate, or in any way allude to North or South as adversaries. This ten-sentence speech, often compared to the Sermon on the Mount, took Lincoln four minutes to deliver. It was preceded by a two-hour speech by the well-known orator Edward Everett Hale, who was, needless to say, outdone.

Four score and seven years ago our fathers brought forth on this continent a new nation, conceived in liberty, and dedicated to the proposition that all men are created equal.

Now we are engaged in a great civil war, testing whether that nation, or any nation so conceived and so dedicated, can long endure. We are met on a great battlefield of that war. We have come to dedicate a portion of that field, as a final resting place for those who here gave their lives that that nation might live. It is altogether fitting and proper that we should do this.

But in a larger sense, we cannot dedicate, we cannot consecrate, we cannot hallow, this ground. The brave men, living and dead, who struggled here have consecrated it, far above our poor power to add or detract. The world will little note, nor long remember, what we say here, but it can never forget what they did here. It is for us the living, rather, to be dedicated here to the unfinished work which they who fought here have thus far so nobly advanced. It is rather for us to be here dedicated to the great task remaining before us— that from these honored dead we take increased devotion to that cause for which they gave the last full measure of devotion—that we here highly resolve that these dead shall not have died in vain— that this nation, under God, shall have a new birth of freedom—and that government of the people, by the people, for the people, shall not perish from the earth.

ᏳᎲᎲᎧ

MEMORIAL TABLET
HONORING THE BRITISH, AUSTRALIAN, AND NEW ZEALAND
SOLDIERS KILLED IN THE 1915 DARDANELLES CAMPAIGN,
GALLIPOLI, TURKEY

by

KEMAL PASHA ATATÜRK
(1881–1938)

In World War I, the Allies unsuccessfully attempted to wrest control of the Dardanelles and the Bosporus Strait from Turkey. Engraved upon a stone monument on a Gallipoli hillside covered with soldiers' graves are the following words written by Kemal Atatürk, the father of modern Turkey, whose troops successfully resisted the disastrous British-led invasion. The "Johnnies" are the British soldiers, the "Mehmets" the Turks.

Those heroes that shed their blood
and lost their lives . . .
You are now lying in the soil of a friendly country.
Therefore rest in peace.
There is no difference between the Johnnies
And the Mehmets to us where they lie side by side
Here in this country of ours.
You the mothers
Who sent their sons from faraway countries
Wipe away your tears.
Your sons are now lying in our bosom
And are at peace.
After having lost their lives on this land they have
Become our sons as well.

◦◦◦◦◦

"He is my brother. I knew him, though never well. We were both too young to know each other well. The world was too young to know him well, or what he might have done, had he not had to do something quite different. But this is destiny. And dust."

A VALEDICTORY TO THE UNKNOWN SOLDIERS
OF WORLD WAR II

by

JAMES O'NEILL JR.
(1920–1967)

James O'Neill was a journalist at the Washington Daily News. *He wrote this valedictory after Memorial Day, 1958.*

Unknown?
    I know them well.
    Each one is an old, old friend.
    One, for instance, is an old bald-headed master sergeant, with hash clear up to his third rocker. He died in Italy, alone, but known by countless thousands of infantrymen who owe their lives to what

173

he cursed them into doing and being.

Or, he is the gentle, quiet kid who flew with me in Texas. I watched him die one morning, in a clear, bright sun-washed sky.

Or he is the bluff, arrogant boy from Milwaukee, who drilled all day in the hot sun like an automaton and wrote to his mother every night. He read his *Soldier's Handbook* and did push-ups while we were drinking PX beer.

He is the thoughtful, curious one who spoke of Nietzsche and Spinoza and cried himself to sleep at night on a GI pillow.

He's one of those older fellows. The one, I think, who had four grown sons in the Navy. He was a master plumber and was blown to shreds in his workshop outside Bizerte.

He is the pink-cheeked farm kid whose mother signed for him. The Navy wired and told her he died so bravely. So well; so finally. In the Coral Sea. He had just turned eighteen. The name Blanche was tattooed beneath a heart on his left forearm. Blanche is his twin sister. He had never known any other girls.

He's that poor, bedraggled little guy in the oversized fatigues, sweat-stained and dirty, standing in a Georgia chow line, swearing eternal hatred for all warriors. But God how he could shoot.

He was the one who always got to the PX just after it closed.

He couldn't dig a hole, but he could lob a grenade like Walter Johnson. He died by that sword he wielded so well.

His daughter just turned sixteen. She was one when he died. She has his eyes and her mother's memory of him.

He pressed his pants on a footlocker, covered with a blanket. He sent his pay home to a faithless child bride and spent his last three seconds on earth falling across the muzzle of a German machine gun just this side of a place called Bastogne.

He was the best crapshooter in the Bronx, and the greatest lover in Louisville, Kentucky.

He planned to be a rabbi.

He held a doctorate in English and abhorred the crudities of the latrine balladeers.

He left a line of healthy illegitimate children in a Detroit slum and died heroically in Belgium.

He, whose grandfather had been born in slavery, saw Inchon through tired eyes and bled to death on its beach.

He died as nobly as he could on the Yalu River. Weeping, he died, for it was all so futile and such a waste. He was twenty-two and very much in love. His wife still weeps.

He is my brother. I knew him, though never well. We were both too young to know each other well. The world was too young to know him well, or what he might have done, had he not had to do something quite different. But this is destiny. And dust.

He carried an onionskin Shakespeare through a lush Pacific jungle. All that was left of it when they found him were some torn pages; a few sonnets, Anthony's brief eulogy to dead Brutus. The Japanese had demolished both the onionskin Shakespeare and the man who bore it bravely into battle.

Ernie Pyle knew him. They damned the war together in a ditch on Je Shima. He wept at Ernie's funeral and died the day after in yet another ditch.

Bill Mauldin knew him. George Baker knew him. Ray Clapper knew him.

The fancy girls in Honolulu knew him and the old French priest who heard his last confession in a monastery beyond Cherbourg knew him.

> So how, then, are they unknown,
> When you think of them today, as all the
> days of your life, think of them as I do.
> Unknown?
> I know them well.
> Each one is an old friend.

⟨⟩

"We think of the victims and we learn that despair is not the solution. Despair is the question. And that is why we gather year after year—to fight despair; and not only mine—ours."

DAYS OF REMEMBRANCE

by

ELIE WIESEL
(1928–)

Elie Wiesel, who survived a Nazi death camp, has dedicated his life to telling the story of the "Holocaust," a word he is credited with first apply-ing to the slaughter of the Jews and Jewish sympathizers by the Germans in World War II. This speech was delivered in the Rotunda of the U.S. Capi-tol on April 30, 1984.

Mr. Vice President, Congressman Yates, distinguished members of the House and Senate, fellow survivors, friends:

For some of us, this is the most solemn and awesome day of the year. We delve into the darkest recesses of our memory only to con-front and evoke a vanished universe surrounded by flames and pen-etrated by silence. The living and the dead locked together as they are during Kol Nidre services, young and old, pious and secular, princes and madmen, sages and wanderers, beggars and dreamers. On this day, Mr. Vice President and friends, we close our eyes and we see them—an eerie procession which slowly, meditatingly, walks toward angels of death carried on wings of night into night. We see them as you see us. We are the link between you and them. . . .

It is symbolic that our commemoration takes place in this august hall of legislation and commitment to law, and commitment to humanity. What we are teaching the world from this room, thanks to you, members of the House and the Senate, is that laws must be human. Laws are to serve humanity and not destroy it. Laws are given to human beings to perfect life and not to profane it. Laws, too, became corrupt once upon a time. And here with your deed and our words, we shall shield laws in the future.

And so once more, as we have done since 1979, on this Day of Remembrance we gather from all the corners of exile to tell tales— tales of fire and tales of despair and tales of defiance—tales that we must tell lest we are crushed by our memories. In remembering them, remembering the victims in the ghettos and camps and the prisons, we become aware of man's singular vulnerability but also of his stunning ability to transcend it.

We remember the killers and we lose our faith in humanity. But then we remember the victims, and though scarred, our faith is restored—it must be. The fact that the Jewish victims never became executioners, that they never victimized others, that they remained Jewish to the end—human to the end—that inside ghettos and death camps, my God, inside gas chambers, they could speak to God, to God. They could say: *"S'hma Yisroael Adonai Elohenu, Adonai Echad"*—God is God and God is One and God is the Lord to Creation. To say those words there on the threshold of death and oblivion must restore our faith in them and therefore in humankind. We think of the victims and we learn that despair is not the solution. Despair is the question. And that is why we gather year after year— to fight despair; and not only mine—ours.

As a son of the Jewish people, as a citizen who is proud to be a member of the American people, I live with the memory of Jewish children and their parents. It has been our task, it will remain our task, to maintain that memory alive. But then we remember not because we seek vengeance; we don't believe in it. We only seek justice. We do not aim to hurt, only to sensitize. We believe that by retelling our tales we might help our contemporaries by making them aware of what could happen to human beings when they live in an inhuman society surrounded and penetrated by indifference on one hand, evil on the other, with so few opposing evil and indifference. That is why I allow myself at times to see in the Holocaust an analogy only to itself, meaning that nothing should be compared to it but that everything must be related to it. It is because of what we endured that we must try to help victims everywhere today: the Bahais in Iran who are being murdered by the dictatorship in Iran; the Miskitos on the border of Nicaragua; we must help the Boat People who are still seeking refuge; the Cambodian refugees; and the prisoners, so many of them, in Communist jails. It is because we remember what has been done to our people that we must plead at every opportunity, in this House and in all other houses, for Anatoly Scharansky, Iosif Begun, Vladmir Slepack, and all the dissidents and prisoners who are in jail waiting for someone to shake off humankind's indifference. If they were to lose faith in us, we should be damned. It is because we remember the solitude of Jews in those times that we feel so linked to and proud of the state of Israel today. We survivors, our friends and allies, are grateful to Israel, grateful to a people simply for existing, for inspiring us to keep faith in a certain form of humanity and tradition.

While we remember the victims, we also remember those who tried to help us—the Raoul Wallenbergs and the Oskar Shindlers. . . .

They were so few and they were so alone. It breaks my heart to think of their solitude, of their sacrifice. Memory is not exclusive. Memory is inclusive. It is because we remember the singular aspect of the tragedy that we remember its universality. We must also think of tomorrow as though it would be part of our memory. I think the world unleashed madness forty years ago and that madness is still dominating spirits and minds of too many countries. There are too many signals of danger—racism, anti-Semitism, bigotry, fanaticism. We are scared of what humankind could do to itself. Therefore, we tell the story.

In conclusion, Mr. Vice President, may I quote to you a legend of the great masterwork of human civilization and culture, the Talmud. The Talmud tells us that when God gave the law to the people of Israel, he lifted up Mount Sinai over the heads of the Jewish people and said, "If you accept the law, you shall live. If not, you shall die." And so, we accepted the law.

I have the feeling today, Mr. Vice President and friends, that God has lifted above our heads a mountain of fire, and it is as though God were to say to us: If you obey the law—if you remember that we are all children of one father, if you remember that whatever happened to one people must affect all other people, if you remember that stupid cruelty is absurd and grotesque, and it is not in hurting people that one can redeem oneself—if you remember, you shall live, and if not—but we must remember.

⟨✦⟩

CHAPTER SEVEN

THE EULOGY
AS SOCIAL COMMENTARY

Assembled here are a half dozen eulogies that have such a wide-angle lens that the reader is able to see a great deal more than the individual being commemorated. They are not all flattering portraits. Sarah, Duchess of Marlboro's reminiscence of Queen Anne is really a wicked character sketch, the writing of which was a small cottage industry in the seventeenth century. Sinclair Lewis's portrait of the Reverend Henry Ward Beecher is an indirect diatribe against the society that floated Beecher to the top.

In the same vein, only with more acid in it, is H. L. Mencken's "eulogy" for William Jennings Bryan, the three-time Democratic candidate for president who died just after winning the Scopes evolution case in Dayton, Tennessee, against Clarence Darrow.

Mencken compares him to a human flytrap, who "set his traps and spread his bait" in the swampy backwaters of rural America, which Mencken populates with all the evils of American society, from the Ku Klux Klan to Baptist preachers who "dammed the brooks with the saved."

At the time of its publication, it was a shocking piece of journalism that inspired a flurry of "how could you?"–type letters to the newspaper in which it was printed, but Mencken—who actually toned down his first version and then reinstated what he had left out when it reappeared in his *American Mercury*—was unrepentant. "We killed the son of a bitch" was his only comment. So did Darrow, who won the Scopes case on appeal.

By contrast, Victor Hugo's tribute to Voltaire is a passionate accolade from the greatest writer in the nineteenth century to the greatest writer of the eighteenth. But Hugo delays introducing Voltaire until he has sketched in enough ghastly injustices of eighteenth-century France—people being broken on the wheel, having their tongues ripped out—to make one cry out for a champion. It is a masterful way to set the stage.

Voltaire was a rationalist and Hugo a romantic, but there were enough similarities between them to understand why Hugo felt himself the rightful inheritor of Voltaire's spirit. Both defied the authorities, civil and religious, which sporadically imprisoned them or sent them into exile, both used their pen to correct injustices, and both were beloved by the French people, who buried them in the Pantheon, where its most revered citizens are interred.

Joseph Brodsky takes us inside the Soviet Union to the city of Pskov, where the widow Nadezhda Mandelstam lived with the poetry of her late husband, Osip, and the poet Anna Akhmatova stuffed inside her head—the only safe place for it to be. It is a portrait of a difficult and loyal woman who did something extraordinary. At the end of her life she sat down and wrote a memoir that pinned the Soviet Union and all the artists who collaborated with it against the wall.

"There is something quite breathtaking in the realization that she wrote those two volumes of hers at the age of sixty-five," writes the poet Joseph Brodsky. "In the Mandelstam family it is Osip who was the writer; she wasn't." But under the influence of the poetry she had stored in her head, she wrote a powerful book that, as Brodsky said, "turns out to be capable of slowing down, if not averting in the long run, the cultural disintegration of a whole nation."

Finally, we move "inside" as Diana Trilling takes us on a tour of Marilyn Monroe's psyche. It is an unlikely and brilliant pairing of an intellectual woman analyzing a self-taught actress whose hunger for education was culturally suspect. "The notion," writes Trilling, "that someone with Marilyn Monroe's sexual advantages could have wanted anything except to make love robbed us of a prized illusion, that enough sexual possibility is enough everything."

It is a long and riveting exploration of what it was about Monroe that made her such an astonishing phenomenon—and why she did not survive. Innocence, concludes Trilling, "lay at the heart of her gift," which also made her fatally vulnerable. Unable to connect with her own history, so as not to repeat it, Monroe finally succumbed.

"Her memory was exceeding great, almost to a wonder, and had these two peculiarities very remarkable in it, that she could, whenever she pleased, forget what others would have thought themselves obliged by truth and honor to remember, and remember all such things as others would think it a happiness to forget."

QUEEN ANNE OF ENGLAND
(1665–1714)

by

SARAH, DUCHESS OF MARLBORO
(1660–1744)

In the seventeenth century, the custom of penning character sketches was extremely popular. Sarah, Duchess of Marlboro, was a childhood friend of Queen Anne's, and when Anne ascended to the throne in 1702, Sarah wielded enormous influence over her. However, the queen was a weak-minded woman and gradually Sarah was supplanted.

About Queen Anne, whose reign is known primarily for good furniture and superior silver, there is little to counter or add to the Duchess of Marl-boro's portrait, which was presumably written upon her death and not before. But one historian wrote that Queen Anne "died so slowly and was rumored to be dead so often before she ceased to breathe that for many years the words 'Queen Anne is dead' made a sick joke."

Queen Anne had a person and appearance not at all ungraceful, till she grew exceeding gross and corpulent. There was something of majesty in her look, but mixed with a sudden and constant frown, that plainly betrayed a gloominess of soul and a cloudiness of disposition within. She seemed to inherit a good deal of her father's moroseness, which naturally produced in her the same sort of stubborn positiveness in many cases, both ordinary and extraordinary, as well as the same sort of bigotry in religion.

Her memory was exceeding great, almost to a wonder, and had these two peculiarities very remarkable in it, that she could, whenever she pleased, forget what others would have thought themselves obliged by truth and honor to remember, and remember all such things as others would think it a happiness to forget. Indeed, she chose to retain in it very little besides ceremonies and customs of courts and such like insignificant trifles. . . .

Her friendships were flames of extravagant passion, ending in indifferences or aversion. Her love to the prince seemed in the eye of the world to be prodigiously great; and great as was the passion of her grief, her stomach was greater, for that very day he died she ate three very large and hearty meals, so that one would think that as other persons' grief takes away their appetites, her appetite took away her grief. . . .

She loved fawning and adoration, and hated plain dealing, even in the most important cases. She had a soul that nothing could so effectually move as flattery or fear. A sudden surprise, in an unguarded moment, would make the truth sometimes discover itself in her look or in some unlucky word; but if she had time and warning enough to learn her lesson, all the arguments and reason in the world could extort nothing from her that she had not a mind to acknowledge. In such cases she seemed to have the insensibility of a rock, and would resolutely dissemble or disown anything in the world. . . .

She had no native generosity of temper, nor was often known of herself to do a handsome action either as a reward or as a piece of friendship. The diligence and faithfulness of a servant signified but little with her, where she had no passion for the person. . . . In a word, she had little zeal for the happiness of others . . . and at last preferred her own humor and passion before the safety and happiness of her own people and of all Europe, which she had either not sense enough to see or not goodness enough to regard. Whether her memory will be celebrated by posterity with blessings or curses, time will show.

⁂

"If the magistracy calls itself torture, if the Church calls itself Inquisition . . . then philosophy rises in wrath, and arraigns the judge before justice, and the priest before God!
    This is what Voltaire did. It was grand."

VOLTAIRE
(1694–1778)

by

VICTOR HUGO
(1802–1885)

Voltaire, the prolific eighteenth-century philosopher and writer of "the Enlightenment," used his pen to attack the moral wrongs of French society. He was a cynic who loved life; in chronic poor health, he was a volcano of creative energy. When he died, he left the statement "I die adoring God, loving my friends, not hating my enemies, and detesting persecution."

In Victor Hugo's tribute, delivered at the Paris Exhibition one hundred years after Voltaire died, arguably the greatest writer of the nineteenth century pays tribute to the man he considered his spiritual father.

A hundred years ago today a man died. . . . When he was born, Louis XIV still reigned; when he died, Louis XVI already wore the crown; so that his cradle saw the last rays of the great throne, and his coffin the first gleams from the great abyss. . . .

Before the Revolution the social structure was this:

At the base, the people;

Above the people, religion represented by the clergy;

By the side of religion, justice represented by the magistracy.

And at that period of human society, what was the people? It was ignorance. What was the religion? It was intolerance. And what was justice? It was injustice. Am I going too far in my words? Judge.

I will confine myself to the citation of two facts, but decisive.

At Toulouse, October 12, 1761, there was found in the lower story of a house a young man hanged. The crowd gathered, the clergy fulminated, the magistracy investigated. It was a suicide; they made of it an assassination. In what interest? In the interest of religion. And who was accused? The father. He was a Huguenot, and he wished to hinder his son from becoming a Catholic. There was here a moral monstrosity and a material impossibility; no matter! This father had killed his son; this old man had hanged this young man. Justice travailed, and this was the result. In the month of March 1762, a man with white hair, Jean Calas, was conducted to a public place, stripped naked, stretched upon a wheel, the members bound upon it, the head hanging. Three men are there upon a scaffold, a magistrate named David, charged to superintend the punishment, a priest to hold the crucifix, and the executioner with a bar of iron in his hand. The patient, stupefied and terrible, regards not the priest, and looks at the executioner. The executioner gives him the coup de grâce; that is to say, crushes in his chest with the thick end of the bar of iron. So died Jean Calas.

That lasted two hours. After his death the evidence of the suicide came to light. But an assassination had been committed. By whom? By the judges.

Another fact. After the old man, the young man. Three years later, in 1765, at Abbeville, the day after a night of storm and high wind, there was found upon the pavement of a bridge an old crucifix of worm-eaten wood, which for three centuries had been fastened to the parapet. Who had thrown down this crucifix? Who committed this sacrilege? It is not known. Perhaps a passerby. Perhaps the wind. Who is the guilty one? The bishop of Amiens launched a *monitoire*. Now what a *monitoire* was: it was an order to all the faithful, on pain of hell, to declare what they knew or believed they knew of such or such a fact; a murderous injunction, when addressed by fanaticism to ignorance. The *monitoire* of the bishop of Amiens does its work; the town gossip assumes the character of the crime charged. Justice discovers, or believes it discovers, that on the night when the crucifix was thrown down, two men, two officers, one named La Barre, the other D'Etallonde, passed over the bridge of Abbeville, that they were drunk, and that they sang a guardroom song.

The tribunal was the Seneschalcy of Abbeville. The Seneschalcy of Abbeville was equivalent to the court of the Capitouls of Toulouse. It was not less just. Two orders for arrest were issued. D'Etallonde escaped, La Barre was taken. Him they delivered to judicial examination. He denied having crossed the bridge; he confessed to having sung the song. The Seneschalcy of Abbeville condemned him; he appealed to the Parliament of Paris. He was conducted to Paris; the sentence was found good and confirmed. He was conducted back to Abbeville in chains. I abridge. The monstrous hour arrives. They begin by subjecting the Chevalier de la Barre to the torture ordinary, and extraordinary, to make him reveal his accomplices. Accomplices in what? In having crossed a bridge and sung a song. During the torture one of his knees was broken; his confessor, on hearing the bones crack, fainted away. The next day, June 5, 1766, La Barre was drawn to the great square of Abbeville, where flamed a penitential fire; the sentence was read to La Barre; then they cut off one of his hands, then they tore out his tongue with iron pincers; then, in mercy, his head was cut off and thrown into the fire. So died the Chevalier de la Barre. He was nineteen years of age.

Then, O Voltaire; thou didst utter a cry of horror, and it will be thine eternal glory!

Then didst thou enter upon the appalling trial of the past; thou didst plead, against tyrants and monsters, the cause of the human race, and thou didst gain it. Great man, blessed be thou forever!

The frightful things which I have recalled were accomplished in the midst of a polite society; its life was gay and light; people went and came; they looked neither above nor below themselves; their indifference had become carelessness; graceful poets, Saint Aulaire, Boufflers, Gentil-Bernard, composed pretty verses; the court was all festival; Versailles was brilliant; Paris ignored what was passing; and then it was that, through religious ferocity, the judges made an old man die upon the wheel and the priests tore out a child's tongue for a song.

In this presence of this society, frivolous and dismal, Voltaire alone, having before his eyes those united forces, the court, the nobility, capital; that unconscious power, the blind multitude; that terrible magistracy, so severe to subjects, so docile to the master, crushing and flattering, kneeling upon the people before the king; that clergy, vile mélange of hypocrisy and fanaticism; Voltaire alone, I repeat, declared war against that coalition of all the social iniquities, against that enormous and terrible world, and he accepted battle with it. And what was his weapon? That which has the lightness of the wind and the power of the thunderbolt—a pen.

With that weapon he fought; with that weapon he conquered.

Let us salute that memory.

Voltaire conquered; Voltaire waged the splendid kind of warfare, the war of one alone against all; that is to say, the grand warfare. The war of thought against matter, the war of reason against prejudice, the war of the just against the unjust, the war for the oppressed

THE BOOK OF EULOGIES

against the oppressor, the war of goodness, the war of kindness. He had the tenderness of a woman and the wrath of a hero. He was a great mind and an immense heart.

He conquered the old code and the old dogma. He conquered the feudal lord, the Gothic judge, the Roman priest. He raised the populace to the dignity of people. He taught, pacificated, and civilized. He fought for Sirven and Montbailly, as for Calas and La Barre; he accepted all the menaces, all the outrages, all the persecutions, calumny, and exile. He was indefatigable and immovable. He conquered violence by a smile, despotism by sarcasm, infallibility by irony, obstinacy by perseverance, ignorance by truth.

I have just pronounced the word *smile*. I pause at it. Smile! It is Voltaire.

Let us say it, pacification is the great side of the philosopher; in Voltaire the equilibrium always reestablishes itself at last. Whatever may be his just wrath, it passes, and the irritated Voltaire always gives place to the Voltaire calmed. Then in that profound eye the smile appears.

That smile is wisdom. That smile, I repeat, is Voltaire. That smile sometimes becomes laughter, but the philosophic sadness tempers it. Toward the strong it is mockery; toward the weak it is a caress. It disquiets the oppressor, and reassures the oppressed. Against the great it is raillery; for the little it is pity. Ah, let us be moved by that smile! It had in it the rays of the dawn. It illuminated the true, the just, the good, and what there is of worthy in the useful. It lighted up the interior of superstitions. Those ugly things it is salutary to see, he has shown. Luminous, that smile was fruitful also. The new society, the desire for equality and concession and that beginning of fraternity which called itself tolerance, reciprocal goodwill, the just accord of men and right, reason recognized as the supreme law, the annihilation of prejudices and prescribed opinions, the serenity of souls, the spirit of indulgence and of pardon, harmony, peace—behold what has come from that great smile!

On the day—very near, without any doubt—when the identity of wisdom and clemency will be recognized, when the amnesty will be proclaimed, I affirm it! Up there in the stars Voltaire will smile.

Between two servants of humanity, who appeared eighteen hundred years apart, there is a mysterious relation.

To combat Pharisaism; to unmask imposture; to overthrow tyrannies, usurpations, prejudices, falsehoods, superstitions; to demolish the temple in order to rebuild it, that is to say, to replace the false by the true; to attack a ferocious magistracy, a sanguinary priesthood; to take a whip and drive the money changers from the sanctuary; to reclaim the heritage of the disinherited; to protect the weak, the poor, the suffering, the overwhelmed, to struggle for the persecuted and oppressed—that was the war of Jesus Christ! And who waged that war? It was Voltaire.

The completion of the evangelical work is the philosophical work; the spirit of mercy began, the spirit of tolerance continued. Let us say it with a sentiment of profound respect: Jesus wept; Voltaire smiled. Of that divine tear and that human smile is composed the sweetness of the present civilization.

Did Voltaire always smile? No. He was often indignant. You remarked it in my first words.

Certainly measure, reserve, proportion, are reason's supreme law. We can say that moderation is the very respiration of the philosopher. That effort of the wise man ought to be to condense into a sort of serene certainty all the approximations of which philosophy is composed. But at certain moments the passion for the true rises powerful and violent, and it is within its right in so doing, like the stormy winds which purify. Never, I insist upon it, will any wise man shake those two august supports of social labor, justice and hope, and all will respect the judge if he is embodied justice, and all will venerate the priest if he represents hope. But if the magistracy calls itself torture, if the Church calls itself Inquisition, then Humanity looks them in the face, and says to the judge: I will none of thy law! And says to the priest: I will none of thy dogma! I will none of thy fire upon the earth and thy hell in the future! Then philosophy rises in wrath, and arraigns the judge before justice, and the priest before God!

That is what Voltaire did. It was grand.

♾

"He was a combination of St. Augustine, Barnum, and John Barrymore. He differed from the Reverend Elmer Gantry chiefly in having once, pretty well along in young manhood, read a book, and in being a Beecher, which was a special state of grace."

REV. HENRY WARD BEECHER
(1813–1887)

by

SINCLAIR LEWIS
(1885–1951)

In the last quarter of the nineteenth century the Reverend Henry Ward Beecher was the most sought after public speaker in America. A brilliant orator, Beecher had a big church, a big income, and—at the end of his life— a big lawsuit. The wife of one of his parishioners claimed to have had an affair with him, although it was never proved. Beecher was called "an American prophet of reassurance" for the rising class of nouveau riche who needed to be told that their materialism and embrace of a less demanding form of Christianity were not grounds for damnation. Beecher, who as a young man had confessed, "I like above all things in the world to be loved," set their minds at ease. Beecher today is a footnote to his sister, Harriet Beecher Stowe, who wrote Uncle Tom's Cabin. *But during his lifetime, when Emerson, Whitman, and Thoreau were alive, it was Beecher who drew the biggest crowds.*

America's first Nobel Prize–winning novelist, Sinclair Lewis was a leading social critic of his era who wrote about middle-class Americans in the 1920s whose lives had been ruined by money, conformity, and fear of disapproval. Although he was born into a later generation, Lewis knew who Beecher was, and in this introduction to a biography of Beecher by Paxton Hibben, he paints a portrait of the man—and the country that idolized him.

When the Reverend Henry Ward Beecher was sued on a charge of adultery with the wife of his friend Theodore Tilton, the America of 1871 was ecstatically shocked.

For Mr. Beecher was, till his death in 1887, the archbishop of American liberal Protestantism. He came out for the right side of every question—always a little too late. . . . He was referred to as "the greatest preacher since St. Paul," he was mentioned for the presidency, he was a powerful writer of trash, and all over the land families got out the carryall to drive into town and hear him lecture on everything from "The Strange Woman" to the doozy theory that a worker who didn't rejoice in bringing up five children on a wage of a dollar a day was a drunken gunny-sack.

Plymouth Church, in Brooklyn, paid him $20,000 a year, and in his pocket he liked to carry uncut gems. He would have been an intimate friend of Lincoln except for the detail that Lincoln despised him. He confided to many visitors that he was always glad to pray with Lincoln and to give him advice whenever the president sneaked over to Brooklyn in the dark, and the only flaw is that nobody except Beecher ever saw him sneak.

. . . He was a combination of St. Augustine, Barnum, and John Barrymore. He differed from the Reverend Elmer Gantry chiefly in having once, pretty well along in young manhood, read a book, and in being a Beecher, which was a special state of grace. His father, Lyman Beecher of Litchfield and Cincinnati, was a powerful hellfire preacher and progenitor, and his sister was Harriet Beecher Stowe, whose *Uncle Tom's Cabin* was the first evidence to America that no hurricane can be so disastrous to a country as a ruthlessly humanitarian woman.

At the sunlit height of Beecher's career came Tilton's suit for alienation of affection, and in Brooklyn and Litchfield they are still arguing about it. But its effect upon the whole Protestant church, which might otherwise have taken over the whole government, is only beginning to be seen. . . .

[In Hibben's biography] Beecher is here entire, from his boyhood, blundering, lonely, almost abnormal in the longing for friendly sympathy, through his frantic and fairly phony days as an ambitious young preacher on the Indiana frontier in 1837, up to his antimacassar splendor as a metropolitan pastor filled with pomposity and metaphors and the best oyster stew. He slapped the backs of all men, he tickled the ribs of almost all the current ideas, and he kissed a surprising proportion of the women.

The subtitle of the book is "An American Portrait," and indeed here is the portrait of that blowsy hoyden of an America that existed when Grant was accounted a statesman and Longfellow an epic poet. Although Hibben never wants from his scrupulous portraiture to give highfalutin panshots of the whole country, yet in understanding Beecher we understand everything that was boisterously immature in American religion, American literature, American manners, and the American relationship, ardent but sneaking, between men and women. We understand all the spirited spinsters who wanted to paint water lilies on the backs of the herded buffalos. We understand what we are still living down. Here is the story of our own grandfathers, which is one-quarter of our own stories. Though we speak with the brisk quack of the radio, our words are still too often the lordly lard of Henry Ward Beecher.

In discovering his emptiness, the country discovered its own emptiness and, as Captain Hibben says, "When the social history of the last quarter of the nineteenth century comes to be written, the Beecher case may be found to have had more to do with clearing the intellectual ground and freeing the minds of men from the clutter of the past than any other one episode."

Hibben does not spare his patient. The horsehair hypocrisies of Beecher are set down like fever symptoms on a chart. He does not flinch from the charming melodrama of Beecher's association with the wives of all the backers of his one-man show. Yet the book is never lip-licking and never a tirade. You see that, given the glacial hellfire of old Lyman Beecher, his son Henry would have to be a hypocrite, exactly in ration to his own energy and imagination and desire for affection.

❧

"He liked getting up early in the morning, to the tune of cocks crowing on the dunghill. He liked the heavy, greasy victuals of the farmhouse kitchen. . . . His place in the Tennessee hagiocracy is secure. If the village barber saved any of his hair, then it is curing gallstones down there today."

WILLIAM JENNINGS BRYAN
(1860–1925)

by

H. L. MENCKEN
(1880–1956)

William Jennings Bryan was an Illinois-born lawyer, lecturer, and politician whose fundamentalist-style oratory and convictions earned him the nickname "The Commoner," after the popular weekly he founded. A three-time Democratic nominee for president, he represented the state of Tennessee in its lawsuit against a high school teacher, J. T. Scopes, for teaching Darwin's theory of evolution. Clarence Darrow represented Scopes. Tennessee won in the lower court but that decision was almost immediately reversed upon appeal.

H. L. Mencken, editor of the American Mercury *in Baltimore, admired Darrow as much as he detested Bryan, and when Bryan died the following obituary appeared in the October 1925* Mercury.

Has it been marked by historians that the late William Jennings Bryan's last secular act on this earth was to catch flies? A curious detail, and not without its sardonic overtones. He was the most sedulous fly-catcher in American history, and by all odds the most successful. His quarry, of course, was not *Musca domestica* but *Homo neanderthalensis.* For forty years he tracked it with snare and blunderbuss, up and down the backways of the Republic. Wherever the flambeaux of Chautauqua smoked and guttered, and the bilge of idealism ran in the veins, and Baptist pastors dammed the brooks with the saved, and men gathered who were weary and heavy laden, and their wives who were unyieldingly multiparous and full of Peruna—there the indefatigable Jennings set his traps and spread his bait.

He knew every forlorn town in the South and West, and he could crowd the most remote of them to suffocation by simply winding his horn. The city proletariat, transiently flustered by him in 1896, quickly penetrated his buncombe and would have no more of him; the gallery jeered him for twenty-five years. But out where the grass grows high, and the horned cattle dream away the lazy days, and men still fear the powers and principalities of the air—out there between the corn rows he held his old puissance to the end. There was no need of beaters to drive in his game. The news that he was coming was enough. For miles the flivver dust would choke the roads. And when he rose at the end of the day to discharge his Message, there would be such breathless attention, such a sweet rustle of amens as the world had not known since Johanan fell to Herod's headsman.

There was something peculiarly fitting in the fact that his last days were spent in a one-horse Tennessee village, and that death found him there. The man felt at home in such scenes. He liked people who sweated freely, and were not debauched by the refinements of the toilet. Making his progress up and down the main street of little Dayton, surrounded by gaping primates from the upland valleys of the Cumberland range, his coat laid aside, his bare arms and hairy chest shining damply, his bald head sprinkled with dust—so accoutred and on display he was obviously happy. He liked getting up early in the morning, to the tune of cocks crowing on the dunghill. He liked the heavy, greasy victuals of the farmhouse kitchen. . . . His place in the Tennessee hagiocracy is secure. If the village barber saved any of his hair, then it is curing gallstones down there today.

But what label will he bear in more urban regions? One, I fear, of a far less flattering kind. Bryan lived too long, and descended too deeply in the mud, to be taken seriously hereafter by fully literate men, even of the kind who write schoolbooks. . . . When he began denouncing the notion that man is a mammal, even some of the hinds at Dayton were agape. And when, brought upon Darrow's cruel hook, he writhed and tossed in a very fury of malignancy, bawling against the baldest elements of sense and decency like a man frantic—when he came to that tragic climax, there were snickers among the hinds as well as hosannas.

Upon that hook, in truth, Bryan committed suicide. He staggered from that rustic court ready to die, and he staggered from it ready to be forgotten, save as a character in a third-rate farce, witless and in execrable taste.

Heave an egg out of a Pullman window, and you will hit a fundamentalist almost anywhere in the United States today. They swarm in the country towns, inflamed by their pastors, and with a saint, now, to venerate. They are thick in the mean streets behind the gasworks. They are everywhere that learning is too heavy a burden for mortal minds, even the vague, pathetic learning on tap in little red schoolhouses. They march with the Klan, with the Christian Endeavor Society, with the Junior Order of United American Mechanics, with the Epworth League, with all the rococo bands that poor and unhappy folk organize to bring some light of purpose into their lives. They have had a thrill, and they are ready for more.

Such is Bryan's legacy to his country. He couldn't be president, but he could at least help magnificently in the solemn business of shutting off the presidency from every intelligent and self-respecting man. The storm, perhaps, won't last long, as time goes in history. It may help, indeed, to break up the democratic delusion, now already showing weakness, and so to hasten its own end. But while it lasts, it will blow off some roofs and flood some sanctuaries.

ᏩᎲᏬᎾ

"A frail woman of sixty-five turns out to be capable of slowing down, if not averting in the long run, the cultural disintegration of a whole nation. Her memoirs are something more than a testimony to her times; they are a view of history in the light of conscience and culture. In that light history winces, and an individual realizes his choice: between seeking the light's source and committing an anthropological crime against himself."

NADEZHDA MANDELSTAM
(1898–1980)

by

JOSEPH BRODSKY
(1940–1996)

Nadezhda Mandelstam was the widow of Osip Mandelstam, one of the greatest Russian poets of the twentieth century. Like many other writers during the Stalinist Soviet era, he was arrested and sent to a Siberian labor camp, where he died in 1938, his body thrown into a mass grave. It was decades before either his family or the outside world learned of his fate. Nadezhda Mandelstam's two-volume memoir, Hope Against Hope *and* Hope Abandoned, *was published in 1970 and 1973, respectively.*

Poet Joseph Brodsky, born in Leningrad, was exiled by the Soviet regime for two years to Arkhangel'sk. He emigrated to the United States in 1972, became a citizen in 1977, and was named poet laureate in 1991.

Of the eighty-one years of her life, Nadezhda Mandelstam spent nineteen as the wife of Russia's greatest poet in this century, Osip

193

Mandelstam, and forty-two as his widow. The rest was childhood and youth. In educated circles, especially among the literati, being the widow of a great man is enough to provide an identity. This is especially so in Russia, where in the thirties and in the forties the regime was producing writers' widows with such efficiency that in the middle of the sixties there were enough of them around to organize a trade union.

"Nadya is the most fortunate widow," Anna Akhmatova used to say, having in mind the universal recognition coming to Osip Mandelstam at about that time. The focus of this remark was, understandably, her fellow poet, and right though she was, this was the view from the outside. By the time this recognition began to arrive, Mme. Mandelstam was already in her sixties, her health extremely precarious, and her means meager. Besides, for all the universality of that recognition, it did not include the fabled "one-sixth of the entire planet," i.e., Russia itself. Behind her were already two decades of widowhood, utter deprivation, the Great (obliterating any personal loss) War, and the daily fear of being grabbed by the agents of State Security as a wife of an enemy of the people. Short of death, anything that followed could mean only respite. . . .

She was a small woman, of slim build, and with the passage of years she shriveled more and more, as though trying to turn herself into something weightless, something easily pocketed in the moment of flight. Similarly, she had virtually no possessions: no furniture, no art objects, no library. The books, even foreign books, never stayed in her hands for long: after being read or glanced through they would be passed on to someone else—the way it ought to be with books. In the years of her utmost affluence at the end of the sixties and the beginning of the seventies, the most expensive item in her one-room apartment on the outskirts of Moscow was a cuckoo clock on the kitchen wall. A thief would be disillusioned here; so would those with a search warrant.

There is something quite breathtaking in the realization that she wrote those two volumes of hers at the age of sixty-five. In the Mandelstam family it is Osip who was the writer; she wasn't. If she wrote anything before those volumes, it was letters to her friends or appeals to the Supreme Court. Nor is hers the case of someone reviewing a long and eventful life in the tranquillity of retirement.

Because her sixty-five years were not exactly normal. It's not for nothing that in the Soviet penal system there is a paragraph specifying that in certain camps a year of serving counts for three. By this token, the lives of many Russians in this century came to approximate in length those of biblical patriarchs—with whom she had one more thing in common: devotion to justice.

Yet it wasn't this devotion to justice alone that made her sit down at the age of sixty-five and use her time of respite for writing these books. What brought them into existence was a capitulation, on the scale of one, of the same process that once before had taken place in the history of Russian literature. I have in mind the emergence of great Russian prose, in the second half of the nineteenth century. That prose, which appears as though out of nowhere, as an effect without traceable cause, was in fact simply a spin-off of the nineteenth century's Russian poetry. . . .

Poetry always precedes prose, and so it did in the life of Nadezhda Mandelstam, and in more ways than one. As a writer, as well as a person, she is a creation of two poets with whom her life was linked inexorably: Osip Mandelstam and Anna Akhmatova. And not only because the first was her husband and the second her lifelong friend. . . . What strengthened the bond of that marriage as well as of that friendship was a technicality: the necessity to commit to memory what could not be committed to paper, i.e., the poems of both authors.

In doing so in that "pre-Gutenberg epoch," in Akhmatova's words, Nadezhda Mandelstam certainly wasn't alone. However, repeating day and night the words of her dead husband was undoubtedly connected not only with comprehending them more and more but also with resurrecting his very voice, the intonations peculiar only to him, with a however fleeting sensation of his presence, with the realization that he kept his part of that "for better or for worse" deal, especially its second half. The same went for the poems of the physically often absent Akhmatova, for, once set in motion, this mechanism of memorization won't come to a halt. The same went for other authors, for certain ideas, for ethical principles—for everything that couldn't survive otherwise.

And gradually those things grew on her. If there is any substitute for love, it's memory. To memorize, then, is to restore intimacy.

Gradually the lines of those poets became her mentality, her identity. They supplied her not only with the plane of regard or angle of vision; more importantly, they became her linguistic norm. So when she set out to write her books, she was bound to gauge—by that time already unwittingly, instinctively—her sentences against theirs. The clarity and remorselessness of her pages, while reflecting the character of her mind, are also inevitable stylistic consequences of the poetry that had shaped that mind. In both their content and style, her books are but a postscript to the supreme version of language which poetry essentially is and which became her flesh through learning her husband's lines by heart. . . .

. . . These two volumes by Mme. Mandelstam indeed amount to a Day of Judgment on earth for her age and for its literature—a judgment administered all the more rightfully since it was this age that had undertaken the construction of earthly paradise. . . . The authorities, I must say, were more honest in their reaction than the intelligentsia: they simply made possession of these books an offense punishable by law. As for the intelligentsia, especially in Moscow, it went into actual turmoil over Nadezhda Mandelstam's charges against many of its illustrious and not so illustrious members of virtual complicity with the regime, and the human flood in her kitchen significantly ebbed. . . .

There is something in the consciousness of the literati that cannot stand the notion of someone's moral authority. They resign themselves to the existence of a First Party Secretary, or of a Führer, as to a necessary evil, but they would eagerly question a prophet. This is so, presumably, because being told that you are a slave is less disheartening news than being told that morally you are a zero. After all, a fallen dog shouldn't be kicked. However, a prophet kicks the fallen dog not to finish it off but to get it back on its feet. The resistance to those kicks, the questioning of a writer's assertions and charges, come not from the desire for truth but from the intellectual smugness of slavery. All the worse, then, for the literati when the authority is not only moral but also cultural—as it was in Nadezhda Mandelstam's case. . . .

. . . For a frail woman of sixty-five turns out to be capable of slowing down, if not averting in the long run, the cultural disintegration of a whole nation. Her memoirs are something more than a testi-

mony to her times; they are a view of history in the light of conscience and culture. In that light history winces, and an individual
realizes his choice: between seeking the light's source and committing an anthropological crime against himself. . . .

If she lacked anything, it was humility. In that respect she was
quite unlike her two poets. But then they had their art, and the quality of their achievements provided them with enough contentment
to be, or to pretend to be, humble. She was terribly opinionated, cat-
egorical, cranky, disagreeable, idiosyncratic; many of her ideas were
half-baked or developed on the basis of hearsay. In short, there was
a great deal of one-upwomanship in her, which is not surprising
given the size of the figures she was reckoning with in reality and
later in imagination. In the end, her intolerance drove a lot of people
away, but that was quite all right with her, because she was getting
tired of adulation, of being liked by Robert McNamara and Willy
Fisher (the real name of Col. Rudolph Abel). All she wanted was to
die in her bed, and, in a way, she looked forward to dying, because
"up there I'll again be with Osip." "No," replied Akhmatova, upon
hearing this. "You've got it all wrong. Up there it's now me who is
going to be with Osip."

Her wish came true, and she died in her bed. Not a small thing for
a Russian of her generation. There undoubtedly will surface those
who will cry that she misunderstood her epoch, that she lagged
behind the train of history running into the future. Well, like nearly
every other Russian of her generation, she learned only too well that
the train running into the future stops at the concentration camp or
at the gas chamber. She was lucky that she missed it, and we are
lucky that she told us about its route. I saw her last on May 30, 1972,
in that kitchen of hers, in Moscow. It was late afternoon, and she sat,
smoking, in the corner, in the deep shadow cast by the tall cupboard
onto the wall. The shadow was so deep that the only things one
could make out were the faint flicker of her cigarette and the two
piercing eyes. The rest—her smallish shrunken body under the
shawl, her hands, the oval of her ashen face, her gray, ashlike hair—
all were consumed by the dark. She looked like a remnant of a huge
fire, like a small ember that burns if you touch it.

∽

"There is always this shield of irony some of us raise between our-selves and any object of popular adulation, and I had made my dull point of snubbing her pictures. Then one evening I chanced on a television trailer for *Bus Stop,* and there she was. I'm not even sure I knew whom I was seeing on the screen, but a light had gone on in the room. . . . In a moment's flash of light, the ironies with which I had resisted this sex idol, this object of an undifferentiating pub-lic taste, dropped from me never to be restored."

MARILYN MONROE
(1926–1962)

by

DIANA TRILLING
(1905–1996)

Marilyn Monroe was the embodiment of the American Cinderella story, the orphaned child discovered by Hollywood who went on to become a leg-endary sex symbol and star. She was married and divorced three times—as a teenager to a mechanic, then to baseball hero Joe DiMaggio, and finally to playwright Arthur Miller—and her instability took an increasing toll on her professional and personal life, culminating in her suicide in 1962.

Author, critic, and editor Diana Trilling wrote frequently on literary, social, and political subjects for the country's leading newspapers and peri-odicals.

On a Sunday morning in August 1962, Marilyn Monroe, aged thirty-six, was found dead in the bedroom of her home in Los Angeles, her hand on the telephone as if she had just received or, far more likely, been about to make a call. On the night table next to her bed stood a formidable array of medicines, among them a bottle that had held twenty-five Nembutal pills, now empty. Two weeks later a team of psychiatrists, appointed by the state in conformity with California law, brought in its report on the background and circumstances of her death, declaring it a suicide. There had of course never been any suggestion of foul play. The death was clearly self-inflicted, a climax of extended mental suffering. In fact, it was soon revealed that on Saturday evening Marilyn Monroe had made an emergency call to the psychoanalyst who had been treating her for her acute sleeplessness, her anxieties and depression, and that he had paid her a visit. But the formal psychiatric verdict had to do with the highly technical question of whether the overdose of barbiturates was purposeful or accidental: Had Marilyn Monroe *intended* to kill herself when she took the twenty-five sleeping pills? The jury of experts now ruled it was purposeful: she had wanted to die.

It is an opinion, or at least a formulation, that can bear, I believe, a certain amount of modification. Obviously, I'm not proposing that Marilyn Monroe's death was accidental in the sense that she took so large a dose of pills with no knowledge of their lethal properties. But I think it would be more precise to call this kind of death incidental rather than purposeful—incidental to the desire to escape the pain of living. I am not a psychiatrist and I never knew Marilyn Monroe, but it seems to me that a person can want to be released from consciousness without seeking actual death; that someone can want to stop living without wishing to die. And this is my feeling about Marilyn Monroe, that even when she had spoken of "wanting to die," she really meant that she wanted to end her suffering, not her life. She wanted to destroy consciousness rather than herself. Then, having taken the pills, she realized she might never return from the sleep she craved so passionately and reached for the phone for help.

But this is of course only speculation, and more appropriately engaged in by the medical profession than by the layman. For the rest of us, the motives surrounding Marilyn Monroe's suicide fade in importance before the all-encompassing reality of the act itself: Marilyn Monroe terminated her life. While the medical experts pondered the delicate difference between accident and suicide, the public recognized that the inevitable had at last occurred: Marilyn Monroe had killed herself. Shocked and grieved as everyone was, no one was at all surprised that she had died by her own hand, because for some years now the world had been prepared for just some such tragic outcome to one of the extraordinary careers of our time.

The potentiality of suicide or, at any rate, the threat of extreme mental breakdown had been, after all, conveyed to us by virtually every news story about Marilyn Monroe of recent years. I don't mean that it had been spelled out that she would one day take her life or otherwise go off the deep psychic end. But no one seemed able to write about her without reassuring us that despite her instability and the graveness of her emotional problems, she was still vital and eager, still, however precariously, a going concern. Marilyn Monroe was an earnest, ambitious actress, determined to improve her skill; Marilyn Monroe had failed in several marriages, but she was still in pursuit of fulfillment in love; Marilyn Monroe had several times miscarried, but she still looked forward to having children; Marilyn Monroe was seriously engaged in psychoanalysis; Marilyn Monroe's figure was better than ever; she was learning to be prompter; she was coping, or was struggling to cope, with whatever it was that had intervened in the making of her last picture—so, on the well-worn track, ran all the news stories. Even what may have been her last interview to appear in print (by the time it came out, she was already dead) sounded the same dominant chord of hopefulness, telling us of a Marilyn Monroe full of confidence that she would improve her acting and find her roles, and that between the two therapies, hard work and psychoanalysis, she would achieve the peace of mind that had for so long eluded her.

Where there is this much need for optimism, surely there is great peril, and the public got the message. But what is striking is the fact that throughout this period of her mounting difficulties, with which we were made so familiar, the popular image remained intact. Whatever we were told of her weak hold on life, we retained our image of Marilyn Monroe as the very embodiment of life energy. I think my response to her death was the common one: it came to me with the impact of a personal deprivation but I also felt it as I might a catastrophe in history or in nature; there was less in life, there was less of life, because she had ceased to exist. In her loss life itself had been injured.

In my own instance, it happens that she was already an established star before I knew her as anything except the latest pinup girl. There is always this shield of irony some of us raise between ourselves and any object of popular adulation, and I had made my dull point of snubbing her pictures. Then one evening I chanced on a television trailer for *Bus Stop*, and there she was. I'm not even sure I knew whom I was seeing on the screen, but a light had gone on in the room. Where everything had been gray there was all at once an illumination, a glow of something beyond the ordinarily human. It was a remarkable moment, of a kind I don't recall having had with any other actress, and it has its place with certain rare, cherished experiences of art such as my youthful remembrance of Pavlova, the most perfect of performing artists, whose control of her body was like a radiance, or even the quite recent experience of seeing some photographs of Nijinsky in motion. Marilyn Monroe was in motion, too, which is important, since no still picture could quite catch her electric quality; in posed pictures the redundancy of flesh was what first imposed itself, dimming one's perception of its peculiar alive-ness, of the translucence that infused body with spirit. In a moment's flash of light, the ironies with which I had resisted this sex idol, this object of an undifferentiating public taste, dropped from me never to be restored.

But mine was a minority problem; the world had long since recognized Marilyn Monroe's unique gift of physical being and responded to it as any such gift of life demands. From the start of her public career it had acknowledged the genius of biology or chem-istry or whatever it was that set this young woman apart from the general kind. And once it had admitted her magic, nothing it was to learn of her "morbidity" could weigh against the conviction that she was alive in a way not granted to the rest of us, or, more accurately, that she communicated such a charge of vitality as altered our imag-ination of life, which is of course the whole job and wonder of art.

Since her death it has occurred to me that perhaps the reason we were able to keep these two aspects in which we knew Marilyn Mon-roe—her life affirmation and her impulse to death—in such discreet balance was that they never presented themselves to us as mutually exclusive but, on the contrary, as two intimately related, even expectable, facets of her extraordinary endowment. It is as if the world that loved Marilyn Monroe understood that her superabun-dant biology had necessarily to provoke its own restraint, that this is the cruel law by which nature, or at least nature within civilization, punishes those of us who ask too much of life, or bring too much to life. We are told that when one of the senses is defective, nature fre-quently provides a compensation in another of the senses; the blind often hear better than the seeing, or have a sharper sense of touch. What we are not told but perhaps understand nonetheless is the working of nature's system of negative compensation—the price we pay for gift, the revenge that life seems so regularly to take upon distinction. Certainly our awareness of the more, the plus, in Marilyn Monroe prepared us for some sort of minus. The fact that this young woman whose biological gift was so out of the ordinary was in mental pain seemed to balance the ledger. And one can speculate that had we not known of her emotional suffering, we would have been prepared for some other awful fate for her—an airplane disaster, maybe, or a deforming illness. So superstition may be thought of as an accurate reading of the harder rules of life.

And yet it is difficult to suppose the gods could be all that jealous. Had Marilyn Monroe not been enough punished in childhood to ensure against further misfortune? Once this poor forlorn girl had been so magically brought into her own, the most superstitious of us had the right to ask happiness for her ever after. It was impossible to think of Marilyn Monroe except as Cinderella. The strange power of her physical being seemed best explained and justified by the extreme circumstances of her early life—the illegitimate birth, the mad mother, the orphanage and near-mad foster homes, the rape by one of her early guardians. If there was no good fairy in Marilyn Monroe's life and no Prince Charming, unless Hollywood, this didn't rob her story of its fairy-book miraculousness; it merely assimilated to the old tale our newer legend of the self-made hero or heroine. Grace Kelly had her good Philadelphia family to pave her path and validate her right to a crown. But Marilyn Monroe reigned only by virtue of her beauty and her determination to be raised out of the squalor and darkness, and to shine in the full, the fullest, light. It is scarcely a surprise that the brighter her radiance, the more we listened for the stroke of midnight that would put a limit on such transcendence.

But it was not only the distance Marilyn Monroe had traveled from her unhappy beginnings that represented for us a challenge of reality, to be punished by reality. If her gift is to be regarded not as that of the stage or screen, which I think it primarily was not, but as the gift of biology, she was among those who are greatly touched with power; she was of the true company of artists. And her talent was so out of the range of the usual that we were bound to feel of it that it was not to be contained in society as we know it; therefore it proposed its own dissolution. Like any great artistic gift, Marilyn

Monroe's power of biology was explosive, a primitive and savage force. It had, therefore and inevitably, to be a danger both to herself and to the world in which it did its work. All art is fierce in the measure that it matters, finally, and in its savagery it chooses either to push against society, against the restrictions that hedge it in, or against the artist himself. And no doubt it is the incapacity of most human beings to sustain this inordinate pressure that accounts for the fact that the artist is an exception in any civilized population. To mediate between the assault upon oneself and upon society, to keep alive in the battle and come out more or less intact, is a giant undertaking in which the native endowment of what we call talent is probably but a small element.

Among the very few weapons available to the artist in this monstrous struggle, naïveté can be the most useful. But it is not at all my impression that Marilyn Monroe was a naive person. I think she was innocent, which is very different. To be naive is to be simple or stupid on the basis of experience, and Marilyn Monroe was far from stupid; no one who was stupid could have been so quick to turn her wit against herself, or to manage the ruefulness with which she habitually replied to awkward questioning. To be innocent is to suffer one's experience without being able to learn self-protection from it; as if will-lessly, innocence is at the mercy of experience, unable to mobilize counterforces to fortune.

Of Ernest Hemingway, for example, I feel much as I do of Marilyn Monroe, that he was unable to marshal any adequate defense against the painful events of his childhood, and this despite his famous toughness and the courage he could call upon in war, in hunting, in all the dangerous enterprises that seduced him. He was an innocent man, not a naïve man, though not always intelligent. Marilyn Monroe offers us a similar paradox. Even while she symbolized an extreme of experience, of sexual knowingness, she took each new circumstance of life, as it came to her or as she sought it, like a newborn babe. And yet this was what made her luminous— her innocence. The glow was not rubbed off her by her experience of the ugliness of life because finally, in some vital depth, she had been untouched by it.

From the psychiatrist's point of view, too much innocence, a radical disproportion between what has happened to a person and what he has absorbed from his experience, is a symptom, and alarming. It can indicate a rude break in his connection with himself, and if he is in treatment, it suggests a difficult cure, since, in emotional logic, he will probably be as impervious to the therapy as to the events through which he has passed, and yet without any mitigation of suffering. In the creative spheres, an excess of innocence unquestionably exercises an enormous fascination on us; it produces the purity of expression which leads us to say of an artistic creation or performance that it is "out of this world." But the psychiatric judgment has to pick its way on tiptoe between the gift and the pathology. What constitutes a person's art may eventually spell his emotional undoing.

I can suppose of Marilyn Monroe that she was peculiarly elusive to the psychiatrists or analysts who tried to help her, that emotionally speaking she presented herself to them as a kind of blank page on which nothing had been written, failing to make the connection between herself and them even as she pleaded for it. And yet disconnection was at the heart of her gift, it defined her charm for the world, much as Hemingway's dissociation from his own experience was determinative of his gift.

For several decades, scores of writers have tried to imitate Hemingway's style: the flexibility and purity of his prose, the bright, cogent distance he was able to put between himself and the object under examination. But none has succeeded. And I believe this is because his prose was, among many other things, a direct report of the unbridgeable distance between external reality and his emotions. Just so, Marilyn Monroe was inimitable. Hollywood, Broadway, the nightclubs: they all regularly produce their quota of sex queens, but the public takes them and leaves them, or doesn't really take them; the world is not enslaved as it was by Marilyn Monroe because none but Marilyn Monroe could suggest such a purity of sexual delight. The boldness with which she could parade herself and yet never be gross, her sexual flamboyance and bravado which yet breathed an air of mystery and even reticence, her voice which carried such ripe overtones of erotic excitement and yet was the voice of a shy child—these complications were integral to her gift. And they described a young woman trapped in some never-never land of unawareness.

What I imply here, of course, is a considerable facetiousness in

Marilyn Monroe as a sexual figure. Certainly the two or three men I've known who met her in "real life" were agreed on her lack of direct sexual impact; she was sweet and beautiful and lovely, yes, but somehow not at all the arousing woman they had expected. The nature of sexuality is most difficult to define, so much of what we find sexually compelling has its source in fantasies that have little to do with the primary sexual instinct. Especially in the case of a movie star we enter a realm where dream and biology make their easiest merger. The art of acting is the art of *performing as if*, and the success of this feat of suggestion depends upon the degree to which it speaks to some fantasy of the onlookers.

Marilyn Monroe spoke to our dreams as much as to our animal nature, but in a most unusual way. For what she appealed to was our determination to be rid of fantasy and to get down to the rock-bottom actuality. She gratified our wish to confront our erotic desires without romance, without diversion. And working within a civilization like ours, in which sexuality is so surrounded with restraints and fears and prohibitions, she perhaps came as close as possible to giving us the real thing. But she didn't give us the real thing; she merely acted as if she were giving it to us. She glamorized sexuality to the point at which it lost its terrors for us; and maybe it was this veil that she raised to sexual reality that permitted women, no less than men, to respond to her so generously. Instinctively, I think, women understood that this seemingly most sexual of female creatures was no threat to them.

The myth of Marilyn Monroe was thus even more of a myth than we realized, for this girl who was supposed to release us from our dreams into sexual actuality was in all probability not actual even to herself. Least of all could she have been sexually actual to herself and at the same time such a marvelous public performer of sex, such a conscious artist of sex. And we can conjecture that it was this deep alienation from her own feelings, including her sexual feeling, that enabled her to sustain the disorder of her early years even as long and as well as she did, and to speak of her awful childhood so simply and publicly. For most of us, the smallest "shame" in our past must be kept locked from others. We prefer that the least menacing of skeletons remain in the closet lest our current image of ourselves be violated by its emergence into the open. But Marilyn Monroe had no need for such reserves. She told the public the most gruesome facts of her personal history, for all the world as if we on the outside were worthy of such confidences—except that in some odd, generous response to her innocence, we exceeded ourselves in her instance and didn't take the advantage of her that we might have. Judged from the point of view of what we require of the artist, that he have the will and fearlessness to rise above the conventions which bind those of us with less gift, Marilyn Monroe's candor about her early life was something to be celebrated. But from another point of view her frankness was a warning that the normal barriers of self-protection were down or nonexistent, leaving her grievously exposed to the winds of circumstance.

And indeed the very word *exposed* is a key word in the pattern of her life. She was an actress and she exposed her person and her personality to the public gaze. She was an exposed human being who told the truth about herself too readily, too publicly. And more than most actresses, she exposed her body, with but inadequate understanding of what this involved. We recall, for instance, the awkward little scandal about her having once posed naked for a calendar and the bewildered poise, the really untoward innocence and failure of comprehension, with which she met the dismay of her studio, as if to say, "But that was me yesterday when I needed money. That isn't me today; today I have money." Just as today and yesterday were discontinuous with each other, she was discontinuous with herself, held together, one feels, only and all too temporarily by her success.

And this success was perhaps more intimately connected with her awareness of her physical appeal than we always understood. It may well have been the fact that she was so much and so admiringly in the public eye that gave Marilyn Monroe the largest part of her sense of a personal identity. Not long before her death, we now discover, she had herself photographed in the nude, carefully editing the many pictures as if to be certain she left the best possible record for posterity. The photographs leave, however, a record only of wasted beauty, at least of the famous body—while Marilyn Monroe's face is lovely as ever, apparently unscarred by her intense suffering, her body looked ravaged and ill, already drained of life. Recently the pictures have been published in an expensive magazine devoted to erotica. If their high price, prohibitive to the general buyer, could be interpreted as a precaution against their being too easily available to a sensation-seeking audience, the restraint was not really necessary. At the last, the nude Marilyn Monroe could excite no decent viewer to anything but the gentlest pity, and much fear.

But even before this ultimate moment the public success had been threatened. The great career was already failing. There had not been a Marilyn Monroe movie for a long time, and the last film she had worked on had had to be halted because she was unable to appear. And there was no private life to fall back upon, not even the formal structure of one: no marriage, no family, apparently not even friends. One had come, indeed, to think of her as the loneliest of people, so that it was not without bitterness that, on her death, one discovered that it was not only oneself who had wished to help her but many other strangers, especially women to whose protectiveness her extreme vulnerability spoke so directly. But we were the friends of whom she knew nothing, and among the people she knew it would seem that real relationships were out of reach across the desert emptiness that barricades whoever is out of touch with his feelings. One thinks of her that last evening of her life, alone and distraught, groping for human comfort and finding nothing but those endless bottles of medicine, and one confronts a pathos worse than tragedy.

Certainly it strains justice as well as imagination that the world's most glamorous woman should have been alone, with no date, on a Saturday night—for it was, in fact, a Saturday night when she killed herself. On other nights but Saturday, we are allowed our own company. Saturday night is when all American boys and girls must prove themselves sexually. This is when we must be "out" in the world where we can be seen among the sexually chosen. Yet the American girl who symbolized sexual success for all of us spent her last Saturday night alone in despair. Every man in the country would have wanted to date Marilyn Monroe, or so he would say, but no man who knew her did.

Or, contemplating her loneliness, we think of her funeral, which, contrived to give her the peace and privacy that had so strenuously eluded her throughout her life, yet by its very restraint and limited attendance reminded us of the limitations of her actual connection with the world. Joe DiMaggio, who had been her husband for a few brief months earlier in her career, was the chief mourner. It was DiMaggio to whom, she had told us, it was impossible to be married because he had no conversation; at meals, instead of talking to her, he read the papers or looked at television. The more recent husband, *with* conversation, was not present, no doubt for his own inviolable reasons, but it was saddening. I do not know what, if anything, was read at the service, but I'd like to think it was of an elevated and literary kind, such as might be read at the funeral of a person of the first intellectual rank.

For of the cruelties directed at this young woman even by the public that loved her, it seems to me that the most biting, and unworthy of the supposedly enlightened people who were particularly guilty of it, was the mockery of her wish to be educated, or thought educated. Granting our right to be a bit confused when our sex idol protests a taste for Dostoyevsky, surely the source of our discomfort must yet be located in our suspicions of Dostoyevsky's worth for us and in our own sexual unease rather than in Marilyn Monroe. For what our mockery signifies is our disbelief that anyone who has enough sexuality needs to read Dostoyevsky. The notion that someone with Marilyn Monroe's sexual advantages could have wanted anything except to make love robbed us of a prized illusion, that enough sexual possibility is enough everything.

I doubt that sex was enough anything for Marilyn Monroe, except the means for advancing herself in the world. One of the touching revelations of her early life was her description of how she discovered that somehow she was sexually different from other girls her age; the boys all whistled at her and crowded to her like bears to honey, so she came to realize that she must have something special about her, which she could use to rise above her poor circumstances. Her sexual awareness, that is, came to her from outside herself. It would be my guess that it remained outside her always, leaving a great emptiness, where a true sexuality would have supplied her with a sense of herself as a person with connection and content.

This void she tried to fill in every way available, with worldly goods, with fame and public attention and marriage, and also in ways that turned out to be unavailable, like children and domesticity—nothing could be more moving than the eagerness with which she seized upon a Jewish mother-in-law, even upon Jewish ceremonials and cooking, as if in the home life of her last husband's people she would find the secret of emotional plenitude. She also tried to fill her emptiness with books and learning. How mean-spirited can we be, to have denied her whatever might have added to her confidence that she was really a solid person and not just an uninhabited body?

And that she had the intellectual capacity for education there can be no question, had it but been matched with emotional capacity. No one without a sharp native intelligence could have spoofed herself as gracefully as she did or parried reporters with such finesse. If we are to judge by her interviews, she was as singularly lacking in the endemic offstage dullness of actors and actresses, the trained courtesy and charm that is only another boring statement of their self-love, as she was deficient in the established defenses of her profession: one recalls no instance of even implied jealousy of her colleagues or of censure of others—directors, scriptwriters, husbands—for her own failures. Her generosity of spirit, indeed, was part of the shine that was on her. But unfortunately it spared everyone but herself; she had never studied self-justification. To herself she was not kind. She made fun of herself and of all that she had to go on in life: her biology. Certainly this added to her lovableness but it cut from under her the little ground that she could call her own. When she exhibited her sexual abundance with that wonderful, gay exaggeration of hers, or looked wide-eyed upon the havoc she wrought, it was her way of saying, "Don't be afraid. I don't take myself seriously so you don't have to take me seriously either." Her talent for comedy, in other words, was a public beneficence but a personal depredation, for, far more than most people, she precisely needed the assurance that she weighed in the scheme of human life, that she had substance and reality, that she had all the qualifications that make for a person we take seriously. Herself a supplicant, she gave us comfort. Herself a beggar, she distributed alms.

At her death, several writers of goodwill who undertook to deal with the tragedy of her suicide blamed it on Hollywood. In the industry that had made millions from her and in the methods by which Hollywood had exploited her, they found the explanation of her failed life; they wrote about her as the sacrificial lamb on the altar of American vulgarity and greed. I share their disgust with Hollywood and I honor their need to isolate Marilyn Monroe from the nastiness that fed on her, but I find it impossible to believe that this girl would have been an iota better off were Hollywood to have been other than what we all know it to be, a madness in our culture.

The self-destructiveness that Marilyn Monroe carried within her had not been put there by the "system," however overbearing in its ugliness. Just as her sweetness was her own, and immune to the influences of Hollywood, her terrors were also her own. They were not implanted in her, though undoubtedly they were increased, by the grandiosity of being a star. Neither for better nor worse, I feel, was she essentially falsified or distorted by her public role, though she must often have suffered cruelly from the inescapability of the public glare. In fact, it would be my conjecture that had she never gone into the movies and become rich and world-famous, her troubled spirit would long since have had its way with her. She would have been equally undone, and sooner, and with none of the many alleviations and compensations that she must have known in these years of success.

This doesn't mean that I don't think she was a "victim." But she was not primarily a victim of Hollywood commercialism or exploitation or of the inhumanity of the press. She was not even primarily a victim of the narcissistic inflation that so regularly attends the grim business of being a great screen personality. Primarily she was a victim of her gift, a biological victim, a victim of life itself. It is one of the excesses of contemporary thought that we like to blame our very faulty culture for tragedies that are inherent in human existence—at least, inherent in human existence in civilization. I think Marilyn Monroe was a tragedy of civilization, but this is something quite else again from, and even more poignant than, being a specifically American tragedy.

CHAPTER EIGHT

DEATH BE NOT SOLEMN

Within this chapter is a gambler whose luck ran out, a writer who couldn't think of anything nice to say and said it, a mother who raised her sons to entertain her, and a nun who had all the time in the world. With the possible exception of the Marx Brothers' mother, none of them thought their life was a laughing matter. But somebody else did.

William Knickerbocker's eulogy for the gambler Riley Grannan is elegant but noncommittal ("He was born in the Sunny Southland— in Kentucky. *He died in Rawhide.* . . . Here is the beginning and the end"). Between these two facts, Mr. Knickerbocker manages to say absolutely nothing absolutely beautifully. Perhaps Mr. Grannan's mother was in the crowd.

Florence King's view of Ambrose Bierce, a fellow misanthrope, is a view of him we do not usually have. Minnie Marx is one of the great, unambitious stage mothers. And Sister Beatrice of Jesus, whose inability to be rushed was legendary, deserves to be appreciated beyond the cloister in which she lived for the last sixty years of her life. Thanks to Sister Robin Stratton, the convent's boundaries have been redrawn to include the reader within its walls.

"He was born in the Sunny Southland—in Kentucky. *He died in Rawhide.*

Here is the beginning and the end. I wonder if we can see in this a picture of what Ingersoll said at the grave of his brother—'Whether it be near the shore or in the midocean or among the breakers, at the last a wreck must mark the end of one and all.' "

RILEY GRANNAN
(1868–1908)

by

WILLIAM HERMAN KNICKERBOCKER

The eulogy below was delivered over the bier of a gambler who died in the mining town of Rawhide, Nevada. Knickerbocker was a well-educated Southerner and former minister turned prospector. His eulogy for Grannan is a brilliant garland of smoke woven around one truth, that Grannan wasn't worth talking about. Knickerbocker solves that problem by talking about everything else.

I feel that it is incumbent upon me to state that in standing here I occupy no ministerial or prelatic position. I am simply a prospector. I make no claims whatever to moral merit or to religion except the religion of humanity, the brotherhood of man. I stand among you today simply as a man among men, feeling that I can shake hands and say "brother" to the vilest man or woman that ever lived. If there should come to you anything of moral admonition through what I may say, it comes not from any sense of moral superiority, but from the depths of my experience.

Riley Grannan was born in Paris, Kentucky, about forty years ago. I suppose he dreamed all the dreams of boyhood. They blossomed into phenomenal success along financial lines at times during his life. I am told that from the position of a bellboy in a hotel he rose rapidly to be a celebrity of worldwide fame. He was one of the greatest plungers, probably, that the continent has ever produced.

He died day before yesterday in Rawhide.

This is a very brief statement. You have the birth and the period of the grave. Who can fill the interim? Who can speak of his hopes and fears? Who can solve the mystery of his quiet hours that only himself knew? I cannot.

He was born in the Sunny Southland—in Kentucky. *He died in Rawhide.*

Here is the beginning and the end. I wonder if we can see in this a picture of what Ingersoll said at the grave of his brother— "Whether it be near the shore or in the midocean or among the breakers, at the last a wreck must mark the end of one and all."

He was born in the Sunny Southland, where brooks and rivers run musically through the luxuriant soil; where the magnolia grandiflora like white stars grow in a firmament of green; where crystal lakes dot the greensward and the softest summer breezes dimple the wave-lips into kisses for the lilies on the shore; where the air is resonant with the warbled melody of a thousand sweet-voiced birds and redolent of the perfume of many flowers. This was the beginning. He died in Rawhide, where in winter the shoulders of the mountains are wrapped in garments of ice and in summer the blistering rays of the sun beat down upon the skeleton ribs of the desert. Is this a picture of universal human life?

Sometimes when I look over the circumstances of human life, a curse rises to my lips, and, if you will allow me, I will say here that I speak from an individual point of view. I cannot express other than my own views. If I run counter to yours, at least give me credit for a desire to be honest.

When I see the ambitions of man defeated; when I see him struggling with mind and body in the only legitimate prayer he can make to accomplish some end; when I see his aim and purpose frustrated by a fortuitous combination of circumstances over which he has no control; when I see the outstretched hand, just about to grasp the flag of victory, take instead the emblem of defeat, I ask, What is life? Dreams, awakening, and death; "a pendulum 'twixt a smile and a tear"; "a momentary halt within the waste and then the nothing we set out from"; "a walking shadow, a poor player that struts and frets his hour upon the stage and then is heard no more"; "a tale told by an idiot, full of sound and fury, signifying nothing"; a child-blown bubble that but reflects the light and shadow of its environment and is gone; a mockery, a sham, a lie, a fool's vision; its happiness but Dead Sea apples; its pain the crunching of a tyrant's heel. I feel as Omar did when he wrote:

We are no other than a moving row
Of magic Shadow-shapes that come and go
Round with the Sun-illumined lantern held
In midnight by the Master of the show
But helpless pieces of the game He plays
Upon the checker-board of nights and days;
Hither and thither moves, and checks and slays
And one by one back in the closet lays.
The ball no question makes of Ayes and Noes,
But here and there as strikes the player goes;
And He that tossed you down into the field—
He knows about it all—He knows—He knows.

But I don't. This is my mood.

Not so with Riley Grannan. If I have gauged his character correctly, he accepted the circumstances surrounding him as the mystic officials to whom the universe had delegated its whole office concerning him. He seemed to accept both defeat and victory with equanimity. He was a man whose exterior was as placid and gentle as I have ever seen, and yet when we look back over his meteoric past, we can readily understand, if this statement is true, that he was absolutely invincible in spirit. If you will allow me, I will use a phrase most of you are acquainted with. He was a "dead game sport." I say it not irreverently, but fill the phrase as full of practical human philosophy as it will hold, and I believe that when you say one is a "dead game sport," you have reached the climax of human philosophy.

⟋⟍⟍⟍⟍

"[Ambrose Bierce] penned the shortest and most lethal book review on record: 'The covers of this book are too far apart.' "

AMBROSE BIERCE
(1842–1914?)

by

FLORENCE KING
(1936–)

Journalist, short-story writer, and satirist, Ambrose Gwinnett Bierce is best known today as the author of a collection of sardonic definitions, The Devil's Dictionary. *After serving in the Civil War, he moved to San Francisco, where his columns for William Randolph Hearst's* Sunday Examiner *made him the preeminent literary critic of the West Coast. According to one biographical source, "disillusionment and sadness pervaded the latter part of his life," and in 1913 he went to Mexico and was never heard from again.*

Florence King, author of With Charity Toward None: A Fond Look at Misanthropy, *contests the view that Bierce was a bitter, lonely man. "Bitter Bierce," she writes, "had a ball. He also had what today's pundits lack: two." Ms. King is herself a misanthrope, which affords her an insider's view.*

The most famous question mark in American literature is "1842–1914(?)," which would be on Ambrose Bierce's tombstone if he had one. Unfortunately, his disappearance in revolution-torn Mexico has overshadowed his reputation as a writer. In his own time critics rated his Civil War fiction superior to Stephen Crane's *Red Badge of Courage,* but today Bierce is known only as the author of *The Devil's Dictionary.* . . .

Ambrose Bierce was born in Horse Cave Creek, Ohio, which explains much. He later immortalized his boyhood home in a poem that begins, "The malarial farm with the scum-covered duck pond/ The foul-smelling barnyard beside it." A voracious reader, he longed for escape and found it in 1861. Among the first Union volunteers, he fought at Shiloh and Chickamauga, winning a battlefield commission for carrying a wounded officer to safety under fire. One of only two future writers to serve in the Civil War (Confederate Sidney Lanier was the other), he always regarded Twain, Adams, James, and Howells as shirkers, describing the latter as "two eminent triflers and cameo-cutters-in-chief to Her Littleness the Bostonese small virgin."

Footloose after Appomattox, he went to San Francisco and began writing for newspapers and magazines, eventually becoming an editorial columnist for Hearst's *Examiner.* His columns "Prattle" and "Town Crier" won him the sobriquets of "Bitter Bierce," "the wickedest man in San Francisco," and from radical feminist Charlotte Perkins Gilman, "public tormentor." A blond Adonis, Bierce enjoyed attracting women—sort of. "Oh, that we could fall into a woman's arms without falling into her hands" pretty well sums it up.

He penned the shortest and most lethal book review on record: "The covers of this book are too far apart." As well as the shortest and most savage obituary: "Here lies Frank Pixley—as usual." Evangelists were "a he-harlotry of horribles," and do-gooders were advised: "If you find a man starving, the least you can do is loan him your umbrella."

Going after the railroad tycoons, he dubbed Leland Stanford "$tealand" and Collis P. Huntington "a promoted peasant." Of Charles Crocker he wrote: "His tendency to make improvements is merely a natural instinct inherited from his public-spirited ancestor, the man who dug the postholes on Mount Calvary."

As he approached seventy, Bierce's pronouncements began to bristle with more than the old invective. He seemed to be planting hints, as when he announced: "I see no point in remaining in a country that is on the verge of Prohibition and women's suffrage." Always fascinated by death, he now laid it on the line: "To be a Gringo in Mexico—ah, that is euthanasia!" He left for Mexico in 1913, ostensibly as an observer of the Pancho Villa revolution, and was never seen or heard from again.

<hr />

"She had done more than bear her sons, bring them up, and turn them into play actors. She had invented them. They were just comics she imagined for her own amusement . . . and their reward was her ravishing smile."

MINNIE MARX
(1864–1931)

by

ALEXANDER WOOLLCOTT
(1887–1943)

In this appreciation of the mother of the Marx Brothers, drama critic Alexander Woollcott tracks the talent of Harpo, Groucho, Chico, Zeppo, and Gummo Marx back to the source.

Last week the Marx Brothers buried their mother. On the preceding Friday night, more from gregariousness than from appetite, she had eaten two dinners instead of the conventional one and, after finishing off with a brief, hilarious game of Ping-Pong, was homeward bound across the Queensboro Bridge when paralysis seized her. Within an hour she was dead in her Harpo's arms. Of the people I have met, I would name her as among the few of whom it could be said they had greatness.

She had done more than bear her sons, bring them up, and turn them into play actors. She had invented them. They were just comics she imagined for her own amusement. They amused no one more, and their reward was her ravishing smile.

She herself was doing sweatshop lacework when she married a tailor named Sam Marx. But for fifty years her father was a roving magician in Hanover, and as a child she had known the excitement of their barnstorming cart rides from one German town to another.

Her trouble was that her boys had got to Broadway. They had arrived. Thereafter, I think she took less interest in their professional lives. When someone paid them a king's ransom to make their first talkie, she only yawned. What she sighed for was the zest of beginnings. Why, I hear that last year she was caught hauling her embarrassed chauffeur off to dancing school, with the idea of putting him on the stage. In her boredom she took to poker, her game being marked by so incurable a weakness for inside straights that, as often as not, her rings were missing and her bureau drawer littered with sheepish pawn tickets. On the night *Animal Crackers* opened, she was so absorbed that she almost forgot to go at all. But at the last moment she sent her husband for her best wig, dispatched her chauffeur to fetch her new teeth, and assembling herself on the way downtown, reached the theater in time to greet the audience. Pretty as a picture she was as she met us in the aisle. "We have a big success," she said.

Minnie Marx was a wise, tolerant, generous, gallant matriarch. In the passing of such a one, a woman full of years, with her work done, and children and grandchildren to hug her memory all their days, you have no more of a sense of death than you have when the Hudson—sunlit, steady, all-conquering—leaves you behind on the shore on its way to the fathomless sea.

She was in this world sixty-five years and lived all sixty-five of them. She died during rehearsals, in the one week of the year when her boys would be around her—back from their summer roamings, that is, but not yet gone forth on tour. Had she foreseen this—I'm not sure she didn't—she would have chuckled, and combining a sly wink with her beautiful smile, she would have asked, "How's that for perfect timing?"

⟐

"On one occasion about ten years before her death we were sitting in the [convent] parlor listening to a noted European scholar. He had spoken for nearly two hours when Beatrice whispered to the Sister next to her, 'He's finished, but he doesn't know it.' "

SISTER BEATRICE OF JESUS, OCD
(1894–1991)

by

SISTER ROBIN STRATTON, OCD
(1940–)

Beatrice Bacchelli, born in Bologna, was the only daughter of a distinguished Italian family. Educated privately at home, she was eleven when Alfredo Oswald, son of a Brazilian diplomat, fell in love with her. When she was eighteen, she received her father's consent to marry the distinguished concert pianist. After her marriage, they traveled around the world, finally settling in Baltimore, Maryland, where Alfredo was offered a teaching position at the Peabody Conservatory of Music. Then, after they had been married fifteen years, he confided to Beatrice his desire to enter the religious life. After seeking counsel from their Jesuit spiritual director, they were told that if Oswald entered the religious life, Beatrice must do so, too. Thus it was that until her death sixty years later, Beatrice was a sister at the Carmelite Monastery in Baltimore. The following is excerpted from an appreciation written of Sister Beatrice upon her death.

Seventeen years after they married, on September 18, 1930, Alfredo drove to Carmel with his wife. He then continued his own journey to the Jesuit novitiate in Wernersville, Pennsylvania, where he gave himself to God as a Brother. After his novitiate, he was sent to

Georgetown Preparatory School in Rockville, Maryland, where he was sacristan, conducted the choir, and taught piano for many years. Brother Oswald once joked that his biography could be entitled *From Brahms to Brooms*. Every month through his life, he visited Beatrice at the monastery and claimed he always called ahead "to be sure she would be at home." After a long and distinguished life of teaching, and in the midst of one of the worst hurricanes this area has ever known, he died on June 22, 1972.

Beatrice chose Carmel because she felt that here she would be giving everything to God. But she worried about the persons she and Ozzie had supported financially. The mother of one large family consoled her, saying, "Do not worry. You will be poor and you will be one of us." Among the very few items Beatrice brought with her to Carmel were a large worn Italian Bible and an equally worn copy of *The Divine Comedy*. These were to be her cherished companions through the years.

The adjustment to her new life was enormous, but Beatrice maintained her sense of humor. One morning soon after she entered, Beatrice and another postulant were hanging the wash, one of many simple tasks they were given as "beginners." The second postulant muttered under her breath, "And to think, I had a good job," to which Beatrice responded, "And I had a good husband!" One evening at recreation, the question arose as to what Beatrice might call Ozzie. One of the nuns quipped that it really didn't matter, so long as she didn't refer to him as "*our* husband."

Beatrice was always good-humored. She was relaxed, unhurried, and imperturbable, a woman of prayer filled with wisdom and grace. She left us a refreshing sense of freedom and flexibility. Our favorite descriptive word for Beatrice was *elasticity*. This was the word she herself claimed had to be a "principle" of our life after Vatican II. At community meetings she could be counted upon to introduce another side of the issue at hand, often just at the point when we thought we had reached a consensus.

Beatrice was in no way rigid. Even her physical movement was leisurely. When Brother Oswald had wanted her to hurry up or to get something done, he would call her "tranquillitate." Anyone who assisted her in work had to adjust to Beatrice's unhurried pace. She could graciously discuss a hundred ways of accomplishing a needlework project without feeling any need to hurry the decision, while her assistant became acutely aware of the urgent need to decide immediately if the task were ever to be finished. But finished it would be for Beatrice was a night owl who could sit up sewing long after the rest of us had retired.

In the mid-1960s after the Lay Sisters received the black veil and many of us took turns preparing the meals, Beatrice would occasionally offer to make dinner. She was a talented cook and enjoyed preparing good Italian cuisine. We were assured of a gloriously prepared first portion—but an "assistant" was needed if the rest of the meal were to arrive at the table on time. Beatrice would have required more hours than were at her disposal to accomplish everything. In her later years, she could sit at the kitchen table patiently picking every scrap from a turkey carcass that already looked stripped to anyone else's eyes.

Beatrice is remembered for apt and often very funny expressions. She had her own name for deviled eggs, calling them "proud eggs" because, she said with a laugh, "they are full of themselves." On one occasion about ten years before her death we were sitting in the parlor listening to a noted European scholar. He had spoken for nearly two hours when Beatrice whispered to the Sister next to her, "He's finished, but he doesn't know it."

In her last years Beatrice, for a reason unknown to all of us, spoke in French (rather than her native Italian) unless we prompted her to speak in English. One day Maryellen (one of our Associates), thinking to please her, initiated a conversation in French. After a few exchanges, Beatrice turned to the Infirmarian and asked politely, "Doesn't this woman speak English?"

Beatrice's body was returned to the monastery on Friday, March 15, and laid out in the chapel. . . . A table nearby contained a picture of Sister Beatrice alone, and one of herself and Brother Oswald taken after he had had a stroke. . . . That evening we celebrated her wake and told stories.

We laid her to rest among our Sisters at New Cathedral Cemetery and hold her memory close to our hearts until we meet again in the paradise of Dante and his Beatrice.

PART II

PRIVATE
LIVES

⟊ጠጠ⟊

CHAPTER NINE

PARENTS

ᘒᘉᘉᘉᘒ

If there is one truth that all parents must embrace sooner or later, it is that no matter how much they love their children they must learn to let them go. Eventually the child must learn the same thing. When a parent dies, we do not say good-bye as much as we release them—from our continuing need for their love and confirmation, even if we have never received it. In all of the eulogies below, there is a sense of sons and daughters gently untying the bonds, of struggling to let their parents go.

They are twentieth-century children, conversant with the psychological landscape and the language of human development, aware of what their parents have given them, as well as what has been denied. "I am the little girl looking for my mother," writes Betsy Cooper. "Over the years, I have pulled from my unconscious fragmented images, like old half-torn photos, of empty rooms from which my mother is conspicuously absent."

They are aware, as well, of what their own parents went without. "My father," observes Michael Saltz, "was a complex, cantankerous man whose parents neither wanted nor understood him. . . . At the age of thirteen he was paying them for his room and board."

These are the thoughts of middle-aged children, whose lives were complicated by parents whose own parents complicated theirs.

Parents are judged by how well or badly they did by their children, by what kind of an example or trail worth following they left behind. The second is far more difficult to get right. The fact is that all parents hurt their children—an occupational hazard for which the only insurance is the child's capacity to forgive. The counterfact, or miracle, is that nearly all children do.

"She tried me at times to the top of my bent," acknowledged Laurie Lee of his mother. "But I absorbed from birth, as now I know, the whole earth through her jaunty spirit."

"He could be rigid," concedes Catharine MacKinnon of her father, "but his stubbornness was also a steadfastness and as such a form of principle."

In David Cook's eulogy for his mother he writes, "The perfect mother and the perfect father do not exist in this life, and I am glad for that. No child could stand them or get free from them."

There are no perfect parents here. But to see them through the eyes of their children is to admire who they were and to have compassion—that late-blooming virtue that waits until we are old enough to need it ourselves—for what they could not be.

"She fed our oafish wits with steady, imperceptible shocks of beauty."

LAURIE LEE

(1914–)

on

HIS MOTHER, ANNIE LEE

In his autobiography, The Edge of Day, *English writer Laurie Lee writes of his mother, who was abandoned by his father and had to raise a family on her own.*

My first image of my mother was of a beautiful woman, strong, bounteous, but with a gravity of breeding that was always visible beneath her nervous chatter. She became, in a few years, both bent and worn, her healthy opulence quickly gnawed away by her later trials and hungers. It is in this second stage that I remember her best, for in this stage she remained the longest. I can see her prowling about the kitchen, dipping a rusk into a cup of tea, with hair loose-tangled and shedding pins, clothes shapelessly humped round her, eyes peering sharply at some revelation of the light, crying "Ah" or "Oh" or "There," talking of Tonks or reciting Tennyson and demanding my understanding.

With her love of finery, her unmade beds, her litters of unfinished scrapbooks, her taboos, superstitions and prudishness, her remark-able dignity, her pity for the persecuted, her awe of the gentry, and her detailed knowledge of the family trees of all the Royal Houses of Europe, she was a disorganized mass of unreconciled denials, a servant girl born to the silk. Yet in spite of all this, she fed our oafish wits with steady, imperceptible shocks of beauty. Though she tortured our patience and exhausted our nerves, she was, all the time, building up around us, by the unconscious revelations of her loves, an interpretation of man and the natural world so unpretentious and easy that we never recognized it then, yet so true that we never forgot it.

Nothing now that I ever see that has the edge of gold around it—the change of a season, a jeweled bird in a bush, the eyes of orchids, water in the evening, a thistle, a picture, a poem—but my pleasure pays some brief duty to her. She tried me at times to the top of my bent. But I absorbed from birth, as now I know, the whole earth through her jaunty spirit.

ᏫᏳᏞᎧ

"When it came, that last breath, it was as though a lamp in whose circle of light I had lived all my life had been extinguished. Now I was free to live anywhere. In the dark."

RICHARD SELZER
(1928–)

on

HIS MOTHER, GERTRUDE SELZER
(WITHHELD)

This reminiscence about his mother, Gertrude Selzer, first appeared in Richard Selzer's memoir, Down from Troy. *A surgeon and professor at Yale Medical School for twenty years, Selzer left to become a writer. Among his books are* Mortal Lessons, Rituals of Surgery, *and* Taking the World in for Repairs.

About Mother, she is what some call dead. I suppose I should have known. There were omens, had I been receptive: a line of migrating geese that wavered and broke like a sudden arrhythmia on an electrocardiogram. And the day before, I had run over a cat.

How old was she? In our family, it had always been considered bad manners to know the exact age of one's mother. But "entre nous" she was just a girl of eighty-eight. Sometimes, secure in the knowledge that I would lie in her favor, she would put the question "How old do you think I am?"

"Oh, I don't know. Somewhere in the sixties."

"Right on the button," she would marvel, then lift that famous forefinger to scold. "But it is wicked of you to know. Tell it not in Gath."

"Why not?"

"Lest the daughters of the uncircumcised find out and rejoice."

. . . And then there was last Sunday. I called her up.

"Autumn," she said. "I wasn't expecting it so soon." And with studied nonchalance: "I've decided to turn over an old leaf."

"What's that supposed to mean?" But I already knew.

"You'll see," she said.

"Don't! I am not ready!"

"Oh, you! You'll never be ready. You have got to be more philosophical. Death is the prize to which we can all aspire." I could just see her scratching in her hair with a pencil and looking out the window at the foliage. An hour later I was in the car and headed upstate. . . . By the time I got to Troy, she was in the intensive-care unit, having achieved a myocardial infarction big enough to turn her nose blue. But sizing me up, I could tell.

"You're holding your belly button," she said. It took her six breaths to get it out.

"I've got a pain in it," I told her. She responded by rolling up her eyes the way she did, commercing with the skies.

"You'll get over it," she gasped.

In the corridor, Billy, the doctor, and I discussed the case. Soberly, sensibly, like professionals.

"No," Billy answered him. "No resuscitation, no tubes, no respirator. Let her be."

"That is wise," said the doctor. "She has been wanting to die for fifteen years that I know of."

Billy and I stood on either side of the bed all night. Toward dawn, she opened her eyes.

"Ivy," she said. It was her last word.

"IV," said Billy. "The intravenous is bothering her." He went to get the nurse. But I knew better. Ivy in a cemetery takes care of itself; there's no need to plant flowers every little while and you need not worry about it being the wrong color.

"Yes," I said. "Ivy would be best." But she was already out of earshot. When it came, that last breath, it was as though a lamp in whose circle of light I had lived all my life had been extinguished. Now I was free to live anywhere. In the dark.

The day of the funeral it rained. I wasn't surprised. The town knew what it had lost. All about us the cemetery was doing what it does, gravely regarding. No stone but bowed its head in welcome. From the road, we watched the men carry her toward Father. It was not smooth sailing, what with the path all muddy and rutted. The coffin swam jerkily like some blind homing creature that would have to find its way by instinct. Never mind—she knew where to go. . . . Then the ancient spectacle, full of murmuring and slow gestures. The village of black umbrellas . . .

That night I fell asleep thinking about the Sunday afternoon last June when Mother and I had gone for a stroll downtown. She was wearing white gloves and carrying her parasol. Believe you me, she could have given master classes in how to open and twirl that thing. At the corner of Congress and River Streets she paused. "Do you think Troy has changed much since your last visit?"

I had been there only six weeks earlier. "Eternal Troy," I said. "Jerusalem of my soul." And waited for what I knew was coming.

"There are many Athens," she said, "but only one Troy." It was her favorite joke. We sauntered on to the Hendrik Hudson Tea Room, where for the umpteenth time she introduced me to Gloria, the waitress. "This is my son," she announced. "With a *u*."

Gloria beamed on cue. "What'll you have today, Gertrude? The usual?"

"Hot, hot tea and two ladyfingers. . . . The water must be boiling when it strikes the tea leaves."

"And sunny boy?"

"Bourbon," I said. "Cold, cold. And skip the ladyfingers." When Mother laughed, there was that white mouse still ringing a silver bell.

My having been born of her did not shut the gate between us as friends. We each knew to expect lies from the other—benevolent, colorful lies about the past. No grown-up proper view of what had once been, but a romantic fiction. Now we looked forward to hearing it for the hundredth time. And underneath the banter and nostalgia lay the confidence that no matter what the folly or miscalculation, we would find motives for each other—to excuse, to exculpate. Above all, we offered each other the opportunity to behave well. Such a thing is to be found only once, if ever, in any lifetime.

Before heading back to New Haven the day after the funeral, I thought, Well, why not? And drove up to the cemetery. There was the clatter of cold metal as I turned the big old key in the iron gate. The path was still muddy from yesterday's rain but there were islands for hopping. I stopped before the fresh mound of earth. "Okay," I said aloud. I was all business. "I've got my notebook and my pencil and now I am ready." I opened the notebook on the flat top of Father's gravestone. It was a congenial height for writing. As though he approved.

"No more fooling around," I said to her. "All that jauntiness, while all the time you were unhappy and only I didn't know. Or wouldn't. Well, thank you for that, but now it's my turn. I'm going to reinvent your life. For a writer no life is beyond repair. How would you like it to go? I can start from the beginning or pick it up anywhere along the line. . . . All you have to do is tell me what you would have wanted, what sorrows avoided, what joys fulfilled. Don't worry about style. That's my department, as music, you always said, was yours, thank you. And not to worry, it isn't going to be any mausoleum of words. If you cooperate, I'll reconsider the working title: *Memoirs of a Girl of Eighty-Eight.* I'll be back in a few weeks with the rough draft."

The ride home through those beloved counties was surprisingly lighthearted. How gentle the countryside near Troy, with much farming everywhere. Farming gives a sense of health to the land. It is replenishing to watch at dusk while a herd of cattle flows toward the barn. First one cow advances. She pauses. Another thrusts ahead, pulling the others behind it, until the last one, trailing milk, is inside the barn. Along the banks of the Hudson River the locust trees have grown very tall. Their bark is thrown into deep folds coated with lichen and moss. So old are these trees that, without the least wind, one will drop off a quite large branch as if to shed part of its burden. This letting-fall doesn't seem to do the tree any harm. . . . How clever of these locust trees to require no surgeon for their trimmage, only their own corporeal wisdom.

⌀〰〰〰〰୨

"Over the years, I have pulled from my unconscious fragmented images, like old half-torn photos, of empty rooms from which my mother is conspicuously absent."

231

BETSY MCCULLY COOPER
(1951–)

on

HER MOTHER, ELOISE SIMMONS MCCULLY
(1918–1995)

The following is from the eulogy delivered by the daughter of Eloise Simmons McCully, who had Alzheimer's disease.

Some shred of her still remains—a fragment of the woman who is my mother. Yet what remains after memory has been mercilessly stripped away? What remains after the insidious disease called Alzheimer's has done its work—like a cat burglar slipping inside the brain, cutting the wires, and setting to its silent task of robbing the house of its contents?

"This is Betsy—your daughter in Brooklyn," I hear my father on the other end of the telephone in Los Angeles, speaking to my mother next to him, beckoning her to come to the phone. "Who? Who?" she says, and getting on the line she cheerfully greets me, "Hello, Betsy in Brooklyn." But I know she does not connect the name to me, to a face remembered, and is merely parroting my father's words. "It's hot here," I say, "in the nineties every day." She responds gaily, "Hotsy, totsy!"

There is the ghost: that gaiety, that musical inflection in her voice, that slightly risqué humor. Her favorite songwriter was Cole Porter, whom she loved, she once told me, for his double entendres. I recall years ago—I was twenty-two and she was fifty-five—sitting with her and my father at a landmark café on the waterfront in San Francisco. It was ten in the morning, and we had stopped there to sample their famous gin fizz. We were the only customers there, and while the bartender mixed the frothy concoction in front of us, my mother began to joke with him. He was French, and I must have mentioned to him my mornings in Paris, going for a café au lait and croissants. "*Café au lit* [coffee in bed]?" he joked. As usual, I was a little slow on the uptake, but Mother got it immediately. She threw back her head and laughed with delight: "*Au lait au lit? Olé!*" giving a Spanish inflection to the last word, tossing her head and clicking her fingers like a flamenco dancer. She and the bartender had a good laugh together. She always had a hearty laugh, throwing back her head and opening her mouth wide with the sheer pleasure of laughing.

"Be prepared," my sister warns me on the phone, "Mother's gotten much worse, she may not recognize you." When I arrive with my six-year-old son at my parents' apartment in Pasadena, I greet my mother with a hug. She seems to recognize me, though she does not address me by name. She struggles to get the words of greeting out, managing a few brief sentences: "It's been a—long—time. . . . It's good—to—see you!" She will repeat the phrases a number of times through the afternoon. . . . I sit with her, hold her hand, tell her how glad I am to see her, laugh with her. "So good so far," she says to me; "So far so good," I respond. "Here's as far as we go!" she exclaims. Laughter has become our way of communicating.

A college-educated woman, Mother always loved a well-turned phrase. Now, she struggles to form words into complete sentences and express the simplest abstract concepts. She speaks in the present tense. My son, pretending to be a plane, accidentally bumps into her leg. "They're funny," she comments, and imitates his movements. "They don't know—what—they're doing, they don't—think." Then she turns to me, tears in her eyes. "They grow. So fast." She gestures tall. "Then—worries—you want to"—she gestures a hug—"help them—but—they don't want help."

Seeing her triggers painful memories. I am the little girl looking for my mother. Over the years, I have pulled from my unconscious fragmented images, like old half-torn photos, of empty rooms from which my mother is conspicuously absent. I am the third of six children. Following the closely spaced births of the fifth and sixth child, Mother suffered from bouts of postpartum depression. Her depression was manifested in withdrawal, silence, and sleep. She told me, in more articulate days, that she believed depression was a genetic trait, that her own mother had what she called "blue periods," when she would not speak for days. . . .

She clutches my hand and turns to me with weepy eyes. "It's good to find you," she says. "I like you, you're my friend—I—don't—have—many; we're friends—you and me—that's *good!*" The words strike me with painful irony. The friendship I had longed for as a girl is now declared to one she does not know to be her daughter. . . .

When it is time to leave, I walk with my mother and father to the car. In a burst of tears I embrace my mother and tell her I love her. My father embraces both of us and with a shaking hand reaches into his pocket and slips something into my hand . . . it is the topaz she brought back from Brazil years ago, which I admired as a child and always associated with her. Clutching the topaz, I get into the car and turn back one last time to say good-bye. To my astonishment Mother looks directly at me and says in a trembling voice, "I love you, Betsy."

I am shaken to the core. It is not the words, for she had said them before in earlier days, but her recognition of me in that moment, responding to my pain, and my own acknowledgment—denied for years—of my need to hear the words. I get in the car, fumble with the ignition, and drive away. The moment has vanished in the irreversible stream of time, yet the feelings of love and need, the sense of the unseverable connection between mother and daughter, has crystallized—like the topaz which I can retrieve from my pocket and hold up to the light.

⁂

"He wants to talk business, the business of the hereafter, after his departure for the Big Canada in the Sky. It's bravado, a form of mental distraction, a proxy for good-bye."

CHARLES TRUEHEART
(1951–)

on

HIS FATHER, WILLIAM C. TRUEHEART
(1918–1992)

At the same time that Washington, D.C., journalist Charles Trueheart was preparing to leave home for a new post in Canada, his father was preparing to die. Charles Trueheart wrote of that double leave-taking in this essay that first appeared in the Washington Post Magazine.

Every day, in the month before Christmas, when I visited my father in the hospital, I said good-bye to him with the false lilt of an inevitable tomorrow. . . . I told him about the new house in Toronto and that there would be a room for him on the third floor when he came to visit. Did my voice lack conviction? He knew the score. He was suddenly sick and might just as suddenly be gone. When I chattered on about Canada and the future, his eyes gently reminded me: he was the one who was leaving, not me. . . .

We make the smallest talk imaginable. Even the newspapers, our point of reference through the years, fail us. He's not reading them anymore, as serious a sign as any the doctors can read of this man's trajectory to closure. There's not anything remotely worth getting outraged about. My chronic admirer has stopped reading my articles, too. When I ask him about one I was proud of, he smiles shyly and shakes his head.

I'm not good at guessing what's important to him, or how he'll react. He tends to be more cynical than I've seen him—even if it's surprising, one needn't wonder why—and given to brittle gibes about my brother and me "fighting over the loot." One day I tried to give him a telephone number where he could reach me, and he insisted on storing it in his pocket calculator, in a little computerized address book he adores. In his weakened state he flubbed the operation, started over, flubbed it again, started over. It took time, more time than I thought I could spare in my very important and busy day. He and I both heard me sigh. Without taking his eyes off the gadget, he said, dry as dust, "I know this must be trying for you."

The next morning he has an agenda. He wants to talk business, the business of the hereafter, after his departure for the Big Canada in the Sky. It's bravado, a form of mental distraction, a proxy for good-bye. I've been engaging in a little of the same myself.

The family lawyer has been in to see him and the will is in order. Check. He wants no heroic measures and has done the paperwork already. Check. He wants no memorial service, no eulogies—but he says he wouldn't object to a couple of newspaper obituaries. I try to tell him the memorial service is not for him, it's for his family and friends, but I don't have the heart to persist, and he doesn't have the patience to listen. Picturing myself weeping in a church, I wonder if I will defy his last request. . . .

One day, as I was ending a visit to his hospital room, I sat down on the bed and leaned over his big old body and hugged him for a while, saying into the bedcovers that I wished there was something I could do for him.

He had an answer. "Just love me," he said. I do.

⌒ထ၅

"His life was leaving him but Life would not."

MICHAEL SALTZ
(1940–)

on

HIS FATHER, JEROME SALTZ
(1907–1994)

Michael Saltz is a television producer for the NewsHour with Jim Lehrer. *He delivered a version of this eulogy for his father, the budget director for the Federation of Jewish Philanthropies in New York, at his father's memorial service at Riverside Memorial Chapel in New York on September 1, 1994.*

My father was a complex, cantankerous man whose parents neither wanted nor understood him or thought that any of his achievements were meaningful—even as an adult. Unfortunately, there was nothing that I ever observed or was told about my grandparents which demonstrated that Dad was wrong in this understanding.

Early on, my father learned that there was little he could expect from his parents. At the age of thirteen he was paying them for his room and board. His most prized possessions, his roller skates and a BB gun, were not gifts but things which he had bought himself. When he turned eighteen, he bought a car, and these three things stayed with him, he stayed with them, for over forty years.

I don't think one can underestimate the importance that those three possessions had for him. They symbolized his freedom, his ability to get what mattered to him, and the keeping of essential parts of himself so private and well-guarded that it put limits on the things he could talk about, even to his closest friends.

This winter, I asked Dad if he had ever had a friend, as an adult, whom he felt comfortable enough with, safe enough with, to confide everything or anything he might feel. He said no. Not even Mother? No, not even her.

"It must have been very lonely," I said.

"Yes," he replied.

Despite the fact that he worked on Wall Street, my father was never comfortable in the presence of serious money, of wealth. To be in the presence of too much money might make you want things. It might lead you to do things which you would later regret. It might lead you to take things for granted. It might lead you to destroy your values. It is ironic that in a career in which serious money was a vital tool, in which he was constantly associating with some of the wealthiest men in America, he never felt comfortable with its trappings or with them.

He found his destiny, at least professionally, when he went to work at the Federation of Jewish Philanthropies where he became a master of understanding how the allocation of resources could be made to promote socially desirable goals. He found that through the manipulation of numbers he could make them dance to his tune. These were the happiest years of his life.

After that began the deterioration of his body—the aneurysms, the operations, the gradual loss of hearing, of sight, movement, and failing memory. If his pleasure in work was voluntarily eliminated, the other pleasures he got through living were being taken away, involuntarily, one by one. He could no longer listen to music, he could no longer read, he could no longer hold a complex thought, he could no longer find his way back home. It was painful for all of us to watch, but most of all it was painful for him. Prepared as he thought he was to die, he kept hanging on beyond his own expectations, locked inside his own chaotic mind, unable, unwilling, to share that pain and loneliness with anyone. His life was leaving him but Life would not.

The one person who mattered most to him remained. Finally, she left, too.

Though he knew Mother had died, there was a corner of his mind in which he thought that maybe, just maybe, it was a mistake. In June we took him on his final trip to his beloved summer home. He asked, "Will Mother be waiting for us?"

"No."

This time he knew it was true.

In the apartment where they had shared their lives for fifty years, there is a bust of Mother sculpted by Grandma, her mother. Now, every time he trod the carpet with faltering steps, he would stop, place a hand on top of her head, and continue on.

Once again, Dad was alone, too far gone for even the memory of the skates and the BB gun and the car to matter. Perhaps even the memory of them was gone, too. Clearly, the time had come to die.

And he did.

My wife, Lee, with whom I've been for eleven years, used to say about my mother that she deserved a Purple Heart for putting up with my father. That may be true, but she never really had a chance to know my father because by the time she came into my life, Dad was well on the way out of his.

How could she know that if you told this man that you loved him, he would cry.

⌖

"In the absence of this woman . . . we could see how clearly she had spent a lifetime puttying in the gaps between us before they had a chance to widen."

JULIE HOUSTON
(1944–)

on

HER MOTHER, RUTHEDA HUNT D'ALTON
(1919–1984)

Julie Houston is a freelance editor and writer who lives in Brooklyn, New York.

When my mother swam in the ocean—in the 1950s when the five of us were under ten—my sisters and I would sit at the edge of the surf calling, "Come back! Come back!" But she couldn't hear us over the waves, and as our eyes fixed on that white-bathing-capped head getting smaller and smaller, we pressed together and struggled as one with the rising fear of losing her. All we could do was wait.

She swam straight out toward the horizon, undaunted by the currents and cutting through the waves with the long, easy strokes of a distance swimmer. When she got far enough out from the shore and into the wide trough of water between the breakers and the sandbar, she would float over onto her back, treading water and waving to us all reassuringly. This was the moment we hoped for. We could not see her face but we knew she was smiling, and that strong, confident arm making wide arcs above the water seemed to relay a solemn, motherly promise that she would return. She always did, of course, but as we watched her helplessly from the shore, she seemed to be playing it awfully close.

As children we didn't know she was a strong, capable swimmer and that we shouldn't have worried about her. Even when there was an undertow and big, strong waves broke at jagged angles against the shore, she knew how to get in and out of them with ease, perfectly timing her exit and running up onto the beach smack into her children, swarming around her with relief and joy, rewarded for our trust by her wet, sandy hugs and salty kisses.

In time we joined her daredevil swims. Spending summer after summer at our beach house on the dunes, we grew up to become a family of ocean swimmers, five sisters and their mother in a fearless camaraderie that must have contributed, in some way, to the simple pleasure we always felt when we got together, long into adulthood and at least until the ordeal of her death was over. The telephone call came early one Sunday morning. . . . My father, his voice too loud and trembling, was summoning us immediately to Connecticut. Mom had had a massive cerebral hemorrhage. . . . As we held on to each other around that huge, high bed, the black, starry sky filling the big glass window in the hospital room . . . suddenly my mother did not seem like a person at all but rather a huge ocean vessel, navigation haywire, alone and adrift on the winter sea. . . . We were sisters reunited and helpless once again, her loving children tempted to hope and pray for a miracle, that somehow she'd recover, trying to survive on our own uncharted sea of confusion about what it means to be alive. . . .

During the months after Mom's death, my sisters and I splintered apart. Sibling animosities and resentments spilled over into trembling emotional skirmishes that divided us first into rival camps and, eventually, into grudging, humorless alliances "for the sake of appearances." During one tedious round of fighting, it suddenly became clear why things had gotten so out of hand. She who had been the glue that kept us all together—the mother bolstering each child's individual needs, giving encouragement and praise to shore up confidence; the clever behind-the-scenes mediator; the diplomat able to smooth over petty frictions—was gone. In the absence of this woman who'd given us a motherly love and energy no husband or father or lover could provide, we could see how clearly she had spent a lifetime puttying in the gaps between us before they had a chance to widen.

. . . Her children knew her faults well; there were many of them. But this complicated, often exasperating woman who was my mother was also a feeling, sharing, funny human being whose greatest joy was her children. In her brief and struggling lifetime, she was happiest during those golden Fire Island summers, free to excel at the two things she did best—nurturing her offspring and swimming in the ocean. In both she thrived where my father floundered. How we cheered when he'd perform the yearly ritual of standing waist-deep in the ocean, holding his nose, and dunking his head under, and racing back to the house! He preferred the beach in winter, dressed in combat clothes to check the eroding dunes in front of our house. And now, with no wifely buffer zone to retreat to, how uncomfortable he is when his grown-up daughters fight! He wrings his hands, incapable of diving in as she did, headlong into the fray, to elbow a space between us with her direct and outspoken love.

. . . Time will cool the anger at losing her in such a cruel and sudden way, and it will soften the intense sadness of missing her so. This is nature's plan for those who must continue to live, and while we have yet to discover if some distance from the events of death will also heal the wounds of our sisterly squabbles, there are signs it probably will. Sorting ourselves out takes time.

Adjusting to losing her, there is another, unexpected process under way as well. Where once I would not have stopped to notice, now when I look in the mirror, I see my mother's face in mine. I hear the soft, distinctive pace of her footsteps as I climb the stairs, feel the rhythm of her hands as I pick up my knitting at the end of the day.

The unmistakable pitch and tone of her laughter rings out and surprises me when my children and I play happily together. Some of her returns, slowly but surely reclaiming a place in our lives.

ᏩᎳᏯ

"Before she became our mother . . . she was simply her father's joy. . . ."

MARIE HARRIS
(1943–)

on

HER MOTHER, MARIE MURRAY HARRIS
(1919–1994)

Marie Harris, a poet, essayist, and editor, lives in Barrington, New Hampshire. Her reminiscence first appeared in The Granite Review.

Every June her family retreated from Brooklyn to Southampton, where their Catholic houses and stables and cottages sat like dowagers above the Atlantic.

The sun was served up daily as though the best specimen of fruit in season had been delivered from Herbert's Market on a Spode plate. Breezes bent the dunegrass, sowed salt and sand onto striped summer slipcovers, into drawers of summer towels and summer silver. Seersucker nannies fussed past shirtsleeved gardeners and grooms. Linen cooks and laundresses tended to clergy in sport shirts. Weekend uncles came by rail, loosening ties. Aunts arranged zinnias by day and read stories at twilight to little cousins in cotton pajamas who turned brown as the rotogravure.

She rode horseback in the fields. She played tennis and golf. She practiced French. She dreamed romantic dreams, fixed her hair, and danced the foxtrot with young men called "beaux." Nightly, she said her prayers and sometimes she prayed for someone.

I want to remember her before I was there to remember, before she would turn to the handsome man on her left and realize he was the one who would usher her into her next life where there would be no doting father to order cut flowers be planted in the cooling September soil, one by one, down to the seawater swimming pool for the debutante party of which, on principle, he disapproved.

Before she became our mother, when she was simply her father's joy, she "received the guests gowned in a bouffant evening frock of white tulle. She carried orchids and six hundred guests were present for dinner and two hundred more came in for the dancing. . . . Fireworks climaxed the evening, ending with Miss Murray's picture and name done in lights."

꩜

"I have never met you, yet I will never forget you. . . ."

A EULOGY TO MY UNKNOWN FATHER

by

ROSA ORDAZ
(1964–)

The author of this eulogy was abandoned by her father when she was eleven months old. He left behind a wife and four children and formed a new family. "What I write," says Ms. Ordaz, "is not endearing, but it is honest and I know many fatherless children must harbor similar feelings. How do I say good-bye to a man who helped give me life but who, by the same token, made that life an arduous exercise? In writing out these feelings, I was freeing my soul."

*My God says I should forgive you
Something I've tried to do my whole life
I have never met you, yet I will never forget you
Your walk on earth has ended.
You no longer breathe nor think
You are no longer.
What am I now?
You were the passion that lived inside of me,
What you did or failed to do is who I became.
The love you never gave me,*

The visit you never paid me,
The letter you never wrote me,
The book you never read me,
The song you never sang me,
The explanation you never gave me,
All of this is who I am.
A passion
An anger
A hunger
A yearning
A pride
A rebellious sorrow
A shielded heart
An ambitious spirit.
You take again from me
First, my rights as your child
Now, my soul's foundation.
I feel as if I've reached the edge of a cliff on a moonless night
I no longer see who I am
Am I me
Or am I what you did to me?
Once again you leave me with no answers.
I never knew why you left me. For, in my eyes, you left me not my mother
Now I clutch bewildered feelings.
Does your exit grant my soul peace
or does it steal from it?
Will I be whole again? Do I want to be that again?
Will I be a better person, wife, mother
Or will I lack the passion that has driven my course?
My God says I should forgive you. I do.
I pray you can forgive yourself. And I sincerely hope you find peace,
FATHER.

ᏫᎳᎧ

"He could be rigid, but his stubbornness was also a steadfastness and as such a form of principle. He moved slowly, even glacially, to some of the more urgent among us. But he moved."

CATHARINE A. MACKINNON
(1946–)

on

HER FATHER, GEORGE E. MACKINNON
(1906–1995)

George E. MacKinnon was a judge on the D.C. Circuit Court of Appeals. Catharine MacKinnon is a lawyer, teacher, writer, and human rights advocate. She delivered her eulogy, from which this is excerpted, at a memorial service for her father on May 5, 1995, in Potomac, Maryland.

We celebrate this day the uncommon life of a common man. George Edward MacKinnon lived into his ninetieth year—a man of common sense, common courage, and uncommon perseverance. Every day, he simply put one foot in front of the other on a path that describes a slow, simple arc upward.

Dad was all one person. "Judge" and "George" sound so much alike, as if the baby born in 1906 was named to foreshadow his appointment to the bench in 1969, a role that fit him like a glove. This was the same man our family knew as father and husband. . . .

He wrote his opinions the way he made his Christmas cookies: systematically, carefully, methodically, deliberately, following a recipe he found, then modified, then rewrote as he tested it against experience until it became his own. His point was to produce a consistent result that anyone could follow. His idea of a Saturday was to show his children how a neighbor made sausage—the best sausage in the world. People Dad knew were always "the best oil geologist in the world" or whatever they were or did. Once, after he lost the race for governor of Minnesota in 1958 (this was also the only time I ever saw him cry; he said he didn't mind losing, but he did mind losing to someone like Orville Freeman), he took two hours to show me the proper way to prepare a grapefruit. He did not read fiction.

Competency mattered to him; brilliance did not especially. . . . He spoke plainly, directly, bluntly. "Very interesting" was what he said of ideas he did not particularly understand as well as of food he did not particularly like. He was deeply suspicious of intellectuals as a category, connecting them with communists and other low forms of life. He was more than quietly gratified to note that much of the world had recently seemed to come around to his evaluation of communism vintage 1935.

His politics were rooted in a deep populism and an utter indifference to status. His father, whom he worshiped, worked his way up from telegraph operator to division superintendent on the railroad. . . . He was as likely to bark at a Supreme Court justice as a waitress, but as Nina Totenberg put it, his bark was worse than his bite. As I put it, his bark was his bite. And he always left good tips. He told me when I was little that waitresses "worked hard and didn't get paid much." Without fanfare, one hot July afternoon in about 1961, he taught his daughter to throw the javelin, a sport in which he was an Olympic alternate for the Amsterdam games in 1928. . . . As traditional as he was about roles, it was so obvious to him that women could do anything that he never needed to say it. And he never said anything he didn't need to say. . . .

George MacKinnon had his own inner compass and his own pace. He could not be pushed, as everyone who ever tried to threaten, bribe, persuade, interview, or change him learned—from organized crime in Minneapolis where he was U.S. district attorney . . . to lawyers making even slightly unconventional arguments before the D.C. Circuit, on which he sat for twenty-five years, to his children seeking to move some of his views into the twentieth century. He had his take and would not be moved. This made his sudden open-mindedness surprising, but it was equally real. His openness to people and ideas increased with age and with his experience in Washington, as did the diversity of his friends, which kept growing until the moment he died. He could be rigid, but his stubbornness was also a steadfastness and as such a form of principle. He moved slowly, even glacially, to some of the more urgent among us. But he moved.

Tenacity, his fierce determination to stay the course, may have been Dad's most uncommon quality. It marked everything he did: as a successful prosecutor of white-slave cases few others were even bringing, to, as he put it, "get Hoffa," which he was part of more or less doing; as a four-term state and one-term federal legislator, where he did the dogged behind-the-scenes drafting of legislation and pursuit of evidence in investigations. . . . As a judge it made him the only one nearly to outlive *D.C. Transit*, a case that makes *Bleak House*'s *Jarndyce and Jarndyce* look swift and sure. Dad played football for Minnesota by never giving up, and as a six-foot-one-inch, 157-pound center back when, as he put it, "center was a skill position," he became an all-American that way. He played golf by sticking at it. Toward the end of his life, Mother had a minister come to the hospital, and when Dad spotted the clerical collar as the poor man came through the door, he reared up in bed and said, "Not by a long shot." He lived seven more weeks.

He loved his wife, one remarkable woman, from the day they met to the day he died. He stuck by his friends . . . he kept his many loyalties—to the U.S. Navy, the Scots, Congress, the Republican Party, and anything connected with the state of Minnesota. As he lay in the hospital toward the end and I thought I was seeing him for what might be the last time, he asked me to open the window. I noticed it had a fine metal frame and smooth works. Then he motioned me to lean down and spoke with difficulty what could have been his last words to me: "Minnesota company."

When he was in intensive care in one of his later crises and almost died, Dad later said he had had a dream in which he learned that death was a choice. This most earthbound of men said he had gone through a long tunnel with a bright light at the end of it. There he was in court and someone was trying to get him to sign an affidavit. He declined at the time and, impossibly, recovered. I remembered Dad's focused restlessness all my life. He was always up and going off somewhere, fully dressed, with tie, taking us if we wanted to go, to do something he wanted to do or see something he wanted to see. Mother used to call it "the old hat trick." On May 1, 1995, George MacKinnon signed that great affidavit and pulled the old hat trick on us one last time.

୧ᴍᴍ୨

"I believe that Mother's life was a testimony to struggle to rise above the limitations of her childhood. She was emotionally rejected by her father, whom she remembers saying to her as a little girl, with a snap of his fingers, 'You aren't worth five cents.' "

DAVID R. COOK
(1928–)

on

HIS MOTHER, NELLE REED COOK
(1897–1991)

This eulogy for Nelle Reed Cook was delivered at her funeral on August 10, 1991, by her son, a retired professor of counseling and psychology at the University of Wisconsin at Stout.

We are gathered to celebrate a fulfilled life. Our mother, grandmother, great-grandmother, and friend, Nelle Reed Cook, lived out her life with courage, determination, joy, and purpose. So if tears come, they will be the tears of feeling the loss of a mighty presence in our lives but not tears of sadness for her death.

I believe that Mother's life was a testimony to struggle to rise above the limitations of her childhood. She was emotionally rejected by her father, whom she remembers saying to her as a little girl, with a snap of his fingers, "You aren't worth five cents." But her father was a man of great honesty, respected in his community and loyal to his family . . . and before he died many years ago, he apologized to her and asked for forgiveness. He did the best he knew.

But Mother suffered a lifelong insecurity about her core sense of self-worth. I believe it was that insecurity that led her to be such a controlling person. Mother told me that she learned from her critical and criticizing father as a child that being critical was the way you were supposed to be. In my mother it took the form of strong opinions, some rigid ideas, judgments about things, and a sometimes unnerving directness that could be hurtful, although I am convinced never intentionally. Mother was not an easy person to live with. All of us children and many of the grandchildren have felt at one time or another the frustration, the sting of her personality.

I share these things with you on the occasion of Mother's funeral because to honor and celebrate her life means to celebrate and honor all of it. Our parents invested us with a deep sense of honesty and integrity. . . . Honesty makes it important to me that my mother not be simply regarded as a "saint," as I'm sure some people feel she is. Though such a thought does honor to Mother's memory, to make her a saint in some sense diminishes her considerable humanity.

The religion of Mother's childhood was a dark, vindictive, and judgmental religion that did not seem to hold much in the way of redemption and grace. When, in the middle of her life, she began to encounter a different vision of God, personified for her in Christ Jesus, it began a healing process in her inner life that allowed her in time to feel her own value and worth as a child of God.

Mother tried to live her life, especially the last twenty-five years, in tune with the infinite. She sought God's guidance on all matters in her life. Nothing was excluded from this, and while this could make for some frustrating feelings in dealing with her, what seems remarkable to me is how often her guidance made sense, how often the pieces fell together. Particularly during the last month of her life, I had no problem seeing God's hand in all of it, guiding and beckoning Mother to her final resting place with the Almighty.

The perfect mother and the perfect father do not exist in this life, and I am glad for that. No child could stand them or get free from them. But the mother of whom you can say she loved you unconditionally, she gave you a sense of purpose in life, and she showed you what it means to live faithfully, to age courageously, and to die at peace with herself—that is all the mother any child could hope for. That is the mother we had. Thank you, Mother, for being just who you were, and thanks be to God for her life.

⚬〰〰⚬

CHAPTER TEN

CHILDREN

It is unthinkable that our children should die at all, much less before their time, although lives are not weighed by hours but by accomplishment, and I know of one particular child who had significantly straightened out every life he touched by the time he died at the age of six. What is truly unthinkable is that children should die before *our* time. But below are the words of four parents whose children did.

Mark Twain's essay on the death of his daughter Susy is a brooding meditation upon the inability of mankind to improve itself. Often cited as another proof of his cynicism, it is only partially a description of Susy, by all accounts an original thinker who sought to find out the meaning of things for herself. Twain's thoughts go back and forth between his daughter and his own outlook on what life, at the bottom of it, contains.

Death itself held no terrors for Twain, who often said he envied those who had already gone ahead. But he was incurably interested in life, once confessing in a letter to his daughter Clara that he found it too dangerous to shave while looking out the window at the brilliant fall foliage. "I have to stop and write this postscript to quiet my mind and lower my temperature so that I can go and stand between the windows again and without peril resume." To the end of his life, Twain remained vulnerable to astonishment, although Susy's existential question "Mamma, what is it all for?" remained his own.

Entirely different in tone is respected conservative journalist William Allen White's obituary for his daughter, Mary. Reading it is to witness a time and place so unlike our own that we instantly shed all the cultural junk of the last seventy years to accompany White in his grief. A tomboy who kept her pigtails until the last possible minute, which never came, Mary White, of Emporia, Kansas, was killed in a horseback riding accident. Her father wrote her obituary in his newspaper, *The Emporia Gazette*, and it was immediately picked up by larger newspapers, and later reprinted in countless magazines and anthologies.

Writer Mary-Lou Weisman's account of her son Peter's death brings to mind the words of C. S. Lewis in *The Screwtape Letters*. "You will notice," writes the Devil to his nephew, Wormwood, "that the young are generally less unwilling to die than the middle-aged and the old." Throughout the story of Peter's life, which Weisman tells in her book, *Intensive Care*, fear does not surface except in other people's minds. And in the end, fear dissolves into another dimension, which Peter, in a word, makes clear.

The section ends with a eulogy by John Conrad for his son, John Jr., who was born with a disease that retarded him physically, mentally, and emotionally. "How do you celebrate a life of dead expectations?" asked his father. How, in other words, do you love with a broken heart? To a greater or lesser degree, all the eulogies attempt to answer that second question.

"She was at times much given to retiring within herself and trying to search out the hidden meanings of the deep things that make the puzzle and pathos of human existence, and in all the ages have baffled the inquirer and mocked him."

SUSY CLEMENS
(1872–1896)

by

MARK TWAIN
(1835–1910)

In 1895, at the peak of his celebrityhood, Mark Twain went bankrupt, the result of investing in a publishing house that left him penniless. He embarked upon a three-year lecture tour of Europe to recoup his losses, and on April 15, 1896, while he and his wife and daughter Clara were in London, news came to the couple that their elder twenty-four-year-old daughter, Susy, was ill. Mrs. Clemens and Clara immediately left for the United States, but three days later Twain received a cablegram that said, "Susy was peacefully released today." Writing of that day in his autobiography, Twain observed, "It is one of the mysteries of our nature that a man, all unprepared, can receive a thunderstroke like that and live."

The summer seasons of Susy's childhood were spent at Quarry Farm on the hills east of Elmira, New York; the other seasons of the year at the home in Hartford. Like other children, she was blithe and happy, fond of play; unlike the average of children, she was at times much given to retiring within herself and trying to search out the hidden meanings of the deep things that make the puzzle and pathos of human existence, and in all the ages have baffled the inquirer and mocked him. As a little child aged seven, she was oppressed and perplexed by the maddening repetition of the stock incidents of our race's fleeting sojourn here, just as the same thing has oppressed and perplexed maturer minds from the beginning of time. A myriad of men are born; they labor and sweat and struggle for bread; they squabble and scold and fight; they scramble for little mean advantages over each other. Age creeps upon them; infirmities follow; shames and humiliations bring down their prides and their vanities.

Those they love are taken from them, and the joy of life is turned to aching grief. The burden of pain, care, misery, grows heavier year by year. At length ambition is dead; pride is dead; vanity is dead; longing for release is in their place. It comes at last—the only unpoisoned gift earth ever had for them—and they vanish from a world where they were of no consequence; where they achieved nothing; where they were a mistake and a failure and a foolishness; where they have left no sign that they have existed—a world which will lament them a day and forget them forever. Then another myriad takes their place, and copies all they did, and goes along the same profitless road, and vanishes as they vanished—to make room for another and another and a million other myriads to follow the same arid path through the same desert and accomplish what the first myriad, and all the myriads that came after it, accomplished—nothing!

"Mamma, what is it all for?" asked Susy, preliminary stating the above details in her own halting language, after long brooding over them alone in the privacy of the nursery.

A year later, she was groping her way alone through another sunless bog, but this time she reached a rest for her feet. For a week, her mother had not been able to go to the nursery, evenings, at the child's prayer hour. She spoke of it—was sorry for it, and said she would come tonight, and hoped she could continue to come every night and hear Susy pray, as before. Noticing that the child wished to respond, but was evidently troubled as to how to word her answer, she asked what the difficulty was. Susy explained that Miss Foote (the governess) had been teaching her about the Indians and their religious beliefs, whereby it appeared that they had not only a god, but several. This had set Susy to thinking. As a result of this thinking she had stopped praying. She qualified this statement—that is, she modified it—saying she did not now pray "in the same way" as she had formerly done. Her mother said, "Tell me about it, dear."

"Well, Mamma, the Indians believed they knew, but now we know they were wrong. By and by it can turn out that we are wrong. So now I only pray that there may be a God and a heaven—or something better."

I wrote down this pathetic prayer in its precise wording, at the time, in a record which we kept of the children's sayings, and my reverence for it has grown with the years that have passed over my head since then. Its untaught grace and simplicity are a child's, but the wisdom and the pathos of it are of all the ages that have come and gone since the race of man has lived, and longed, and hoped, and feared, and doubted.

⟑⟑⟑

"She was mischievous without malice, as full of faults as an old shoe. No angel was Mary White, but an easy girl to live with for she never nursed a grouch five minutes in her life."

MARY WHITE
(1905–1921)

by

WILLIAM ALLEN WHITE
(1868–1944)

William Allen White, a populist Republican journalist in Emporia, Kansas, defended the existence and virtues of small-town America at the same time that such writers as Sinclair Lewis and Theodore Dreiser were debunking them. The editor in chief of The Emporia Gazette, *White had the grim duty of writing the obituary for his own daughter, Mary, when she was killed in a horseback riding accident at the age of sixteen. His eulogy was picked up by Franklin P. Adams and reprinted in the* New York Tribune *and has been much reprinted since.*

In his autobiography, White conceded that "probably if anything I have written . . . survives more than a decade beyond my life's span, it will be the thousand words or so that I hammered out on my typewriter that bright May morning under the shadow and in the agony of Mary's death."

The Associated Press reports carrying the news of Mary White's death declared that it came as the result of a fall from a horse. How she would have hooted at that! She never fell from a horse in her life. Horses have fallen on her and with her—"I'm always trying to hold 'em in my lap," she used to say. But she was proud of few things, and one of them was that she could ride anything that had four legs and hair. Her death resulted not from a fall but from a blow on the head which fractured her skull, and the blow came from the limb of an overhanging tree on the parking.

The last hour of her life was typical of its happiness. She came home from a day's work at school, topped off by a hard grind with the copy of the High School Annual, and felt that a ride would refresh her. She climbed into her khakis, chattering to her mother about the work she was doing, and hurried to get her horse and be out on the dirt roads for the country air and the radiant green fields of the spring. As she rode through the town on an easy gallop, she kept waving at passersby. She knew everyone in town. For a decade the little figure in the long pigtail and the red hair ribbon has been familiar on the streets of Emporia, and she got in the way of speaking to those who nodded at her. She passed the Kerrs, walking the horse in front of the Normal Library, and waved at them; passed another friend a few hundred feet farther on, and waved at her.

The horse was walking, and as she turned into North Merchant Street she took off her cowboy hat, and the horse swung into a lope. She passed the Tripletts and waved her cowboy hat at them, still moving gaily north on Merchant Street. A *Gazette* carrier passed—a High School boy friend—and she waved at him, but with her bridle hand; the horse veered quickly, plunged into the parking where the low-hanging limb faced her, and while she was still looking back waving, the blow came. But she did not fall from the horse; she slipped off, dazed a bit, staggered, and fell in a faint. She never quite recovered consciousness.

But she did not fall from the horse, neither was she riding fast. A year or so ago she used to go like the wind. But that habit was broken, and she used the horse to get into the open, to get fresh, hard exercise, and to work off a certain surplus energy that welled up in her and needed a physical outlet. The need has been in her heart for years. It was back of the impulse that kept the dauntless little brown-clad figure on the streets and the country roads of the community and built into a strong, muscular body what had been a frail and sickly frame during the first years of her life. But the riding gave her more than a body. It released a gay and hardy soul. She was the happiest thing in the world. And she was happy because she was enlarging her horizon. She came to know all sorts and conditions of men; Charley O'Brien, the traffic cop, was one of her best friends. W. L. Holtz, the Latin teacher, was another. Tom O'Connor, farmer-politician, and the Reverend J. H. Rice, preacher and police judge, and Frank Beach, music master, were her special friends; and all the girls, black and white, above the track and below the track, in Pepville and Stringtown, were among her acquaintances. And she brought home riotous stories of her adventures. She loved to rollick; persiflage was her natural expression at home. Her humor was a continual bubble of joy. She seemed to think in hyperbole and metaphor. She was mischievous without malice, as full of faults as an old shoe. No angel was Mary White, but an easy girl to live with for she never nursed a grouch for five minutes in her life.

With all her eagerness for the out-of-doors, she loved books. On her table when she left her room were a book by Conrad, one by Galsworthy, *Creative Chemistry* by E. E. Slosson, and a Kipling book. She read Mark Twain, Dickens, and Kipling before she was ten—all of their writings. Wells and Arnold Bennett particularly amused and diverted her. She was entered as a student in Wellesley for 1922; was assistant editor of the High School Annual this year, and in line for election to the editorship next year. She was a member of the executive committee of the High School YWCA.

Within the last two years she had begun to be moved by an ambition to draw. She began as most children do by scribbling in her schoolbooks, funny pictures. She bought cartoon magazines and took a course—rather casually, naturally, for she was, after all, a child with no strong purposes—and this year she tasted the first fruits of success by having her pictures accepted by the High School Annual. But the thrill of delight she got when Mr. Ecord, of the Normal Annual, asked her to do the cartooning for that book this spring was too beautiful for words. She fell to her work with all her enthusiastic heart. Her drawings were accepted, and her pride—always repressed by a lively sense of the ridiculous figure she was cutting—was a really gorgeous thing to see. No successful artist ever drank a deeper draft of satisfaction than she took from the little fame her work was getting among her schoolfellows. In her glory, she almost forgot her horse—but never her car.

For she used the car as a jitney bus. It was her social life. She never had a "party" in all her nearly seventeen years—wouldn't have one; but she never drove a block in her life that she didn't begin to fill the car with pickups! Everybody rode with Mary White—white and black, old and young, rich and poor, men and women. She liked nothing better than to fill the car with long-legged High School boys and an occasional girl, and parade the town. She never had a "date," nor went to a dance, except once with her brother, Bill, and the "boy proposition" didn't interest her—yet. But young people—great spring-breaking, varnish-cracking, fender-bending, door-sagging carloads of "kids"—gave her great pleasure. Her zests were keen. But the most fun she ever had in her life was acting as chairman of the committee that got up the big turkey dinner for the poor folks at the county home; scores of pies, gallons of slaw, jam, cakes, preserves, oranges, and a wilderness of turkey were loaded into the car and taken to the county home. And, being of a practical turn of mind, she risked her own Christmas dinner to see that the poor folks actually got it all. Not that she was a cynic; she just disliked to tempt folks. While there, she found a blind colored uncle, very old, who could do nothing but make rag rugs, and she rustled up from her school friends rags enough to keep him busy for a season. The last engagement she tried to make was to take the guests at the county home out for a car ride. And the last endeavor of her life was to try to get a rest room for colored girls in the High School. She found one girl reading in the toilet because there was no better place for a colored girl to loaf, and it inflamed her sense of injustice and she became a nagging harpy to those who she thought could remedy the evil. The poor she always had with her and was glad of it. She hungered and thirsted for righteousness; and was the most impious creature in the world. She joined the church without consulting her parents, not particularly for her soul's good. She never had a thrill of piety in her life, and would have hooted at a "testimony." But even as a little child, she felt the church was an agency for helping people to more of life's abundance, and she wanted to help. She never wanted help for herself. Clothes meant little to her. It was a fight to get a new rig on her; but eventually a harder fight to get it off. She never wore a jewel and had no ring but her High School class ring, though she was nearly seventeen. "Mother," she protested, "you don't know how much I get by with, in my braided pigtails, that I could not with my hair up." Above every other passion of her life was her passion not to grow up, to be a child. The tomboy in her, which was big, seemed loath to be put away forever in skirts. She was a Peter Pan who refused to grow up.

Her funeral yesterday at the Congregational was as she would have wished it; no singing, no flowers except the big bunch of red roses from her brother Bill's Harvard classmen—heavens, how proud that would have made her!—and the red roses from the *Gazette* forces, in vases, at her head and feet. A short prayer; Paul's beautiful essay on "Love" from the Thirteenth Chapter of First Corinthians; some remarks about her democratic spirit by her friend John H. J. Rice, pastor and police judge, which she would have deprecated if she could; a prayer sent down for her by her friend Carl Nau; and, opening the service, the slow, poignant movement from Beethoven's *Moonlight* Sonata, which she loved; and closing the service a cutting from the joyously melancholy first movement of Tchaikovsky's *Pathetic* Symphony, which she liked to hear, in certain moods, on the phonograph; then the Lord's Prayer, by her friends in High School.

That was all.

For her pallbearers only her friends were chosen: her Latin teacher, W. L. Holtz; her High School principal, Rice Brown; her doctor, Frank Foncannon; her friend W. W. Finney; her pal at the *Gazette* office, Walter Hughes; and her brother Bill. It would have made her smile to know that her friend Charley O'Brien, the traffic cop, had been transferred from Sixth and Commercial to the corner near the church to direct her friends who came to bid her good-bye.

A rift in the clouds in a gray day threw a shaft of sunlight upon her coffin as her nervous, energetic little body sank to its last sleep. But the soul of her, the glowing, gorgeous, fervent soul of her, surely was flaming in eager joy upon some other dawn.

<hr />

"I shall never know myself to be so good again."

PETER BENJAMIN WEISMAN
(1964–1980)

by

MARY-LOU WEISMAN
(1937–)

Peter Weisman was born with muscular dystrophy. In her account of his life (Intensive Care), *his mother writes of his final moments as she and her husband watched him go.*

We stand at his side, each of us holding a hand, each with a hand on his heart, our fingers laced, listening with our touch to the tiny thump and flutter of his life. Go ahead, Peter, you can die now. Go gentle, darling, go.

His eyes are shut. They twitch like curtains behind which the players are busily taking their places. I can see each vein on the lid, each lash where it meets, enters, and disappears, as if the secret of life lay luminous as a tableau beneath that pale, fragile membrane.

The freckles on his nose, splotched and merged by fifteen summers in the sun, seem to fade before my eyes as his skin bleaches to the color of ash.

His lips, still pink and finely delineated by the perfection of innocence, are parted.

I look at his face never to forget, to take it inside me, indelible, still living, to have forever; memorized, but not a memory.

Peter, will you, in death, come and live inside me, never to be born and never to die again, never to become a fading memory? I don't want a fading memory. I want a real, live you, secreted inside me. I want to be able to conjure you up, all the faces of you—laughing, pouting, sticking your tongue out for a cookie—whenever I want to.

And your voice. I want to hear your voice. I want to have it. I don't want to have to invent it out of filaments of wispy recollections, summoned lost chords, stilled vibrations, thin air.

But that won't happen. I can tell already, just by standing here, watching. I can tell that you are going away from me.

"Daddy?" Peter's whisper sounds so far away, so lost. Quickly! I must start memorizing right now. I must get it all by heart. "Daddy? What does *impudent* mean?"

Bewildered, frightened, I look to Larry. He answers matter-of-factly, while tears stream from his eyes, "*Impudent.* It means bold. Shamelessly bold."

"Then put me in an impudent position."

Tenderly Larry takes his hand from Peter's heart, takes Peter's right arm and wraps it around [his stuffed hippo] Soft Gray. Then he looks up at me. I can see from the look in his eyes that he is as bewildered and frightened as I am. Peter isn't making sense.

All at once I understand. He must not be getting enough oxygen to his brain. "He's hallucinating," I whisper, touching Larry's hand.

No, I can tell. I won't be able to keep you. I can see that you are going away already. Your words, your breath, are already slipping out of your body, running free, escaping.

See? See that stain of urine growing round and warm on the starched white sheet? That's death. Oh my God, that's all there is to it. Just a breakdown of the body, a failure of the systems, a mechanical event. Funny. I had expected so much more of death, so much bigger a deal.

I get it now. Now, at the last moment, I get it. It's not for you I will mourn, who, dying when you were done but not defeated, died on time.

But what about me? What about me, sentenced for life to be free of the literal burden of you, yet condemned and exalted to never forgetting. The burden of having you will turn into the burden of missing you.

I won't be able to remember your face! All your living faces will merge into the photograph we will place on the mantel in the living room, and try as I may, soon I will not be able to pull apart a frown from a smile, and little by little I will stop trying and begin to believe that the photo on the mantel is really you because I will have no choice. You will not live inside me. You are going away.

And even after I have unplugged the intercoms, yours from your room, mine from mine, wrapped the brown rubber cord around the white plastic boxes and put them in the attic, will I still hear you calling me in the night, "Mom?" your voice gravelly with sleep?

I suppose I shall. For a while. For a while I will marvel at this macabre, confluent neural circuitry, this phantom pain of a connection that keeps a soldier feeling his amputated leg, that keeps me hearing you.

But soon I will not be able to conjure up your voice, not even your voice telling me that you love me, from the homunculus of you I would, but cannot, sustain within me. Life will not have it. Inevitably, wounds turn into scars, life into memory, or the memory of a memory. This is called healing. It happens in time. They say it is a blessing.

Little will be left, just a permanent soreness and swelling about the heart. But missing you will never heal into a memory. At least I will have that; that and the sad reassurance that it brings, like some fabled time of perfect grace, some Camelot of the spirit, the understanding that I shall never know myself to be so good again.

I feel Peter's heart falter under my fingers—a flutter, like feeling life. Larry clasps my hand. Peter's lips move, and he speaks just one word: "Deliverance." Then the exquisite skin under his eyes twinkles wildly, fracturing like a mosaic, flashing out electric currents as if there were a fire in his brain. His eyes open wide, staring, sightless, yet intent. His head arches back and falls.

⚭

"How do you celebrate a life like John's? How do you celebrate a tragic life and death? How do you find any redeeming value to the life of a retarded boy who suffered from severe and bizarre emotional problems? How do you celebrate a life of dead expectations?"

JOHN CONRAD JR.
(1979–1993)

by

JOHN CONRAD SR.
(1951–)

John Conrad Jr. was born on July 26, 1979. At the age of ten months symptoms of a progressive disease called tuberous sclerosis were discovered. In a letter accompanying this eulogy, his father wrote: "With the exception of Christmas, 1992, John lived the last five Christmas Eves of his life in a padded cell, sometimes in a straitjacket. When I visited him, during the first of these five horrible Christmas Eves, John was the only child in the entire children's hospital. I found him locked in a padded cell, in a straitjacket, asleep and exhausted from his self-injurious behavior. When I took John in my arms and woke him up, he looked up at me with his hands tied to his back and said, 'Daddy, I want to be good. I just want to be good.' It was John's ability to bounce back from this hopeless life with this undying spirit of hopefulness that inspired my wife, Kathy, and me."

The following eulogy was delivered by John Conrad Sr. on August 29, 1993, at his son's funeral at St. James Episcopal Church in Richmond, Virginia.

How do you celebrate a life like John's? How do you celebrate a tragic life and death? How do you find any redeeming value to the life of a retarded boy who suffered from severe and bizarre emotional problems? How do you celebrate a life of dead expectations?

When John was born, we were ecstatic to have two bouncing twin babies. We had all the arrogant expectations of the best and the brightest. Then we learned that John was a victim of tuberous sclerosis. Tuberous sclerosis is a genetic disease which affects one in ten to fifteen thousand people. Eighty-five percent of the cases are new mutations, like John. TS causes a dysfunction in the cells that exist in virtually every tissue in your body: your skin, brain, heart, lungs, kidneys, and eyes. These cells become sclerotic, or hard, and cease to operate normally. John had these tumors throughout his brain, skin, and in his heart.

At first Kathy and I hoped that John would have a mild case. We hoped at one point that John could go to St. Christopher's. We hoped that he would run and play. We hoped that he could continue to live at home with us. But over the years, gradually it became apparent that he had a full-blown case. His was one of the worst-case scenarios. As John grew, so did the tumors and dysfunctions. He got progressively worse.

No one writes a book that describes or defines the parameters of normality in terms of psychiatric behavior, but after five years of sleepless nights, and three more years of bizarre, violent behavior, we learned that we simply could not handle John at home. And so our deepest expectation, that John could live at home, was dead. We committed John, through the legal system, at age eight, to a life of five years of institutionalization, first at a state psychiatric hospital, then at a residential school, and finally at a private hospital in Florida. Taking your eight-year-old child to the locked ward of a psychiatric facility, notwithstanding his sobbing pleas to the contrary, is like death, too.

So how do you celebrate a life like John's? They say that expectations die hard. John's life was full of expectations which died hard, but John taught us many lessons. They have certainly been expensive lessons, and we would never have voluntarily paid this dear price, but the value of these lessons and John's life, to us, is very profound.

We learned to live life after death; after the death of our expectations. We learned to love our child, the child that we sometimes had thought would be better off dead. We learned to love our child although he was perceived to be of no value. We found that John had great value. We learned to accept him on his terms. We learned not to discount his life because he was handicapped. We learned to respect John's right to live.

John loved his life after he returned to a group home here in Richmond in May 1992. He loved his freedom. He loved the freedom of living in an unlocked building. He loved to go out in public: to the malls, the movies, the Braves games and the batting cage. He loved to go up to strangers and introduce himself. He loved to come home every Sunday for dinner at five o'clock. When I brought him home, he loved to burst through the door and call his mother's, sister's, and brother's names. He loved eating dinner with us and having his father give him a shave afterwards. And for the first time in five years, we saw John smile and laugh and sing again.

And so despite the Christmases which John spent in padded cells, injuring himself, and our thoughts that he would be better off dead, we learned to respect his right to live and gave him all the love and support humanly possible. We learned to respect the differences in people. We learned to respect people of lower functioning. We learned there is life after the death of a "normal" life. We learned that once a tragedy occurs, it redefines your life and that your life before that tragedy is no longer possible. We learned we had to build a new life with different expectations. We learned to develop positive responses to overcome tragedy. We learned to build a new life based on love, faith, and hope. We learned to live life a week at a time. We learned to find redeeming value in life. We learned to appreciate the daily beauty and joys of life. And we do. We learned to be as healthy and happy as possible and to have fun and to limit our grief. And so, in the end, we got nothing that we wanted in our child John and everything that we could have ever needed. John gave us love that gives life a new meaning, that gives us an agenda, that gives us courage and strength and never leaves us alone.

John had his good days and his bad days. When his behavior was bad, he was very violent and abusive to his staff. When he had good days and his behavior was good, he always said he was having a "thumbs-up" day. On the last day of his life, as he sat in his bed with his shaved head, an IV in each arm, and his hands tied to the bed by restraints, when asked how he felt, John told his doctors he was having a "thumbs-up" day. He told his mother, "Mom, do you know what I like?" She said, "No, John," and he said, "You!"

Today our hearts are broken, but we have learned to live life with a broken heart and to enjoy life anyway. We have been inspired by John's love and positive, persevering spirit. And we will live our lives with as many thumbs-up days as possible.

CHAPTER ELEVEN

BROTHERS AND OTHERS

The most famous words in this section belong to Robert Ingersoll, whose words for his brother, Clark, flow with the easy grace of carved figures across the surface of an urn: "This brave and tender man in every storm of life was oak and rock, but in the sunshine he was vine and flower." Like all nineteenth-century orators, Ingersoll was entirely at home with the metaphor. Today we tend to be less poetic, more anecdotal and to the point.

"She was born Kitty O'Donnell," writes Anna Quindlen of her grandmother, "and she had what the nuns in school used to call a smart mouth. The older she got, the smarter it got."

"She was great minded," said H. G. Wells of his wife, Amy. ". . . Her life was a star."

"We are none of us surprised," said Father Joseph Gallagher of his brother Francis, "that his great heart gave out . . . that was the part of himself he used the most."

In a letter accompanying his eulogy for his brother, Father Gallagher wrote that theirs was a family wounded by alcoholism, prison, mental illness, and the early death of three out of four children. In the same family, one brother was eulogized in a cathedral with a cardinal in attendance, while another brother lay unclaimed for months in a city morgue.

The mystery—and the miracle—is not that there was so much suffering in one family but why some collapse beneath it while others manage to convert their pain into creativity and survive. Each family contains the answers to that question within its specific history, but in the beginning the survivors and the casualties cannot be told apart.

"It may be best, just in the happiest, sunniest hour of all the voyage, while eager winds are kissing every sail, to dash against the unseen rock, and in an instant hear the billows roar above a sunken ship. For, whether in midsea or 'mong the breakers of the farther shore, a wreck at last must mark the end of each and all."

CLARK INGERSOLL
(D. 1879)

by

ROBERT GREEN INGERSOLL
(1833–1899)

Robert Ingersoll's brother, Clark, had been his law partner. This eulogy was delivered by Clark's grave.

My friends, I'm going to do that which the dead oft promised he would do for me.

The loved and loving brother, husband, father, friend, died where manhood's morning almost touches noon, and while the shadows still were falling toward the west.

He had not passed on life's highway the stone that marks the highest point, but being weary for a moment, he lay down by the wayside and, using his burden for a pillow, fell into that dreamless sleep that kisses down his eyelids still. While yet in love with life and raptured with the world, he passed to silence and pathetic dust.

Yet, after all, it may be best, just in the happiest, sunniest hour of all the voyage, while eager winds are kissing every sail, to dash against the unseen rock, and in an instant hear the billows roar above a sunken ship. For, whether in midsea or 'mong the breakers of the farther shore, a wreck at last must mark the end of each and all. And every life, no matter if its hour is rich with love and every moment jeweled with joy, will, at its close, become a tragedy as sad and deep and dark as can be woven of the warp and woof of mystery and death.

This brave and tender man in every storm of life was oak and rock, but in the sunshine he was vine and flower. He was the friend of all heroic souls. He climbed the heights and left all superstitions far below, while on his forehead fell the golden dawning of the grander day.

He loved the beautiful, and was with color, form, and music touched to tears. He sided with the weak, and with a willing hand gave alms; with loyal heart and with purest hands he faithfully discharged all public trusts.

He was a worshiper of liberty, a friend of the oppressed. A thousand times I have heard him quote these words: "For justice all places, a temple, and all seasons, summer." He believed that happiness was the only good, reason the only torch, justice the only worship, humanity the only religion, and love the only priest. He added to the sum of human joy, and were everyone to whom he did some loving service to bring a blossom to his grave, he would sleep tonight beneath a wilderness of flowers.

Life is a narrow vale between the cold and barren peaks of two eternities. We strive in vain to look beyond the heights. We cry aloud, and the only answer is the echo of our wailing cry. From the voiceless lips of the unreplying dead there comes no word; but in the night of death hope sees a star, and listening love can hear the rustle of a wing.

He who sleeps here, when dying, mistaking the approach of death for the return of health, whispered with his last breath, "I am better now." Let us believe, in spite of doubts and dogmas, and tears and fears, that these dear words are true of all the countless dead.

And now to you who have been chosen, from among the many men he loved, to do the last sad office for the dead, we give this sacred dust. Speech cannot contain our love. There was, there is, no greater, stronger, manlier man.

ᏇᎷᏜᎧ

"When my heart's dearest died, the light went from my life forever."

ALICE LEE ROOSEVELT
(1861–1884)

by

THEODORE ROOSEVELT
(1858–1919)

President Theodore Roosevelt's first wife, Alice, was not mentioned by him in his autobiography. But upon her death, he wrote this memorial.

She was born at Chestnut Hill, Massachusetts, on July 29, 1861; I first saw her on October 18, 1878, and loved her as soon as I saw her sweet, fair young face; we were betrothed on January 25, 1880, and married on October 27th of the same year; we spent three years of happiness such as rarely comes to man or woman; on February 12, 1884, her baby girl was born; she kissed it, and seemed perfectly well; some hours afterward she, not knowing that she was in the slightest danger, but thinking only that she was falling into a sleep, became insensible, and died at two o'clock on Thursday afternoon, February 14, 1884, at 6 West Fifty-seventh Street, in New York; she was buried two days afterward, in Greenwood Cemetery.

She was beautiful in face and form, and lovelier still in spirit; as a flower she grew, and as a fair young flower she died. Her life had been always in the sunshine; there had never come to her a single great sorrow; and none ever knew her who did not love and revere her for her bright, sunny temper and her saintly unselfishness. Fair, pure, and joyous as a maiden; loving, tender, and happy as a young wife; when she had just become a mother; when her life seemed to be but just begun, and when the years seemed so bright before her— then, by a strange and terrible fate, death came to her.

And when my heart's dearest died, the light went from my life forever.

⧞

"Never was a single word of ungracious judgment passed by her. 'Poor dears,' she would say, 'poor silly dears,' if when some ugly story or report of some vindictive quarrel came to her, for it seemed to her that evil acts must be painful and shameful even to the doer."

AMY CATHERINE WELLS
(1872–1927)

by

H. G. WELLS
(1866–1946)

English author, historian, and social thinker Wells is best known today for
his science fiction novels, which include The Invisible Man, The Time
Machine, *and* The War of the Worlds.

The following is an excerpt from the eulogy by H. G. Wells, which was
read by Dr. T. E. Page at the funeral service for Wells's wife, Amy.

. . . We meet in great sadness, for her death came in the middle season of her life when we could all have hoped for many more years
of her brave and sweet presence among us. . . . Nevertheless, though
we are reminded today of the terrible shortness and swiftness of
human opportunity, we may still learn from such lives as this that a
precious use can be made of brief days and that the courage of a loving stoicism is proof against despair.

This was a life freed from all supernatural terrors and superstitious illusions. Today few are troubled by evil imaginations of what
may lie beyond this peace and silence that has come upon our friend.
This dear career is now like a task accomplished, a tale of years lived
bravely and generously and gone now beyond reach of any corrup-
tion. And though the dark shadow of her interruption lies athwart
our minds today, it is a shadow out of which we can pass. There is
much wisdom and comfort for us in these words of Spinoza's: "The
free man thinks of nothing so little as of death and his wisdom is a
meditation not upon death but upon life."

. . . Some lives stand out upon headlands and are beacons for all
mankind. But some, more lovely and more precious, shine in nar-
rower places and come only by chance gleams and reflections to the
knowledge of the outer world. So it was with our friend. The best
and sweetest of her is known only to one or two of us; subtle and
secret, it can never be told. Faithful, gentle, wise, and self-forgetful,
she upheld another who mourns her here today. To him she gave her
heart and her youth and the best of her brave life, through good
report and evil report and the stresses and mischances of our difficult and adventurous world. She was a noble wife, a happy mother,
and the maker of a free and kindly and hospitable home. She was
perhaps too delicately unaggressive for wide and abundant friendships, but her benevolence was widespread and incessant. She
watched to seize opportunities for unobtrusive good deeds. No one
could give the full record of her tender half-apologetic gifts, her gen-

erous help, her many benefactions, for no one knows them all. She thought that a good deed talked about or even held in memory lost half its worth. She was great minded. . . . Truth was in her texture; never did she tell a lie nor do an underhand act. Never was a single word of ungracious judgment passed by her. "Poor dears," she would say, "poor silly dears," if when some ugly story or report of some vindictive quarrel came to her, for it seemed to her that evil acts must be painful and shameful even to the doer. She was a fountain of pity and mercy, except to herself. . . . And now her dear body must pass from our sight toward the consuming flames. Her life was a star; fire goes to fire and light to light. She returns to the furnace of material things from which her life was drawn. But within our hearts, she rests enshrined, and in the woven fabric of things accomplished, she lives forever.

⚭

"She was born Kitty O'Donnell, and she had what the nuns in school used to call a smart mouth. The older she got, the smarter it got."

KITTY O'DONNELL QUINDLEN
(1898–1987)

by

ANNA QUINDLEN
(1953–)

Anna Quindlen was a columnist for the op-ed page of the New York Times. *In 1992 she won the Pulitzer Prize for commentary. A best-selling novelist, she wrote this essay about her grandmother in 1987 for her* New York Times *column, "Life in the 30's."*

My grandmother was rather vain, and I loved her for it. Her favorite stories concerned her own charms: how she weighed ninety-six pounds until the third of her eight children was born, how some man tried to pick her up on the street even though she was pushing a baby carriage with a toddler on either side of it, how the nicest boys clamored to date her, particularly August LaForte, he of the wonderful manners and fine clothes. Once I asked her why she had chosen instead the rather dour young man, as she described him, who was my grandfather. "I don't know," she said with a sigh. "I don't think I could have hardly stood him at all if he hadn't played the piano."

She was born Kitty O'Donnell, and she had what the nuns in school used to call a smart mouth. The older she got, the smarter it got. "How do you think your brother looks?" she asked my father several weeks ago, lying with her eyes closed in a hospital bed set up in her bedroom. "He looks fine, Mother," my father said. "He should," she shot back, "he doesn't do anything all day."

She would have been eighty-nine years old last week, but she died on April Fools' Day. The joke is on me. I accepted the inevitable disintegration of age without realizing how bereaved her death would leave me. She was the last of my grandparents to die. Concetta was gone before I really knew her. Caesar left me with only the enduring feeling that it was possible to not have much money or education, and yet to be a gentleman to the starched tips of one's white shirt collar. My grandfather Eugene, the one who bested the natty Mr. LaForte, died when I was in college. He was often stern and always undemonstrative. I loved him blindly. I remember sitting at the kitchen table with him as he read my first newspaper story, a serviceable feature about someone's hundredth birthday. I watched him run his finger over my name, at the top of the story, and I felt as though I might keel over with happiness.

Perhaps no four people have meant as much to me as they have, not only because they persuaded me that I had a past and a future, but because their affection and pride were rarely tinged with the perils of ownership. They were close enough to feel the satisfaction of blood in my successes, but not so close that my failures made them doubt themselves. This is the familiar dance of the generations, the minuet in which the closer we are the more difficult relations become. We are able to accept, even love, things in our grandparents that we find impossible to accept in their children, our parents. The reverse is true, too: in us they can take the joys without the responsibilities. In the family sandwich, the older people and the younger ones can recognize one another as the bread. Those in the middle are, for a time, the meat.

I realized this when I had children of my own. When I began to think of my father as my children's grandfather, I began to look at him differently. And he began to behave differently. During the summer he took my three-year-old fishing, a pursuit my father finds sacramental. It was a great rite of passage. But the ocean was rough, the boat dipped, plunged, rolled, and the little boy cried and turned pale. His grandfather turned back immediately to the quiet of the bay, not to embarrass the child by putting him ashore, but to find a quiet backwater where he could go crabbing and save face. It was a lovely thing done in a lovely fashion, and I am ashamed to say that I tried to cajole my son to remain out in the rough waters, for two reasons: I had more of my ego tied up in his behavior, and I could remember a small girl who didn't want to stay at sea, either, but whose father insisted she do so. That father is cut out to be a wonderful grandfather. He is funny, irreverent, rather eccentric, and a bit childish. He is a character.

My grandmother was a character, too. Despite the rosaries and the little clicking sound she made when someone told an off-color joke, she was no saint. I loved her for that. I never tired of hearing the story of my grandmother's career as a world-class shopper, of how one of my uncles was amazed to find himself first on line outside my grandmother's favorite department store the day of a big sale, then flabbergasted to hotfoot it up to the menswear department only to discover his mother peeking at him from the end of a rack of suits. Or the one about my parents bringing my grandmother home after a night on the town and trying to convince her that there was no place to get a nightcap at that hour. My grandmother grandly led them to the Irish War Veterans headquarters and knocked on the door. "Hello, Ms. Quindlen," said the son of a friend she had known would be in charge that night. He let them in.

Now I am the meat in this family sandwich. Already, my elder son has invested his grandparents with a special aura; they are people who are very close to him in some magical way, but not too close for comfort. They get all the calls on his play telephone. That was what my grandparents always were to me.

"I'm going to be in heaven for my birthday," my grandmother told her eldest daughter, who had tended her tirelessly as she weakened. "Sing 'Happy Birthday' to me." She had buried her husband

and two of her children. She left two daughters, four sons, thirty-two grandchildren, twenty-nine great-grandchildren, and so many anecdotes that we were still telling them three hours after we left the cemetery. She always gave me the cherry from her manhattan. In my mind, she'll live forever.

⚭

"Inside me, she lives in our old house. The predominant part of her left to me is her image as a child, the perspective only I have, and that her children and mine ask me about now."

ROBERTA MARGET SCHULTZ
(1937–1989)

by

MADELINE MARGET
(1943–)

Madeline Marget is a writer from Newtonville, Massachusetts. A longer version of this piece, called "Life After Death," originally appeared in Commonweal *magazine.*

My sister died this past summer. Ever since, the house we lived in as children, and the loss of it, have been on my mind. My mother and sister and I left that house after my father died. He came home from work one morning in late August with what he thought was a stomachache and was dead from a heart attack before the ambulance my terrified mother tried to call could arrive. He was an insurance agent, and a passionate man. He loved gardening, and music. I remember him playing the cello and listening to the hi-fi inside our old house, and outside it, unbaling peat moss and raking loam. He died at forty-six—the age I am now—when my sister, Roberta, was fifteen and I was nine. His funeral was on a bright, hot day. The temple was packed, and the rabbi, referring to my father by his nickname, Eddie, wept delivering the eulogy.

My mother felt she could not bear to live without my father in the place he had been, and so, right away, she sold the house and gave away the rugs and lamps and furniture. We moved into a new and newly decorated apartment, and three years later, when my mother married again, into a house in another town. When, shortly after Roberta died, I sat in my mother's living room, the only things I recognized from our old life were a pair of bookends, kneeling Chinese figures that hold up, now as always, two leather-bound volumes of poetry. When I was a child, I wondered about the significance of the content of those books; objects so set apart from the rest, and I worried about my inability to understand it.

Judaism teaches us that we live on in our deeds, and in the minds and hearts of those who knew us. I have heard these words as far back as I can remember, and because death came early in my life, I have always been alert to them. But it is only now, with my sister gone, that they are real to me. I will never see Roberta again. Although I believe that to be true, I cannot comprehend it. Inside me, she lives in our old house. The predominant part of her left to me is her image as a child, the perspective only I have, and that her children and mine ask me about now. . . .

To my mother, the love between sisters is sacred. She was devoted to hers, and she expected the same of Roberta and me. This was a heavy burden, and through our lives both of us sometimes failed to carry it, although Roberta always said she loved me. When I was a newborn baby, she used to tell me, she would wash her hands and then sit by my crib, patting mine. But I had displaced her, as second children do; our personalities and ideas—similar, I think now, at the core—developed differently, and rivalry grew. We reenacted some of the history we had absorbed too well, and in adulthood we suffered and instigated tensions and rifts between us.

They passed, surmounted mostly by the contingencies of her illness. There was, first, her bravery, which she expressed as a longing and need to live, through all the terrible treatments she underwent, and the great physical problems and limitations with which she was left. There was her gratitude to me, maintained in the face of my fear and anger at her plight, for what I did to help her.

In the last months of her life Roberta achieved a great sweetness, and at the very end, peace. She died at home, as she wanted. A few minutes before she lost consciousness she said, calmly and firmly, to me, "It's good you are here." I think those were her last words, but

I'm not at all sure; it may simply be that her grace in so saying them finalized our bond.

Roberta died in the middle of the night, and when my mother and I went into the room where she lay, I was not afraid or disturbed by the sight of her body as I had been of other dead people. This was still, in some way, Roberta. My mother bent and kissed her and stroked her hair. "Oh, Roberta," she cried, "how I'll miss you." My mother's heart had broken years before, when Roberta first got sick, but she managed, out of love, a sense of responsibility, and her tragically good understanding of grief, to be wise and strong for her child. She entertained her, fed her, listened to her, and found the words—available to no one else—to reassure her. Roberta was not afraid to die.

Two weeks before it happened, "Allen bought a cemetery plot," she told my mother. My brother-in-law, tireless in his care of her, had gone himself to choose the site. "I know, dear," said my mother, "near me." Roberta did not seem upset. "That's good, Mum," she said. Roberta talked a lot about the possibility of an afterlife. I told her I thought there must be one, in some unimaginable form. That life was too valuable, too important, to just stop. I think her life was witness to that belief.

I have not physically been in our old house since we moved away, but it inhabits me. Images of its rooms and its light, in the evening and during the day, superimpose themselves on places I read about in novels. They flash into my mind as I go about my business and come to me in the night. I can see all ten of the rooms, and the hallways, too. I know where the furniture is placed, and the colors of the upholstery and the carpets and the walls. Roberta's room was blue. I can see her at her desk—my father bought it unfinished and stained it for her. She's knitting, not reading or studying, and the effort is a youthful one, full of holes. But I, out in the hall, am younger still, and when she turns toward me, I see my big sister, full of knowledge, her face troubled with the future that is sure to come.

❧

"What he loved most about people was the chance to befriend them in their need, to ease their pain even though it magnified his own. . . ."

FRANCIS XAVIER GALLAGHER
(1928–1972)

by

FATHER JOSEPH GALLAGHER
(1929–)

*Father Joseph Gallagher's eulogy was delivered at his brother Francis Gal-
lagher's funeral in Baltimore, Maryland. In an accompanying letter, Father
Gallagher wrote: "From childhood my brother had been afflicted with para-
lyzing migraine headaches. . . . He had only two natural brothers, but he
was a brother to everyone who needed help."*

The profoundest wellspring in my brother was a passionate love for
life—despite all its aches and shadows, with which he was not unac-
quainted, and of which I never heard him complain.

What he most loved about life was people, people as people, in
all their wonderfully wild variety—black and white, Protestant,
Catholic, and Jew, believer and unbeliever, "important" people and
just plain people, Democrats and, as he would probably say, "even"
Republicans.

What he loved most about people was the chance to befriend
them in their need, to ease their pain even though it magnified his
own—that pain which he never outwitted, but which he held in
heroic contempt. By the alchemy of his boundless drive, resource-
fulness, generosity, and availability, he transmuted his own sufferings into a soothing medicine for countless others.

The truest comfort to be found in our present pain is the astonishing and blazing witness of the healing use to which he always
cheerfully put his own.

We are none of us surprised that his great heart gave out, for his
heart was giving out all his short life long, and that was the part of
himself he used the most.

After big holiday meals, my brother loved to quote the words:
"We thank you, Lord, for this brief repast; many a man would have
called it a meal." Grateful for the feast of him, we might aptly say
today as our Grace After Him: "We thank you, Lord, for his brief
sojourn; many a man would have called it a lifetime."

Perhaps one of his beautiful children spoke most simply and eloquently for us all. Learning of his father's death, he said in a tone of measureless loss, "He was so nice." So he was. So he truly was.

CHAPTER TWELVE

SUCH GOOD FRIENDS

Every person is born into a particular quadrant of the heavens. Our friends hang like companion stars around us, giving us point and direction. We run to them when we have something to celebrate, fall back upon them when feeling ill-used or ill-defined. And when a friend dies, as Robert Louis Stevenson writes in his tribute to his childhood friend James Ferrier, "there falls along with him a whole wing of the palace of our life."

Stevenson's tribute to Ferrier is an essay on a man who turned a failed life into a successful one without turning it around. It has a cosmic sweep, as if Ferrier's death had catapulted Stevenson high above the ocean where he could see all of us in our self-important little boats tacking this way and that way, none of us bound for the glory we had in mind.

"The first step for all," observes Stevenson, "is to learn to the dregs our own ignoble fallibility. When we have fallen through story after story of our own vanity and aspiration, and sit rueful among the ruins, then it is that we begin to measure the stature of our friends."

In Mary McGrory's tribute to her friend Nance MacDonald, she repeats the maxim that friends are "those relations one chooses for oneself" in life. It could also be said that life is continually preparing us for who our friends will be.

In Alexander Woollcott's tribute to Anne Sullivan Macy, who was blind by the age of seven, he relates the story of how she went to the Perkins Institution for the Blind and met Laura Bridgman, the first deaf-blind child to learn the hand alphabet. She taught the alphabet to Anne, who would have had great difficulty learning it if she had been sighted. Then, through an operation, she recovered her vision. Had she not regained her sight, she would not have been able to be Helen Keller's teacher. This is preparation bordering upon the divine.

"It is part of the endless fascination of Annie Sullivan's tapestry," Woollcott writes, "that in it the threads of destiny are thus so visible." But the threads are no less visible in the lives of any two friends who are unaware, except in retrospect, of how fortuitously well-prepared they were to meet.

"In his youth he took thought for no one but himself; when he came ashore again, his whole armada lost, he seemed to think of none but others."

JAMES FERRIER
(D. 1883)

by

ROBERT LOUIS STEVENSON
(1850–1894)

Robert Louis Stevenson was born in Scotland and died in Samoa. One of the world's great storytellers (among other works, he wrote Treasure Island, Kidnapped, The Strange Case of Dr. Jekyll and Mr. Hyde, *and* The Master of Ballantrae)*, Stevenson led a globe-trotting life that rivaled that of any from his tales, of which there might have been more had chronic ill health not felled him at forty-four. When his childhood friend James Ferrier died of an alcohol-related illness, he wrote to his sister that he "could not see for crying." To another friend he wrote, "Up to now I had rather thought of [death] as a mere personal enemy of my own; but now that I see him hunting after my friends, he looks altogether darker."*

I would fain strike a note that should be more heroical; but the ground of all youth's suffering, solitude, hysteria, and haunting of the grave is nothing else than naked, ignorant selfishness. It is himself that he sees dead; those are his virtues that are forgotten; his is the vague epitaph. Pity him but the more, if pity be your cue; for where a man is all pride, vanity, and personal aspiration, he goes through fire unshielded. In every part and corner of our life, to lose oneself is to be gainer; to forget oneself is to be happy; and this poor, laughable, and tragic fool has not yet learned the rudiments; himself, giant Prometheus, is still ironed on the peaks of Caucasus. But by and by his truant interests will leave that tortured body, slip abroad, and gather flowers. Then shall death appear before him in an altered guise; no longer as a doom peculiar to himself, whether fate's crowning injustice or his own last vengeance upon those who fail to value him; but now as a power that wounds him far more tenderly, not without solemn compensations, taking and giving, bereaving and yet storing up.

The first step for all is to learn to the dregs our own ignoble fallibility. When we have fallen through story after story of our own vanity and aspiration, and sit rueful among the ruins, then it is that we
begin to measure the stature of our friends: how they stand between
us and our own contempt, believing in our best; how linking us with
others, and still spreading wide the influential circle, they weave us
in and in with the fabric of contemporary life; and to what petty size
they dwarf the virtues and the vices that appeared gigantic in our
youth. So that at the last, when such a pin falls out—when there vanishes in the least breath of time one of those rich magazines of life on
which we drew for our supply—when he who had first dawned
upon us as a face among the faces of the city, and still growing, came
to bulk on our regard with those clear features of the loved and living man, falls in a breath to memory and shadow, there falls along
with him a whole wing of the palace of our life.

One such face I now remember; one such blank some half a dozen
of us labor to dissemble. In his youth he was most beautiful in person, most serene and genial by disposition; full of racy words and
quaint thoughts. Laughter attended on his coming. He had the air of
a great gentleman, jovial and royal with his equals, and to the poor-
est student gentle and attentive. Power seemed to reside in him
exhaustless; we saw him stoop to play with us, but held him marked
for higher destinies; we loved his notice; and I have rarely had my
pride more gratified than when he sat at my father's table, my
acknowledged friend. So he walked among us, both hands full of
gifts, carrying with nonchalance the seeds of a most influential life.

The powers and the ground of friendship is a mystery; but, looking
back, I can discern that, in part, we loved the thing he was, for some
shadow of what he was to be. For with all his beauty, power, breeding, urbanity, and mirth, there was in those days something soulless
in our friend. He would astonish us by sallies, witty, innocent,
and inhumane; and by a misapplied Johnsonian pleasantry, demolish
honest sentiment. I can still see and hear him, as he went on his way
along the lamplit streets, *La ci darem la mano* on his lips, a noble figure
of a youth, but following vanity and incredulous of good; and sure
enough, somewhere on the high seas of life, with his health, his
hopes, his patrimony, and his self-respect, miserably went down.

From this disaster, like a spent swimmer, he came desperately ashore, bankrupt of money and consideration, creeping to the family he had deserted; with broken wing, never more to rise. But in his face there was a light of knowledge that was new to it. Of the wounds of his body he was never healed; died of them gradually, with clear-eyed resignation; of his wounded pride, we knew only from his silence. He returned to that city where he had lorded it in his ambitious youth, lived there alone, seeing few; striving to retrieve the irretrievable; at times still grappling with that mortal frailty that had brought him down; still joying in his friends' successes; his laugh still ready but with kindlier music; and over all his thoughts the shadow of that unalterable law which he had disavowed and which had brought him low. Lastly, when his bodily evils had quite disabled him, he lay a great while dying, still without complaint, still finding interests; to his last step gentle, urbane, and with the will to smile.

The tale of this great failure is, to those who remained true to him, the tale of a success. In his youth he took thought for no one but himself; when he came ashore again, his whole armada lost, he seemed to think of none but others. Such was his tenderness for others, such his instinct of fine courtesy and pride, that of that impure passion of remorse he never breathed a syllable; even regret was rare with him, and pointed with a jest. You would not have dreamed, if you had known him then, that this was that great failure, that beacon to young men, over whose fall a whole society had hissed and pointed fingers. Often have we gone to him, red-hot with our own hopeful sorrows, railing on the rose-leaves in our princely bed of life, and he would patiently give ear and wisely counsel; and it was only upon some return of our own thoughts that we were reminded what manner of man this was to whom we disembosomed: a man, by his own fault, ruined; shut out of the garden of his gifts; his whole city of hope both ploughed and salted; silently awaiting the deliverer. Then something took us by the throat; and to see him there, so gentle, patient, brave, and pious, oppressed but not cast down, sorrow was so swallowed up in admiration that we could not dare to pity him. Even if the old fault flashed out again, it but awoke our wonder that, in that lost battle, he should have still the energy to fight. He had gone to ruin with a kind of kingly *abandon* like one who condescended but once ruined, with the lights all out, he fought as for a kingdom. Most men, finding themselves the authors of their own disgrace, rail the louder against God or destiny. Most men, when they repent, oblige their friends to share the bitterness of that repentance. But he had held an inquest and passed sentence: "mene, mene"; and condemned himself to smiling silence. He had given trouble enough; had earned misfortune amply, and foregone the right to murmur.

Thus was our old comrade, like Samson, careless in his days of strength; but on the coming of adversity, and when that strength was gone that had betrayed him—"for our strength is weakness"—he began to blossom and bring forth. Well, now, he is out of the fight: the burden that he bore thrown down before the great deliverer. We

> *in the vast cathedral leave him:*
> *God accept him,*
> *Christ receive him!*

ᴑᴍᴖᴖᴖᴑ

"Perhaps my strongest impression of him was that of sorrow. . . . He smiled, not with the mouth but with his mind—a gesture of the soul rather than of the face."

MARK TWAIN

(1835–1910)

by

HELEN KELLER

(1880–1968)

When the deaf-mute child Helen Keller was fourteen years old, she met the world-famous author Samuel Clemens, who under the pen name Mark Twain wrote The Adventures of Tom Sawyer *and* The Adventures of Huckleberry Finn. *"The instant I clasped his hand in mine," she wrote, "I knew that he was my friend." They visited each other frequently, and after his death, she reflected upon their friendship.*

He knew with keen and sure intuition many things about me and how it felt to be blind and not to keep up with the swift ones—things that others learned slowly or not at all. He never embarrassed me by saying how terrible it is not to see, or how dull life must be, lived always in the dark. He wove about my dark walls romance and adventure, which made me feel happy and important. Once when Peter Dunne . . . exclaimed, "God, how dull it must be for her, every day the same and every night the same as the day," he said, "You're damned wrong there; blindness is an exciting business, I tell you; if you don't believe it, get up some dark night on the wrong side of your bed when the house is on fire and try to find the door."

He thought he was a cynic, but his cynicism did not make him indifferent to the sight of cruelty, unkindness, meanness, or pretentiousness. He would often say, "Helen, the world is full of unseeing eyes, vacant, staring, soulless eyes." He would work himself into a frenzy over dull acquiescence to any evil that could be remedied. True, sometimes it seemed as if he let loose all the artillery of heaven against an intruding mouse, but even then his "resplendent vocabulary" was a delight.

. . . He often spoke tenderly of Mrs. Clemens and regretted that I had not known her.

"I am very lonely sometimes, when I sit by the fire after my guests have departed," he used to say. "My thoughts trail away into the past. I think of Livy and Susy and I seem to be fumbling in the dark folds of confused dreams. I come upon memories of little intimate happenings of long ago that drop like stars into the silence. One day everything breaks and crumbles. It did the day Livy died." . . .

To one hampered and circumscribed as I am, it was a wonderful experience to have a friend like Mr. Clemens. I recall many talks with him about human affairs. He never made me feel that my opinions were worthless, as so many people do. He knew that we do not think with eyes and ears, and that our capacity for thought is not measured by five senses. He kept me always in mind while he talked, and he treated me like a competent human being. That is why I loved him.

Perhaps my strongest impression of him was that of sorrow. There was about him the air of one who had suffered greatly. Whenever I touched his face, his expression was sad, even when he was telling a funny story. He smiled, not with the mouth but with his mind—a gesture of the soul rather than of the face. His voice was truly wonderful. To my touch, it was deep, resonant. He held the power of modulating it so as to suggest the most delicate shades of meaning, and he spoke so deliberately that I could get almost every word with my fingers on his lips. Ah, how sweet and poignant the memory of his soft, slow speech playing over my listening fingers. His words seemed to take strange, lovely shapes on my hands. His own hands were wonderfully mobile and changeable under the influence of emotion. It has been said that my life has treated me harshly; and sometimes I have complained in my heart because so many plea-sures of human experience have been withheld from me, but when I recollect the treasure of friendship that has been bestowed upon me, I withdraw all charges against life. If much has been denied me, much, very much has been given me. So long as the memory of cer-tain beloved friends lives in my heart, I shall say that life is good.

✺

"His attitude to life and art never lost intensity—he was never the amateur."

MAJ. ROBERT GREGORY
(D. 1918)

by

WILLIAM BUTLER YEATS
(1865–1939)

The Irish poet and playwright William Butler Yeats wrote this obituary for his friend Robert Gregory after he was killed in action during World War I. Yeats's poem "In Memory of Major Robert Gregory" is considered one of his first great works.

His very accomplishment hid from many his genius. He had so many sides: painter, classical scholar, scholar in painting and in modern literature, boxer, horseman, airman . . . that some among his friends were not sure what his work would be. To me he will always remain a great painter in the immaturity of his youth, he himself the personification of handsome youth. . . .

Though he often seemed led away from his work by some other gift, his attitude to life and art never lost intensity—he was never the amateur. I have noticed that men whose lives are to be an ever-growing absorption in subjective beauty . . . seek through some lesser gift, or through mere excitement, to strengthen that self which unites them with ordinary men. It is as though they hesitated before they plunged into the abyss. Major Gregory told Mr. Bernard Shaw, who visited him in France, that the months since he joined the army had been the happiest of his life. I think they brought him peace of mind, an escape from that shrinking, which I sometimes saw upon his face, before the growing absorption of his dream, as from his constant struggle to resist those other gifts that brought him ease and friendship.

⁂

"At her funeral, the small ghost I saw beside that blossom-laden coffin was not Mrs. Macy, nor Teacher either. It was Annie Sullivan, a child unkempt, star-crossed, desperate, dauntless—Annie Sullivan from the Tewksbury Almshouse."

ANNE SULLIVAN MACY
(1866–1936)

by

ALEXANDER WOOLLCOTT
(1887–1943)

Anne Sullivan Macy was Helen Keller's teacher and lifelong companion. In this memorial tribute to Macy, Woollcott, a well-known journalist, drama critic, and broadcaster of the time, tells the story of the woman who would be the conduit for Keller's greatness, beginning with her childhood, which would toughen her for the task that lay ahead.

To the great woman who was the daughter of her spirit, Mrs. Macy was always "Teacher," and in the household which grew up around these two, everyone called her that. The secretary who took her dictation, the chauffeur who stood guard, the newsboy at the corner—

they all called her Teacher. And still do, remembering her every hour of every day. "Teacher would have said we should." That posthumous opinion is enough. However unwelcome the burden, they shoulder it and go on.

But it was as Annie Sullivan that I always thought of her, and when at last I came to know her—I count it as one of my great pieces of good fortune that I did come to know her—it amused her vastly that I always called her Annie Sullivan. At her funeral, the small ghost I saw beside that blossom-laden coffin was not Mrs. Macy, nor Teacher either. It was Annie Sullivan, a child unkempt, star-crossed, desperate, dauntless—Annie Sullivan from the Tewksbury Almshouse.

The Sullivans were shanty Irish, and of all their hapless brood only three were still living, if you could call it that, when the frail mother joined the others in the graveyard. The father went on the drink then and, like an unmoored rowboat, drifted out of history, casually leaving his two youngest on the doorstep of the selectmen. Of these, Annie, the elder, was going on eleven. By some fever that had once ravaged the shanty, her eyes were so blighted that she could hardly see at all. Jimmie was seven, a doomed and twisted little boy with a tubercular hip. His sister loved him with all her tremendous might, but the world and the almshouse were too much for Jimmie. He died within the year, and it calls for a young Dickens to describe the time when little orphan Annie crept into the improvised mortuary and crouched all night beside the wasted, misshapen body of the only person she loved in the world. Indeed, you need the wrathful and compassionate Dickens of *Oliver Twist* and *Bleak House* to do justice to the Tewksbury Almshouse as it was in the seventies of the last century, when General Grant was president in Washington and Jim Fisk was riding high in New York. Cripples, epileptics, syphilitics, stranded old folks, marked-down streetwalkers, drug addicts—all the acutely embarrassing mistakes of the community were put there where no one could see them, much as a slapdash housewife will tidy up for company by sweeping the dirt under the sofa. In that almshouse it must have taken a bit of doing to have faith in Massachusetts.

It was from a lively old prostitute who used to read *East Lynne* to her that Annie first heard there was a place somewhere in the world where she, too, might learn to read—a school for the blind called the

Perkins Institution. Thereafter the Overseers of the Poor could not make their periodic inspections in peace, what with this wild child always darting out at them and demanding that they send her to the school. Once she caught hold of the right coattails—a visitor with power to act, who saw the point. In no time a lone and stormy petrel, who could neither read nor write nor see, and to whom such fripperies as a nightgown and a toothbrush and a comb were unfamiliar refinements, was knocking at the door of the Perkins Institution. She was fourteen years old.

This school, the first of its kind anywhere, had been shouldered fifty years before by Samuel Gridley Howe, a gallant and gifted physician who has been overshadowed in the memory of his countrymen by the circumstance that his wife was the Mrs. Howe who wrote "The Battle Hymn of the Republic." He was the first to attempt the education of a child with neither sight nor hearing—little Laura Bridgman, after whom he named one of his own daughters, the Laura who was later to write *Captain January*. Never equipped to do battle with the world, Miss Bridgman lingered in the shelter of the Institution after Dr. Howe's death and was still there, a spinster pensioner, when Annie arrived. Because she, too, had no home to go to in vacation time, Annie was much thrown in old Laura's company and thereby became adept in the use of the hand alphabet. It is part of the endless fascination of Annie Sullivan's tapestry that in it the threads of destiny are thus so visible.

It was after she had run her course at the school that the doctors in Boston, even at a time when ophthalmic surgery was comparatively primitive, decided that the trouble with her shrouded eyes might be operable. It proved to be so. Wherefore she stood at twenty, lovely to look at, toughened by experience, a young woman with clear eyes who yet knew Braille and all the technique of darkness, a woman with sharp ears who yet knew by chance—or what we have the hardihood to call chance—the speech and the feelings of the deaf. At that fateful moment in space and time there arrived at the Institution a letter from a certain Captain Keller of Tuscumbia, Alabama, wherein the pattern of Annie's tapestry first revealed its design.

The letter reported the plight of the captain's daughter. When this child, who had been christened Helen, was nineteen months old, some sickness had left her deaf and blind. Now she was seven, a mutinous, unmanageable animal, and would be needing something special in the way of a governess. In a book Mrs. Keller had read not long before, there was some account of a certain Laura Bridgman. But the book—it was *American Notes* by Charles Dickens—was already forty years old. This Dr. Howe and his protégée, could they still be living? It was a harness salesman from up Massachusetts way who, passing through Alabama, had then told the Kellers that the Perkins Institution, at least, was still in existence. The salesman had supplied its address. Thus Captain Keller's letter. Could the Institution recommend a governess? "Annie, this looks like a job for you."

The nominee invested a month in reading the manuscript of the diary which Dr. Howe had kept when he was learning to lead the Bridgman child out of the dark silence. While she was thus cramming for her first great test, the girls at the Institution clubbed together and bought a doll as a gift for Helen Keller. When old Laura made the clothes for it, that doll became not only a gift but a symbol and a talisman. Then Annie put the doll in her trunk, packed up her few belongings, afflicted herself with some new shoes that were far too tight for her, and started south. That was in March 1887.

It began—this great adventure which soon the whole world was watching—in the cottage where for one racking month the strange teacher and her still stranger pupil were left alone together. In the beginning was the word, and, in memory of Laura Bridgman, the word was *doll*. Our poor imaginations falter in contemplating the feat of first reaching that inaccessible mind with the notion that there *was* such thing as a word. We still find miraculous the indisputable fact that at twenty-four, with girls of her own age or thereabouts, Helen Keller was graduated from Radcliffe—*cum laude*. . . .

But in time it dawned upon us all that if Helen Keller was one of the wonders of the world, this woman who had taught her must be at least as extraordinary, a suspicion born of logic and confirmed when in 1933 there was published Nella Braddy's distinguished and indispensable biography, *Anne Sullivan Macy: The Story Behind Helen Keller*—the record of such a shining triumph of the human spirit as must make any man or woman who reads it thank God and take courage.

It was when that book was new upon the shelf that there was unfolded the substance for its last and as yet unwritten chapter, wherein the wheel comes full round and life is caught in the act of rhyming. It came in the form of news from a little village in Scotland where these now legendary twain had sought refuge. Annie Sullivan was blind again, and in the half century during which she and her eyes had served her well enough, she had forgotten all the ways of blindness. After all these years, she was even having to take lessons in Braille again. It was Helen who taught her.

I first met her after she returned to America for the operation which would restore her sight for a second time—first met her in hospital where I learned that the gift to send a blind person every day from the florist is one small fragrant blossom that can be held in the hand. . . .

But the meetings that I most fondly remember were those when there would be a jabbering circle of us out at the house Helen used to own on Long Island—Annie Sullivan and Helen each tucking away an old-fashioned; Polly Thomson, the Scotch girl who came to them as secretary twenty-five years ago and became, in due course, the rock to which both of them clung in times of storm; and—on one such occasion which I recall—Harpo Marx, entranced at the privilege of performing for such a one as Helen, who is just about the best audience in this world. Only afterwards would a newcomer realize with a start that in that circle had been one who could neither see nor hear, but who, now touching Teacher's cheek with her left hand or holding out her right to Polly Thomson, had got as much as any of us out of the talk. As much or more. Watch Helen at a play and see how—I suppose through senses we have lost or never known—she, in perception and appreciation, is just a hair's breadth *ahead* of the rest of the house. It is *her* laugh, joyous as a sunburst, which leads all the rest.

At Annie Sullivan's funeral there could have been no one who was not quick with a sense of the unimaginable parting which, after nearly fifty years, had just taken place. While I live, I shall remember those services. Not for the great of the land who turned out for that occasion, not for the flowers that filled the church with an incomparable incense, nor for the wise and good things which Harry Emerson Fosdick said from the pulpit. No, what I shall remember longest was something I witnessed when the services were over and the procession was filing down the aisle, Helen walking with Polly Thomson at her side. As they passed the pew where I was standing, I saw the tears streaming down Polly's cheeks. And something else I saw. It was a gesture from Helen—a quick flutter of her birdlike hands. She was trying to *comfort* Polly.

⟨ ∞ ⟩

"Certainly he was an interesting and charming man, but there was some other quality which far exceeded these. I have thought that it might be his ability to receive. . . . In receiving you cannot appear, even to yourself, better or stronger or wiser than the giver, although you must be wiser to do it well."

EDWARD F. RICKETTS
(D. 1948)

by

JOHN STEINBECK
(1902–1968)

Ed Ricketts was a marine biologist on Cannery Row, Monterey, California. He figures prominently, as himself, in Steinbeck's novel Cannery Row *and coauthored* The Log from the Sea of Cortez *with Steinbeck.*

I have tried to isolate and inspect the great talent that was in Ed Ricketts, that made him so loved and needed and makes him so missed now that he is dead. Certainly he was an interesting and charming man, but there was some other quality which far exceeded these. I have thought that it might be his ability to receive, to receive anything from anyone, to receive gracefully and thankfully and to make the gift seem very fine. Because of this everyone felt good in giving to Ed—a present, a thought, anything.

Perhaps the most overrated virtue in our list of shoddy virtues is that of giving. Giving builds up the ego of the giver, makes him superior and higher and larger than the receiver. Nearly always, giving is a selfish pleasure, and in many cases it is a downright destructive and evil thing. One has only to remember some of our wolfish financiers who spend two-thirds of their lives clawing fortunes out of the guts of society and the latter third pushing it back. It is not enough to suppose that their philanthropy is a kind of frightened restitution, or that their natures change when they have enough. Such a nature never has enough and natures do not change that readily. I think that the impulse is the same in both cases. For giving can bring the same sense of superiority as getting does, and philanthropy may be another kind of spiritual avarice.

It is so easy to give, so exquisitely rewarding. Receiving, on the other hand, if it be well done, requires a fine balance of self-knowledge and kindness. It requires humility and tact and great understanding of relationships. In receiving you cannot appear, even to yourself, better or stronger or wiser than the giver, although you must be wiser to do it well.

It requires a self-esteem to receive—not self-love but just a pleasant acquaintance and liking for oneself.

Once Ed said to me, "For a very long time I didn't like myself." It was not said in self-pity but simply as an unfortunate fact. "It was a very difficult time," he said, "and very painful. I did not like myself for a number of reasons, some of them valid and some of them pure fancy. I would hate to have to go back to that. Then gradually," he said, "I discovered with surprise and pleasure that a number of people did like me. And I thought, if they can like me, why cannot I like myself? Just thinking it did not do it, but slowly I learned to like myself and then it was alright."

This was not said in self-love in its bad connotation but in self-knowledge. He meant literally that he had learned to accept and like the person "Ed" as he liked other people. It gave him a great advantage. Most people do not like themselves at all. They distrust themselves, put on masks and pomposities. They quarrel and boast and pretend and are jealous because they do not like themselves. But mostly they do not even know themselves well enough to form a true liking. They cannot see themselves well enough to form a true liking, and since we automatically fear and dislike strangers, we fear and dislike our stranger-selves.

Once Ed was able to like himself he was released from the secret prison of self-contempt. Then he did not have to prove superiority any more by any of the ordinary methods, including giving. He could receive and understand and be truly glad, not competitively glad.

Ed's gift for receiving made him a great teacher. Children brought shells to him and gave him information about the shells. And they had to learn before they could tell him.

In conversation you found yourself telling him things—thoughts, conjectures, hypotheses—and you found a pleased surprise at yourself for having arrived at something you were not aware that you could think or know. It gave you such a good sense of participation with him that you could present him with this wonder.

Then Ed would say, "Yes, that's so. That's the way it might be and besides . . . ," and he would illuminate it but not so that he took it away from you. He simply accepted it.

Although his creativeness lay in receiving, that does not mean that he kept things as property. When you had something from him it was not something that was his that he tore away from himself. When you had a thought from him or a piece of music or twenty dollars or a steak dinner, it was not his—it was yours already, and his was only the head and hand that steadied it in position toward you. For this reason no one was ever cut off from him. Association with him was deep participation with him, never competition.

I wish we could all be so. If we could learn even a little to like ourselves, maybe our cruelties and angers might melt away. Maybe we would not have to hurt one another just to keep our ego-chins above water.

There it is. That's all I can set down about Ed Ricketts. I don't know whether any clear picture has emerged. Thinking back and remembering has not done what I hoped it might. It has not laid the ghost.

The picture that remains is a haunting one. It is the time just before dusk. I can see Ed finishing his work in the laboratory. He covers his instruments and puts his papers away. He rolls down the sleeves of his wool shirt and puts on his old brown coat. I see him go out and get in his beat-up old car and slowly drive away in the evening.

I guess I'll have that with me all my life.

⟨~~~⟩

"His soul rejoiced when he could say yes and mean it to something someone else believed in."

JAMES AGEE
(1909–1955)

by

JOHN HUSTON
(1906–1987)

James Agee, an American writer from Tennessee, died before his novel A
Death in the Family *won the Pulitzer Prize in 1957. John Huston directed
the films* The Maltese Falcon, The Treasure of the Sierra Madre, Key
Largo, The African Queen, The Misfits, Wise Blood, *and* The Dead,
among many others.

It's all to the good that so many of you now know James Agee's writings—his novels, his criticism, his poetry. (In a sense it was all
poetry.) I wish that you could also have known Jim himself.

Let me begin by describing him physically. He was about six-two
and heavy but neither muscular nor fat—a mountaineer's body. His
hair was dark brown, his eyes blue, and his skin pale. His hands were
big and slablike in their thickness. He was very strong, and except for
one occasion, when I only heard about, when he stove a *Time* editor
against the wall, he was always gentle toward his fellow humans with
that kind of gentleness usually reserved for plants and animals. . . .

His regard for other people's feelings was unique in my experience. I don't believe it was because he was afraid of hurting them,
and certainly it had nothing to do with gaining in anyone's estima-
tion. It was simply that his soul rejoiced when he could say yes and
mean it to something someone else believed in.

He never attempted to win anyone to his way of thinking, far less to
try to prove anyone mistaken or in the wrong. He would take a contrary
opinion—regardless of how foolish it was—and hold it up to the
light and turn it this way and that, examining its facets as though it were
a gem of great worth, and if it turned out to be a piece of cracked glass,
why then, he, Jim, must have misunderstood—the other fellow had
meant something else, hadn't he . . . *this*, perhaps? And sure enough Jim
would come up with some variation of the opinion that would make
it flawless as a specimen jewel. And the other fellow would be very
proud of having meant precisely that, and they would go on from there.

I can see him sitting on the edge of a chair, bunched forward, elbows on knees, arms upraised, the fingers of one of the slablike hands pointing at those of the other and working as if they were trying to untie a knot. His forehead is furrowed and his mouth is twisted in concentration. His head is nodding in sympathy and understanding. He is smiling. Gaps show between his teeth. (Jim only went to the dentist to have a tooth pulled, never fixed.)

He is smiling. It stops raining all over the world. A great discovery has been made. He and another are in complete agreement. We who beheld that smile will never forget it.

⟡

"With the possible exception of Robert Kennedy, I have never known a public figure who was so different from his reputation."

H. L. MENCKEN

(1880–1956)

by

WILLIAM MANCHESTER

(1922–)

H. L. (Henry Louis) Mencken was the iconoclastic writer, critic, and cofounder/editor of the American Mercury *magazine in Baltimore, Maryland. His acid eulogy of William Jennings Bryan begins on page 190. After Mencken died, historian William Manchester wrote of his last visit with his old friend and mentor, then living on Hollins Street in Baltimore with his brother, August. It was Mencken's habit to search the alley behind Hollins Street for scrap wood.*

We had a rite; the length of each piece cut was determined by a measuring stick which was the exact width of the fireplace within. A certain percentage of our output had to be backlogs, and if our alley loot didn't include lengths of the proper thickness, we would nail odds and ends together—two mop handles, say, affixed to a broken crucifix, the base of a peach basket, and the wooden remains of a dilapidated plumber's helper. The more absurd the result, the uneasier Mencken grew over the propriety of feeding it to the flames. When

its turn came at the hearth, he would wrestle audibly with his conscience before flinging it on the grate.

Eventually, everything combustible went up in smoke, with one
memorable exception. One morning we were prowling in an alley,
furtively lifting galvanized lids and looking, I'm sure, like refugees
in postwar Europe probing for a scrap of meat, when he saw, standing against a fence, a shabby chest of drawers. The rats had been
at it; we were far from Mencken's back gate; whether it was worth
dragging all that way was questionable. As we were debating, a
third figure joined us—a short, swart man in seedy khaki. He asked
us whether we wanted the dresser. We told him we didn't know. He
explained: his little daughter needed a place to store her clothes. If
we weren't going to take it, he would.

Disconcerted, and beset this time by genuine pangs, Mencken
stammered that we were merely hunting for firewood; by all means
the child should have it. The young man brightened with gratitude.
He would be back shortly, he said. His car was parked across the
street; he would fetch it and whisk the dresser home. As he dashed
off, we reexamined the rat holes. They were really enormous. It was
a marvel that the thing stood. It had seemed worthless; it still did.
Mencken said, "Poor fellow."

In the long silence that followed we contemplated the plight of a
father reduced to scrounging among castoffs for his children's furniture. Then the hush was broken by the deep-throated roar of a finely
tuned engine, and into the lane backed the longest, fattest, shiniest
pink Cadillac I had ever seen. The man leaped out, the chest of drawers disappeared into its cavernous trunk, and then the Cadillac also
vanished, gone in a cloud of exhaust.

Mencken's mouth fell open in amazement. "Jesus *Christ!*" he gasped.
"Did you see *that?*" I told him I could hardly have missed it. "Think of
it," he mused. "Imagine that man raising a family, sending his children
off to learn the principles of Americanism, keeping his mother off the
poor farm, raising money to cure his wife of gallstones—and driving
around in a rose-colored hearse! *August!*" he roared as we neared
home. "We just saw the goddamndest animal in Baltimore!"

With the possible exception of Robert Kennedy, I have never
known a public figure who was so different from his reputation. His
readers thought of him as bigoted, cantankerous, wrathful, and

rude. It was a case of mistaken identity. He was none of those things; he was the elderly friend of Butch and Alvin. He was the cripple who was always solicitous about his brother's health. He was the stricken man who had forced himself to initial the pages of [my] book, surrendering copyright of his letters; who always asked me in the shed whether I was properly clad; who, when he was in the depth of his worst depressions, would excuse himself and retire to his bedroom because he didn't want to burden me with his troubles.

We talked of reunions, but knew we would never meet again. He was rapidly failing now. Yet he rallied gallantly that last afternoon, and as I turned to leave the vestibule, he struck a pose, one foot in front of the other, one hand on the banister and the other, fisted, on his hip. "You know, I had a superb time while it lasted," he said in that inimitable voice. "Heaven is prepared for me now. Very soon, I'll be there. Won't it be exquisite?" We shook hands; he trudged up the stairs into the shadow. I departed carrying two farewell gifts, an Uncle Willie stogie and a piece of the treated firewood. Shortly afterward the Associated Press reporter phoned to tell me that Mencken had died in his sleep. . . . That evening I carefully laid the piece of treated firewood in my own fireplace. I didn't expect much; after all that time, I thought, the chemicals must have lost their potency. But I was wrong. Instantly a bright blue flame sprung up. Blue changed to crimson, and after a few minutes there was another change. It was eerie. From end to end the wood blazed up in a deep green which would have been familiar to anyone who had ever held a copy of the *American Mercury*.

⌒ᨀᨀ⌒

"She had, in her youth, taken upon herself the obligation to be wonderful, and she would not let a wasting disease interfere with her destiny."

NANCE MACDONALD

(1917–1983)

by

MARY MCGRORY

(1917–)

Mary McGrory is a Pulitzer Prize–winning columnist for the Washington Post.

It was fortunate in that, until just this week, I had an incomparable friend. Nance was to friendship what Jane Austen was to the novel and Leonardo da Vinci to painting.

She died last Tuesday after what is euphemistically called "a long illness." It was in her case, eleven years, but Nance would not, until the last weekend of her life, really admit she was sick. She had, in her youth, taken upon herself the obligation to be wonderful, and she would not let a wasting disease interfere with her destiny.

When I first met her a lifetime ago, she was in Stevenson's words, "trusty, dusky, vivid true." She had the blackest hair I ever saw and the highest color. She held her head at an angle, she was ever in motion. We were at school together; when reverses hit her beloved family, she, as the eldest, had to go to work. She accepted it with Celtic fatalism.

She rarely had a job worthy of her brightness. That did not matter. She worked with a perfectionism that often bewildered the nine-to-fivers around her. That was not important. Her letters, even her telephone messages, were of executive-suite quality.

Every day, she rose in the dark to dress as carefully as for lunch at the Ritz. I remember years ago going to a country church in New Hampshire, with her fuming the whole way because she had not pressed her skirt. It did not matter that other women in the congregation would be in jeans. Nance had her standards.

She loved to travel, loved the sea and our crystal mountain lake in New Hampshire. I was a compulsive picnicker, and she would laughingly drag the quilts and the sandwiches through the hills. For a while, we had a typewriter with us. She accepted my delusion that, in the perfect spot, I could find the words, and cheerfully gripped her end of the ancient Underwood.

She loved *The New Yorker*, especially the cartoons. She and our other inseparable friend, Gertrude, who was as blond and serene as she was dark and volatile, would devour them. For years, they regaled each other with the caption under one that showed an overzealous snow-worker: "No, no, Finnegan, just the fluffy white stuff on the top."

Her life may sound sad, as it is recounted, but she transformed it with her elegance and gallantry. She wanted marriage, knowing it would give her mania for administration its fullest scope. She used to say when we were young, "If I could find some nice guy to set me up in a nice little joint, I really wouldn't want anything else." When she married a man whom she loved and revered for his wit and his erudition, they had two happy years.

In her widowhood she went home to care for her aging mother. It was not easy; but she did it with her usual high style. Long after it became apparent that she could not, with her illness and the dreadful treatments entailed, carry on, she persevered. When, finally, after months of anguish, she found a nursing home for her mother, who by then did not greatly care where she was, she was consumed with woe.

She expected little of others. She would have preferred that they set as much store by civility and decorum as she did, but lapses were explained away. "A little hard to take" was about as far as she went in an indictment.

She was a passionate shopper. She was not acquisitive, she was forever pressing the treasures she found on others. "The thrill of the chase," she would say to me when I berated her for rising from her sickbed to brave Boston's Filene's basement. I accompanied her just once, astounded by the possessed creature who plunged from rack to rack, closing in on a designer item she had been eyeing for weeks.

Her genius was for friendship, "those relations one chooses for oneself." No matter what the occasion, even if it was supper in the kitchen, she came perfectly turned out. She never came empty-handed, her basket overflowed with goodies like fresh-baked lemon squares—"I really didn't have anything to do this morning."

She brought with her a near reverence for other people's feelings. If there was grief, she was quiet and watchful, looking for cracks to fill with tender-hearted solicitude. If there was gaiety, she heightened it. If anyone commented on her thinness, she was vague about "those new pills."

The last time I saw her was at our lake. She was as chic as ever, but the bones were starting out of her face. She gamely addressed the cookout fare, although by that time she could not eat at all.

A few weeks later, when she admitted she was sick, I called her up. I suggested that my aunt, her special friend, would come and stay with her. "I'm not dressed—I couldn't," she said brokenly, "entertain her."

"Nannie," I said, "what are friends for?"

No one knew better than Nance MacDonald.

༄

"It is not our hands that make us human, nor our legs. It is not the shape of our noses or the thickness of our hair or the texture of our skin. We are human because of our hearts and the souls that fill our hearts."

LEWIS B. PULLER JR.
(1946–1994)

by

SEN. BOB KERREY
(1943–)

Lewis B. Puller Jr., son of Chesty Puller, the most decorated soldier in the Marine Corps, was severely crippled after stepping on a land mine in Vietnam in 1968. His book, Fortunate Son, *an account of his childhood, service in Vietnam, and life afterward, won the Pulitzer Prize. When he committed suicide, his friend Nebraska senator Bob Kerrey, who was also wounded in Vietnam, wrote this eulogy, which was never delivered.*

We celebrate your life, Lew Puller. You had forty-eight years on God's earth. Born the year the Second World War ended, when America was full of the optimism of a great moral and military victory, we all came to know you: your father, your mother, your sisters, your wife and children, your fellow patients and friends.

You and I first exchanged greetings in a hospital ward. I had just been admitted and you—more seasoned by that time—came to visit. I hope you didn't mind that I stayed in bed. You, beginning twenty-five years in your wheelchair, asked me about my pain, a gesture that impresses me more now than it did then.

In your autobiography, you said you "felt set apart from humanity" by the terrible and visible nature of your injury. Of course you were. I wish you could have seen how you had to be set apart in order to reach us like you did. You reached us with your great dignity and pride and perseverance. You asked us to help carry you up many stairs that sometimes stood in your way; without asking for our help, you lifted us by climbing the mountain that was always in your way.

You made us uncomfortable, Lew. We didn't always find it easy to look at you. Your body reminded us of something we would just as soon forget. It's more than the Vietnam War, much more.

Vietnam is a part of what we don't want to remember, of course. Your final unwillingness to endure life any longer made our friends afraid that we might feel the same. The tragedy of your torment, of never being able to find peace on this earth, reminds us of war's terrible price.

We wish it weren't so, but freedom is won and secured with more than words and promises. Your blood, Lew, your body, Lew, secured it. You secured it even though Vietnam became a terrible mistake and even though you never fought the one battle that would have given you and Chesty a night on the family porch in Saluda drinking bourbon and talking father to son, son to father.

You also remind us that chasing our father's dreams can be a dangerous business. Even as we do it, we deny that is so. Then one day we wake up and realize that we have become the person we never thought we would be.

You remind us of something else, dear friend, Lewis. You remind us that we should take a little time to do the important work of saving the lives of those we love. You didn't die of cancer or a heart attack or an automobile accident. You died because you did not feel your life was worth living.

It *was* worth living. I am angry at you for not seeing that, for leaving all of us behind to search without hope of finding the answer. But when the anger subsides, I must face this question: Could I have saved your life? Oh, I wish the answer were an easy no. I wish the word *yes* didn't float so stubbornly into view.

When I heard the news that you were back on the pills, I was in Nebraska for a political event. I was home when the call came that you were in trouble. When I heard your voice and the state you were in, I was confused and troubled. We talked many times that Saturday, and I—after consulting with friends who suffer the disease alcoholism—talked you into treatment.

I felt proud of myself, secure in the belief I had done all I could. Professionals would take it from here. Like so many of our generation, I turn to professionals a lot. I have grown accustomed to hiring people to take care of my loved ones when they are hurting, alone, and in need of help.

Reminding us of this would be a great legacy, Lew. If you snapped us out of this get-somebody-else-to-do-it stupor, that would be a great legacy. That would be as big a gift as your own splendid example of triumph and accomplishment. And that would be so much better than the story: another tormented Vietnam veteran bites the dust.

You noticed it from your slow-moving wheelchair, Lew. We Americans have gotten too busy to do the important things. Our schedules are too full to help our friends. Our jobs demand that we neglect our families. Our hunger for success leaves us no appetite for loving others.

The great American economic machine that roared to such triumphs during your forty-eight years has left us rich in numbers and poor in spirit. I wish the shock of your death could awaken us. I wish your death could awaken the few hundred thousand veterans of the Vietnam War who still may not have come home, who wander our streets or who walk the same alleys of despair that you walked.

And I wish your death could awaken the millions of Americans who chase their father's dreams, who are asleep to a life of love and personal commitment to others.

I wish your death would awaken us to the liberating truth that only by loving others can we love ourselves. Two days after your death I read a statement by a woman who was describing another woman's beginnings as a scientist: "So, there was no going back; she had to fight for survival among the mysteries of life. And what human beings want more than anything else is to become human beings."

It is not our hands that make us human, nor our legs. It is not the shape of our noses or the thickness of our hair or the texture of our skin. We are human because of our hearts and the souls that fill our hearts.

Lewis Burwell Puller, you had a heart and a soul that was very much human. You were set apart only in your mind. Now I commend your soul to God and pray that you find the peace that eluded you on earth.

ᏹᏚᏚᎧ

"She touched all of our lives. She made us laugh, she astonished us with her bravery, her devotion to God, and most of all her devotion to us. She had a wonderful unique way of looking at life and the mysteries around us."

ELIZABETH LYNGDOH
(1945–1994)

by

ALBERT PINGREE
(1981–)

The following appreciation was written by a fourteen-year-old student who was applying for admission to a private school in Washington, D.C. He was asked to write an essay on "Who is someone you admire?"

Thirteen years ago, when I was one year old, a woman named Elizabeth Lyngdoh came to live with our family. This lady came from India. She had been a United States citizen for fifteen years. She came to our home to work as a housekeeper. She spent most of her time taking care of my sister and I. She was wonderful in many ways and that is why I admire her so. Elizabeth was funny, kind, and she taught us a lot about courage.

A year after she came to our home, she met a man, also from India, by the name of Tony. A few months later they were married. What we didn't know at that time was that her husband was a homosexual and had the HIV virus. He had married Elizabeth to obtain a green card and left her shortly thereafter.

My mother took "Lizzy" to the doctor for an AIDS test. A few weeks later, we found out that she was positive. Because we were a family, she continued to live with us, despite her illness, until just last year when she passed away.

A few times in life, someone walks into your life and you realize that you have been touched by a miracle. Elizabeth Lyngdoh was a miracle. Everyone who knew Lizzy realized this. She was someone you could count on. She touched all of our lives. She made us laugh, she astonished us with her bravery, her devotion to God, and most of all her devotion to us. She had a wonderful unique way of looking at life and the mysteries around us.

We were a family and seemed to understand each other without spoken words. We all miss Lizzy. She taught us so much, that is why I admire her. There will never be a day that goes by that her smile, her love, and her courage will be far from our thoughts.

CHAPTER THIRTEEN

ANIMAL LOVES

꧁꧂

If George Graham Vest had known, on the morning he dressed for a Missouri courtroom in 1869, that he was about to ensure his immortality with a speech about his client's dog, he might have decided to stay home. Vest, who became a U.S. senator known for his eloquence, might have preferred that he be remembered for something slightly more imposing. But anyone who has ever read his eulogy for Old Drum cannot help agreeing with everything Vest says about the faithlessness of the world compared to man's best friend, the dog.

If you are trying to resist your urge to get a cat, you might want to skip over Charles Dudley Warner's tribute to Calvin. Warner's description of Calvin, so wise, so well-bred, and so graceful upon the windowsill, swinging his tail like a pendulum as he eyed the yard, filled me with such longing for a cat of my own that at the first opportunity I adopted a large marmalade male who needed a home and named him Calvin, too. But Warner's Calvin and mine were two separate animals, and after a short, difficult relationship, he read my mind and left town.

E. B. White wrote frequently about animals, real and imagined. The author of *Charlotte's Web* had a feeling for their feelings, and his brief tribute to his dog Daisy is included here.

Finally, the death notice for Coco, a parrot who lived on the island of Martha's Vineyard, is worth reading, if only to understand how exceptionally lovely human beings can be upon occasion. Coco's life could have been longer, but she had consistent support for every day of it until the end. Most human beings cannot claim as much.

"When all other friends desert, he remains. When riches take wings and reputation falls to pieces, he is as constant in his love as the sun in its journey through the heavens. If fortune drives the master forth an outcast into the world, friendless and homeless, the faithful dog asks no higher privilege than that of accompanying him. . . ."

OLD DRUM

by

GEORGE GRAHAM VEST
(1830–1904)

On October 28, 1869, Leonidas Hornsby, a Missouri frontiersman whose sheep were being killed by an unknown animal, saw a dog hanging around the edges of his property in the evening and ordered one of his ranch hands to shoot it. The ranch hand took aim and sent the dog howling off into the darkness.

Several days later, at the edge of a nearby lake, Charles Burden, a neighboring rancher and brother-in-law to Hornsby, found his lead hunting dog, Old Drum, dead of shotgun wounds, alongside another dog, also shot.

Old Drum was known in Johnson County as a dog that never "lied," i.e., gave off false alarms on a hunt. He had been Burden's closest companion for fifteen years. Burden accused Hornsby of killing him and sued for damages. On November 29, 1869, the case went to trial. It resulted in a hung jury.

Burden sued for a new trial. This time the jury decided in his favor, awarding him $25 in damages. But Hornsby appealed the case. Both sides retained new attorneys. This time, the jury decided for Hornsby.

Undaunted, Burden appealed the appeal, on the grounds of having new evidence, and hired yet another law firm, Phillips & Vest, to represent him. Hornsby also hired new counsel. By now the case of Old Drum had become a cause célèbre with friends and strangers choosing sides and coming from all parts of the state to sit in on the trial.

George Vest, the firm's senior partner, was not handling the case, but he agreed to accept a $10 stipend for accompanying his colleague to the trial. After the witnesses from both sides had been heard, Vest's colleague made his closing argument and asked Vest if he wanted to add anything. Vest said that he saw no need, that the case had been argued very well. But his part-

ner pointed out that perhaps he had better say something or risk losing his $10 stipend.

Vest rose without any notes or advance preparation and delivered the following statement.

Gentlemen of the jury: The best friend a man has in the world may turn against him and become his enemy. His son or daughter that he has reared with loving care may prove ungrateful. Those who are nearest and dearest to us, those whom we trust with our happiness and our good name, may become traitors to their faith. The money that a man has he may lose. It flies away from him perhaps, when he needs it most. A man's reputation may be sacrificed in a moment of ill-considered action. The people who are prone to fall on their knees and do us honor when success is with us may be the first to throw the stones of malice when failure settles its cloud upon our heads. The one absolutely unselfish friend a man can have in this selfish world, the one that never proves ungrateful or treacherous, is his dog.

Gentlemen of the jury, a man's dog stands by him in prosperity and poverty, in health and sickness. He will sleep on the cold ground where the wintry winds blow and the snow drives fiercely, if only he may be near his master's side. He will kiss the hand that has no food to offer, he will lick the wounds and sores that come in encounters with the roughness of the world. He guards the sleep of his pauper master as if he were a prince.

When all other friends desert, he remains. When riches take wings and reputation falls to pieces, he is as constant in his love as the sun in its journey through the heavens. If fortune drives the master forth an outcast into the world, friendless and homeless, the faithful dog asks no higher privilege than that of accompanying him, to guard against danger, to fight against his enemies. And when the last scene of all comes, and death takes his master in its embrace and his body is laid away in the cold ground, no matter if all other friends pursue their way, there by his graveside will the noble dog be found, his head between his paws, his eyes sad, but open in alert watchfulness, faithful and true even in death.

In one version of this event, it was reported that "as George Graham Vest finished and resumed his seat, tears were running down the faces of the spectators and jurors alike . . . [and that] one of Hornsby's lawyers then whispered to the other, 'We'd better get out of here before all of us are hanged,' so obvious was the sentiment of the jurors."

The jury deliberated for less than fifteen minutes and returned a verdict for Burden, assessing $500 in damages—$450 more than the court was legally able to award.

George Graham Vest went on to become a U.S. senator, using his powers of persuasion to defend Yellowstone Park against development by entrepreneurs, coal miners against exploitation, and Native Americans against the policies of Theodore Roosevelt. (After spending two days at Fort Shaw, a Crow Indian reservation, Vest was so appalled at the living conditions that he became their advocate for life.) Yet his immortality was secured by a brief, extemporaneous courtroom tribute to a slain hunting dog, which has been passed down the generations as "The Eulogy for Old Drum."

⚭

"Calvin's life seems to me a fortunate one, for it was natural and unforced. He ate when he was hungry, slept when he was sleepy, and enjoyed existence to the very tip of his toes and the end of his expressive and slow-moving tail."

CALVIN

by

CHARLES DUDLEY WARNER
(1829–1900)

Charles Dudley Warner was the editor of the Hartford Courant *and co-author with his friend Mark Twain of* The Gilded Age. *He was a member of the Hartford, Connecticut, literary life, along with Twain and Harriet Beecher Stowe, who gave Calvin to Warner when she moved permanently to Florida.*

Calvin is dead. His life, long to him, but short for the rest of us, was not marked by startling adventures, but his character was so uncommon and his qualities were so worthy of imitation that I have been asked by those who personally knew him to set down my recollections.

His origin and ancestry were shrouded in mystery; even his age was a matter of conjecture. Although he was of the Maltese race, I have reason to suppose that he was American by birth. . . . [He] was exquisitely proportioned, and as graceful in every movement as a young leopard. When he stood up to open a door—he opened all the doors with old-fashioned latches—he was portentously tall, and when stretched on the rug before the fire, he seemed too long for this world—as indeed he was. . . .

He disliked cats, evidently regarding them as feline and treacherous, and he had no association with them. Occasionally there would be heard a night concert in the shrubbery. Calvin would ask to have the door opened, and you would hear a rush and a *pestztk* and the concert would explode, and Calvin would quietly come in and resume his seat on the hearth. There was no trace of anger in his manner, but he wouldn't have any of that around the house. . . .

I hesitate a little to speak of his capacity for friendship and the affectionateness of his nature, for I know from his own reserve that he would not care to have it much talked about. We understood each other perfectly but we never made any fuss about it; when I spoke his name and snapped my fingers, he came to me; when I returned home at night, he was pretty sure to be waiting for me near the gate and would rise and saunter along the walk, as if his being there were purely accidental—so shy was he commonly of showing feeling; and when I opened the door, he never rushed in like a cat, but loitered, and lounged, as if he had no intention of going in, but would condescend to. . . . There was one thing he never did—he never rushed through an open doorway. He never forgot his dignity. If he had asked to have the door opened and was eager to go out, he always went deliberately; I can see him now, standing on the sill, looking about at the sky as if he was thinking whether it were worthwhile to take an umbrella, until he was near having his tail shut in. . . .

He had a habit of coming to my study in the morning, sitting quietly by my side or on the table for hours, watching the pen run over the paper, occasionally swinging his tail round for a blotter, and then going to sleep among the papers by the inkstand. Or, more rarely, he would watch the writing from a perch on my shoulder. Writing always interested him, and until he understood it, he wanted to hold the pen. . . .

[Calvin] had his limitations. Whatever passion he had for nature, he had no conception of art. There was sent to him once a fine and very expressive cat's head in bronze, by Fremet. I placed it on the floor. He regarded it intently, approached it cautiously and crouchingly, touched it with his nose, perceived the fraud, turned away abruptly, and never would notice it afterward. On the whole his life was not only a successful one, but a happy one. He never had but one fear, so far as I know: he had a mortal and reasonable terror of plumbers. He would never stay in the house when they were here. . . . Of course he didn't share our fear about their charges, but he must have had some dreadful experience with them in that portion of his life which is unknown to us. A plumber was to him the devil, and I have no doubt that, in his scheme, plumbers were foreordained to do him mischief. . . .

As I look back upon it, Calvin's life seems to me a fortunate one, for it was natural and unforced. He ate when he was hungry, slept when he was sleepy, and enjoyed existence to the very tip of his toes and the end of his expressive and slow-moving tail. He delighted to roam about the garden, and stroll among the trees, and to lie on the green grass and luxuriate in all the sweet influences of summer. You could never accuse him of idleness, and yet he knew the secret of repose. The poet who wrote so prettily of him that his little life was rounded with a sleep understated his felicity; it was rounded with a good many. His conscience never seemed to interfere with his slumbers. In fact, he had good habits and a contented mind. I can see him now walk in at the study door, sit down by my chair, bring his tail artistically about his feet, and look up at me with unspeakable happiness in his handsome face. I often thought that he felt the dumb limitation which denied him the power of language. But since he was denied speech, he scorned the inarticulate mouthings of the lower animals. The vulgar mewing and yowling of the cat species was beneath him; he sometimes uttered a sort of articulate and well-bred ejaculation, when he wished to call attention to something that he considered remarkable, or to some want of his, but he never went whining about . . . he had a nightly power of purr to express his measureless content with congenial society. There was in him a musical organ with stops of varied power and expression, upon which I have no doubt he could have performed Scarlatti's celebrated cat's-fugue.

Whether Calvin died of old age or was carried off by one of the diseases incident to youth, it is impossible to say; for his departure was as quiet as his advent was mysterious. I only know that he appeared to us in this world in his perfect stature and beauty, and that after a time, like Lohengrin, he withdrew. . . . An alarming symptom was his preference for the warmth of a furnace register to the lively sparkle of the open wood fire. Whatever pain he suffered, he bore it in silence and seemed only anxious not to obtrude his malady. We tempted him with the delicacies of the season, but it soon became impossible for him to eat, and for two weeks he ate or drank scarcely anything. Sometimes he made the effort to take something, but it was evident that he made the effort to please us. The neighbors—and I am convinced that the advice of neighbors is never good for anything— suggested catnip. He wouldn't even smell it. We had the attendance of an amateur practitioner of medicine, whose real office was the cure of souls, but nothing touched his case. He took what was offered, but it was with the air of one to whom the time for pellets was passed. He sat or lay day after day almost motionless, never once making a display of those vulgar convulsions or contortions of pain which are so disagreeable to society. His favorite place was on the brightest spot of a Smyrna rug by the conservatory, where the sunlight fell and he could hear the fountain play. If we went to him and exhibited our interest in his condition, he always purred in recognition of our sympathy. And when I spoke his name, he looked up with an expression that said, "I understand it, old fellow, but it's no use." He was to all who came to visit him a model of calmness and patience in affliction.

I was absent from home at the last, but heard by daily postal card of his failing condition; and never again saw him alive. One sunny morning, he rose from his rug, went into the conservatory (he was very thin then), walked around it deliberately, looking at all the plants he knew, and then went to the bay window in the dining room and stood for a long time looking out upon the little field, now brown and sere, and toward the garden, where perhaps the happiest hours of his life had been spent. It was a last look. He turned and walked away, laid himself down upon the bright spot in the rug, and quietly died.

It is not too much to say that a little shock went through the neighborhood when it was known that Calvin was dead, so marked was his individuality; and his friends, one after another, came to see him. There was no sentimental nonsense about his obsequies; it was felt that any parade would have been distasteful to him. John, who acted as undertaker, prepared a candlebox for him, and I believe assumed a professional decorum; but there may have been the usual levity underneath, for I heard that he remarked in the kitchen that it was the "dryest wake" he ever attended.

When I returned, they had laid Calvin on a table in an upper chamber by an open window. It was February. He reposed in a candlebox, lined about the edge with evergreen, and at his head stood a little wineglass with flowers. He lay with his head tucked down in his arms—a favorite position of his before the fire—as if asleep in the comfort of his soft and exquisite fur. It was the involuntary exclamation of those who saw him, "How natural he looks!" As for myself, I said nothing. . . .

Perhaps I have failed to make appear the individuality of character that was so evident to those who knew him. At any rate, I have set down nothing concerning him but the literal truth. He was always a mystery. I do not know whence he came; I do not know whither he has gone. I would not weave one spray of falsehood in the wreath I lay upon his grave.

⌀⫘⫘⫘9

"Persons who knew her only slightly regarded her as an opinionated little bitch and said so; but she had a small circle of friends who saw through her, cost what it did."

DAISY
(1928–1931)

by

E. B. WHITE
(1899–1985)

E. B. White was one of the early writers for the New Yorker *magazine. A brilliant stylist, White wrote numerous books for adults, including* Quo

THE BOOK OF EULOGIES

Vadimus, One Man's Meat, *and* Is Sex Necessary? *which he coauthored with James Thurber. But White may have secured his immortality with two children's books,* Charlotte's Web *(about a pig and a spider) and* Stuart Little *(about a mouse), which became classics in his lifetime.*

Daisy ("Black Watch Debatable") died December 22, 1931, when she was hit by a Yellow Cab on University Place. At the moment of her death she was smelling the front of a florist's sloop. It was a wet day, and the cab skidded up over the curb—just the sort of excitement that would have amused her had she been at a safer distance. She is survived by her mother, Jeannie; a brother, Abner; her father, whom she never knew; and two sisters, whom she never liked. She was three years old.

Daisy was born at 65 West Eleventh Street in a clothes closet at two o'clock of a December morning in 1928. She came, as did her sisters and brothers, as an unqualified surprise to her mother, who had for several days previously looked with a low-grade suspicion on the box of bedding that had been set out for the delivery, and who had gone into the clothes closet merely because she had felt funny and wanted a dark, awkward place to feel funny in. Daisy was the smallest of the litter of seven, and the oddest.

Her life was full of incident but not of accomplishment. Persons who knew her only slightly regarded her as an opinionated little bitch and said so; but she had a small circle of friends who saw through her, cost what it did. At Speyer Hospital where she used to go when she was indisposed, she was known as Whitey, because, the man told me, she was black. All her life she was subject to moods, and her feeling about horses laid her sanity open to question. Once she slipped her leash and chased a horse for three blocks through heavy traffic, in the carking belief that she was an effective agent against horses. Drivers of teams, seeing her only in the moments of her delirium, invariably leaned far out of their seats and gave tongue, mocking her, and thus made themselves even more ridiculous, for the moment, than Daisy.

She had a stoical nature and spent the latter part of her life an invalid, owing to an injury to her right hind leg. Like many invalids, she developed a rather objectionable cheerfulness, as though to deny that she had cause for rancor. She also developed, without

316

instruction or encouragement, a curious habit of holding people firmly by the ankle without actually biting them—a habit that gave her an immense personal advantage and won her many enemies. As far as I know, she never even broke the thread of a sock, so delicate was her grasp (like a retriever's), but her point of view was questionable, and her attitude was beyond explaining to the person whose ankle was at stake. For my own amusement I often tried to diagnose this quirkish temper, and I think I understand it: she suffered from a chronic perplexity, and it relieved her to take hold of something.

She was arrested once, by Patrolman Porko. She enjoyed practically everything in life except motoring, an exigency to which she submitted silently, without joy, and without nausea. She never took pains to discover, conclusively, the things that might have diminished her curiosity and spoiled her taste. She died sniffing life, and enjoying it.

ᏬᎳ

"Coco had lots of friends on the island. For many years she stayed with Mrs. Jeffrey S. White when Mrs. Blake was traveling, and always returned with a few broken feathers, indicating she had had a good time and had been played with a lot."

COCO
(1971?–1995)

by

VINEYARD GAZETTE EDITORIAL
(VINEYARD HAVEN, MASSACHUSETTS)

Coco, an African grey parrot who belonged to Mrs. Edith G. Blake of Edgartown, died on January 4 after a valiant effort on the part of many people to save her. Coco came to the Island twenty-four years ago next month, and one can only hope had a happy life on the Island with only a few trips ashore.

Throughout the Christmas holidays Coco had showed signs of internal troubles, and Dr. Michelle Gerhard suggested blood tests, but before anything could be accomplished Coco was down on the bottom of her cage on Wednesday morning. Mrs. Edward B. Self volunteered to help with a mad dash to Dr. Gerhard's for sustaining shots and directions to the bird hospital at the Windhover Veterinary Center in Walpole.

The Steamship Authority immediately found space on the ferry and positioned the car so that Coco could leave the boat early in an already heated car. Members of the culinary staff on board warmed rubber gloves filled with water (supplied by Dr. Gerhard) to keep Coco warm on the trip, and filled hot-water bottles.

Everyone did what they could, but it was a case of too little too late. Shortly after her arrival at the hospital Coco revived and the doctors thought she would make it, but then she quietly didn't.

Coco had lots of friends on the island. For many years she stayed with Mrs. Jeffrey S. White when Mrs. Blake was traveling, and always returned with a few broken feathers, indicating she had had a good time and had been played with a lot. In later years she has been staying with Christopher Murphy in Chilmark, where she was never intimidated by Mr. Murphy's macaw, who was three times her size.

Miss Ellen Weise was also one of Coco's friends and would never (regardless of the horrid summer traffic) miss a trip from West Tisbury to give her a much appreciated scratch.

It is particularly sad to lose Coco since she had a life expectancy longer than most humans and only made it to twenty-four. She will be returned to the Island and (when the ground thaws) be buried in Sheriff's Meadow alongside her predecessor.

Mrs. Blake can never express her gratitude to Mrs. Self, Dr. Gerhard, the Steamship Authority, and Windhover for their help and care.

PART III

WORDS
OF CONSOLATION

⌗

When death is imminent or has just happened, we look for words of wisdom on what that great common occurrence signifies. When flooded with suffering, we grab at words of understanding to keep us from falling over the edge.

On the subject of death, most philosophers and poets appear to be in solid agreement: it is a natural and desired end, with much good in its arrival. Buddha sees death as a release, Plato as either the best sleep of one's life or a chance to commune with the gods, and Sir Francis Bacon lists all the weapons that are superior to death: "Revenge triumphs over death; Love slights it; Honour aspireth to it. . . ."

When grief overwhelms, words may prevent the survivor's heart from breaking. When we write letters, essays, poetry, and slide it under a grieving friend's door, we are sliding our own hearts toward another in the hope that in companionship there will be relief.

The men and women who appear here were simultaneously grieving and comforting others. William Sloane Coffin, his son dead less than a fortnight, stands in his church and speaks to his congregation. Barbara Boggs Sigmund was a politician. But when she was stricken with cancer, she turned to poetry for solace and preparation. In a letter of pain and compassion for the family of a victim of the Pan Am 103 terrorist explosion, the Scottish family who found the body on their land writes of their love for "your dear one [who] came to us from the night" and how they tended him as one of their own.

In every selection, whether it is by a poet, a great religious leader, or a young child, one human being is reaching out to console someone and, when possible, press a candle in another's hand.

CHAPTER FOURTEEN

WHAT DEATH MEANS

⟨✺⟩

"Now that at last I emerge from the vast and endless suffering—is that the best time for you to grieve?"

THE LORD BUDDHA ON DYING
(563–483 B.C.)

A sheltered Himalayan prince, Siddhartha Gautama, the founder of Buddhism, was twenty-nine before he left his father's palace grounds and saw, for the first time, the death and misery in the rest of the world. He became a wandering ascetic, seeking enlightenment. He finally achieved it at the age of thirty-five, becoming a Buddha. Just before he died, at the age of eighty, he is said to have delivered the following words to his grieving disciples.

In the hour of joy it is not proper to grieve. Your despair is quite inappropriate, and you should regain your composure. The goal, so hard to win, which for many aeons I have wished for, now at last it is no longer far away. When that is won—no earth or water, fire, wind, or ether present; unchanging bliss beyond all objects of the senses, a peace which none can take away, the highest thing there is; and when you hear of that and know that no becoming mars it and nothing ever there can pass away—how is there room for grief then in your minds? At Gaya, at the time when I won enlightenment, I got rid of the causes of becoming, which are nothing but a gang of harmful vipers; now the hour comes near when I get rid also of this body, the dwelling place of the acts accumulated in the past. Now that at last this body, which harbors so much ill, is on its way out; now that at last the frightful dangers of becoming are about to be extinct; now

323

that at last I emerge from the vast and endless suffering—is that the best time for you to grieve? . . .

It is indeed a fact that salvation cannot come from the mere sight of me. It demands strenuous efforts in the practice of yoga. But if someone has thoroughly understood this my Dharma, then he is released from the net of suffering, even though he never cast his eyes on me. A man must take medicine to be cured; the mere sight of the physician is not enough. Likewise the mere sight of me enables no one to conquer suffering; he will have to meditate for himself about the gnosis I have communicated. If self-controlled, a man may live away from me as far as can be, but if he only sees my Dharma, then indeed he sees me also. But if he should neglect to strive in concentrated calm for higher things, then though he live quite near me, he is far away from me. Therefore be energetic, persevere, and try to control your minds. Do good deeds, and try to win mindfulness!

෴

"There is great hope that death is a blessing."

APOLOGY OF SOCRATES
(469–399 B.C.)

by

PLATO
(CA. 428–CA. 348 B.C.)

Socrates was the Greek philosopher and gadfly who taught that the search for truth was the only proper pursuit. Tried in Athens on charges of corrupting youth and spreading heresies, he was condemned to death, by drinking hemlock. His final words were recorded by Plato, who was his most famous pupil and responsible for all we know about Socrates.

Moreover, we may hence conclude that there is great hope that death is a blessing. For to die is one of two things: for either the dead may be annihilated and have no sensation of anything whatever; or, as it is said, there are a certain change and passage of the soul from one place to another. And if it is a privation of all sensation, as it were a sleep in which the sleeper has no dream, death would be a wonderful gain. For I think that if anyone, having selected a night in which he slept so soundly as not to have had a dream, and having compared this night with all the other nights and days of his life, should be required, on consideration, to say how many days and nights he had passed better and more pleasantly than this night throughout his life, I think that, not only a private person, but even the great king himself, would find them easy to number, in comparison with other days and nights. If, therefore, death is a thing of this kind, I say it is a gain; for thus all futurity appears to be nothing more than one night. But if, on the other hand, death is a removal from hence to another place, and what is said be true, that all the dead are there, what greater blessing can there be than this, my judges? For if, on arriving at Hades, released from these who pretend to be judges, one shall find those who are true judges, and who are said to judge there, Minos and Rhadamanthus, Aeacus and Triptolemus, and such others of the demigods as were just during their own lives, would this be a sad removal? At what price would you not estimate a conference with Orpheus and Musaeus, Hesiod and Homer? I, indeed, should be willing to die often, if this be true.

௸

"Men fear Death, as children fear to go in the dark. . . ."

OF DEATH

by

SIR FRANCIS BACON
(1561–1626)

An English Renaissance philosopher, statesman, writer, and scientific visionary, Sir Francis Bacon was called by Alfred North Whitehead "one of the greatest builders who constructed the mind of the modern world."

Men fear Death, as children fear to go in the dark; and as that natural fear in children is increased with tales, so is the other. Certainly, the contemplation of death, as the wages of sin and passage to another world, is holy and religious; but the fear of it, as a tribute due unto nature, is weak. Yet in religious meditations there is sometimes a mixture of vanity and of superstition. You shall read in some of the friars' books of mortification, that a man should think with himself what the pain is if he have but his finger's end pressed or tortured, and thereby imagine what the pains of death are, when the whole body is corrupted and dissolved; when many times death passeth with less pain than the torture of a limb: for the most vital parts are not the quickest of sense. And by him that spake only as a philosopher and natural man, it was well said, *Pompa mortis magia terret, quam mors ipsa:* (it is the accompaniments of death that are frightful rather than death itself.) Groans and convulsions, and a discoloured face, and friends weeping, and blacks, and obsequies, and the like, shew death terrible. It is worthy the observing, that there is no passion in the mind of man so weak, but it mates and masters the fear of death; and therefore death is no such terrible enemy when a man hath so many attendants about him that can win the combat of him. Revenge triumphs over death; Love slights it; Honour aspireth to it; Grief flieth to it; Fear preoccupateth it . . . ; It is as natural to die as to be born; and to a little infant, perhaps, the one is as painful as the other. He that dies in an earnest pursuit, is like one that is wounded in hot blood; who, for the time, scarce feels the hurt; and therefore a mind fixed and bent upon somewhat that is good doth avert the dolours of death. But above all, believe it, the sweetest canticle is, *Nunc dimmitis* (now is the hour), when a man hath obtained worthy ends and expectations. Death hath this also; that it openeth the gate to good fame, and extinguisheth envy. *Extinctus amabitur idem* (the same man that was envied while he lived, shall be loved when he is gone).

⌒⫟⨳⊙

"Death is beautiful when seen to be a law, and not an accident. . . ."

ON DEATH

by

HENRY DAVID THOREAU
(1817–1862)

Henry David Thoreau's writings on the subjects of individualism, nature, and the need for human beings to be self-sufficient, reflective, and nonmaterialistic continue to grow in influence. A native of Concord, Massachusetts, Thoreau belonged to the important Transcendentalist movement, powered by a small, influential group of men and women in New England. His mentor and closest friend was Ralph Waldo Emerson. The excerpt below is taken from the first letter Thoreau wrote to Emerson, in 1842. Both had recently had deaths in their families.

How plain, that death is only the phenomenon of the individual or class. Nature does not recognize it, She finds her own again under new forms without loss. Yet death is beautiful when seen to be a law, and not an accident—It is as common as life. Men die in Tartary—in Ethiopia—in England—in Wisconsin. And after all what portion of this so serene and living nature can be said to be alive? Do this year's grasses and foliage outnumber all the past?

Every blade in the field—every leaf in the forest—lays down its life in its season as beautifully as it was taken up. It is the pastime of a full quarter of the year. Dead trees—sere leaves—dried grass and herbs—are not these a good part of our life? And what is that pride of our autumnal scenery but the hectic flush—the sallow and cadaverous countenance of vegetation—its painted throes—with the November air for canvas—

When we look over the fields, we are not saddened because these particular flowers or grasses will wither—for the law of their death is the law of new life. Will not the land be in good heart *because* the crops die down from year to year? The herbage cheerfully consents to bloom, and wither, and give place to a new.

So it is with the human plant. We are partial and selfish when we lament the death of the individual, unless our plaint be a paean to the departed soul, and we sigh as the wind sighs over the fields, which no shrub interprets into its private grief.

One might as well go into mourning for every sere leaf—but the more innocent and wiser soul will snuff a fragrance in the gales of autumn, and congratulate Nature upon her health.

After I have imagined thus much will not the Gods feel under obligations to make me realize something as good?

"Your fear of death is but the trembling of the shepherd when he stands before the king whose hand is to be laid upon him in honor."

KAHLIL GIBRAN
(1883–1931)

A Lebanese-born poet, philosopher, and artist, Kahlil Gibran is considered to be the greatest genius of his age in the Arab world. His book The Prophet, *from which this excerpt is taken, is cherished by readers around the world. Gibran considered it his finest work.*

> *Then Almitra spoke, saying, We would
> ask now of Death.
> And he said:
> You would know the secret of death.
> But how shall you find it unless you seek it
> in the heart of life?
> The owl whose night-bound eyes are
> blind unto the day cannot unveil the mystery
> of light.
> If you would indeed behold the spirit of
> death, open your heart wide unto the body
> of life.
> For life and death are one, even as the
> river and the sea are one.
> In the depth of your hopes and desires
> lies your silent knowledge of the beyond;
> And like seeds dreaming beneath the snow
> your heart dreams of spring.
> Trust the dreams, for in them is hidden
> the gate to eternity.
> Your fear of death is but the trembling
> of the shepherd when he stands before the
> king whose hand is to be laid upon him in
> honour.
> Is the shepherd not joyful beneath his*

trembling, that he shall wear the mark of
the king?
  Yet is he not more mindful of his trembling?
  For what is it to die but to stand naked
in the wind and to melt into the sun?
  And what is it to cease breathing, but to
free the breath from its restless tides, that
it may rise and expand and seek God unencumbered?
  Only when you drink from the river of
silence shall you indeed sing.
  And when you have reached the mountain
top, then you shall begin to climb.
  And when the earth shall claim your
limbs, then shall you truly dance.

ᠬᠡᠯᠡ

"Death is nothing at all. . . ."

HENRY SCOTT HOLLAND
(1847–1918)

Henry Scott Holland was a professor of divinity at Oxford University, Oxford, England.

Death is nothing at all—I have only slipped away into the next room. I am I, and you are you. Whatever we were to each other, that we still are. Call me by my old familiar name, speak to me in the easy way you always used. Wear no forced air of solemnity or sorrow.

Laugh as we always laughed at the little jokes we enjoyed together. Play, smile, think of me, pray for me. Let my name be ever the household word that it always was. Let it be spoken without the ghost of a shadow on it. Life means all that it ever meant. . . . There is absolutely unbroken continuity.

What is death but a negligible accident? Why should I be out of mind because I am out of sight?

I am waiting for you—for an interval—somewhere near just around the corner.

All is well.

⊙〰〰〰⊙

A PARABLE OF IMMORTALITY

by

REV. HENRY VAN DYKE
(1852–1933)

Henry Van Dyke, an American clergyman, educator, and author, and a graduate of Princeton Theological Seminary, was best known for his fable The Other Wise Man. *He was one of two clergymen who officiated at the funeral of Mark Twain. These words have been attributed to other people as well, but the majority sides with Van Dyke.*

I am standing upon the seashore. A ship at my side spreads her white sails to the morning breeze and starts for the blue ocean. She is an object of beauty and strength, and I stand and watch until at last she hangs like a speck of white cloud just where the sea and sky come down to mingle with each other. Then someone at my side says, "There she goes!"

Gone where? Gone from my sight . . . that is all. She is just as large in mast and hull and spar as she was when she left my side and just as able to bear her load of living freight to the place of destination. Her diminished size is in me, not in her. And just at the moment when someone at my side says, "There she goes!" there are other eyes watching her coming and other voices ready to take up the glad shout, "Here she comes!"

⊙〰〰〰⊙

"Is it possible that in aging we all receive just such intimations, such 'animal' reconciliations with the fact of dying? . . . Not from weariness of life, not from a tragic protest against life's difficulty, not from a dread of the declining years, but from some deep, purely natural

330

acceptance of the given assignment of youth, maturity, age, and death."

HOW WONDERFUL IT IS THAT PEOPLE DIE

by

Thornton Wilder
(1897–1975)

Thornton Wilder is considered one of the greatest American playwrights and novelists. The plays Our Town *and* The Skin of Our Teeth, *and his novel* The Bridge of San Luis Rey *all won Pulitzer Prizes. When he died, his sister was quoted as saying, "There are those who write of what they don't know they know. They're the men who live their lives inside themselves and reach out. They have the real voice to sing." When Wilder was teaching poetry at Harvard, he wrote about the following dream.*

In all dreams in which my mother appears she is still alive, so alive that on waking I go through a highly conscious moment of bewilderment, like this: "Now let me see . . . she . . . she . . . no, she is dead." In this dream she is across the room, sewing or somehow occupied in domestic work, I am sitting on my father's lap, facing her; yet I somehow seem also to be behind myself and seeing, as it were, the backs of my mother's and my father's head. I think I see myself as full grown. Yet I have no sense of being a weight and encumbrance to my father. The mood of the scene is that of tranquil conversation, but one part of my mind is saying to itself, "We must not say anything that would remind my father that he is dead; it would embarrass him." Thereupon I woke up and rose to a level of consciousness nearer to waking, and the following words rose spontaneously to my mind: "How wonderful it is that people die."

This astonishing sentence was propelled from me, from that atmosphere of contentment, as a joyous moment of illumination, and of course without the faintest shade of resentment or repudiation of the life represented.

When finally awake and considering what I have just described, my thought was: Is it possible that in aging we all receive just such intimations, such "animal" reconciliations with the fact of dying? I—

who have never had any revulsion against the thought of dying—then hoped that that was so: Not from weariness of life, not from a tragic protest against life's difficulty, not from a dread of the declining years, but from some deep, purely natural acceptance of the given assignment of youth, maturity, age, and death.

ᏧᎳᎩ

"When the eyes without my physical eyes shall open upon the world to come, I shall simply be consciously living in the country of my heart."

THE COUNTRY OF MY HEART

by

HELEN KELLER
(1880–1968)

Helen Keller, the world-famous American lecturer and author, was a follower of Emanuel Swedenborg, whose beliefs mirrored her own.

I cannot understand why anyone should fear death. Life here is more cruel than death—life divides and estranges, while death, which is life eternal, reunites and reconciles. I believe that when the eyes without my physical eyes shall open upon the world to come, I shall simply be consciously living in the country of my heart.

ᏧᎳᎩ

"I do not know what I believe about life after death; if it exists, then I burn with interest, if not—well, I am tired."

ON DEATH

by

FLORIDA SCOTT-MAXWELL
(1883–1973)

Florida Scott-Maxwell was a Jungian analyst, actress, and writer. American-born, she lived most of her life in Scotland. This selection comes from her journal, The Measure of My Days, *published in 1968.*

My only fear about death is that it will not come soon enough. Life still interests and occupies me. Happily I am not in such discomfort that I wish for death, I love and am loved, but please God I die before I lose my independence. I do not know what I believe about life after death; if it exists, then I burn with interest, if not—well, I am tired. I have endured the flame of living and that should be enough. I have made others suffer, and if there are more lives to be lived, I believe I ought to do penance for the suffering I have caused. I should experience what I have made others experience. It belongs to me, and I should learn it.

If I suffer from my lacks, and I do daily, I also feel elation at what I have become. At times I feel a sort of intoxication because of some small degree of gain; as though the life that is in me has been my charge, the trust birth brought me, and my blunders, sins, the lacks in me as well as the gifts, have in some long painful transmutation made the life that is in me clearer.

The most important thing in my life was the rich experience of the unconscious. This was a gift life gave me and I only had the sense to honor and serve it. It taught me that we are fed by great forces, and I know that I am in the hands of what seemed immortal. It hardly matters whether I am mortal or not since I have experienced the immortal. This makes me at rest in much of my being, but not in all. It is almost as if the order in me is barely me, and I still have to deal with the chaos that is mine.

⟨∞∞⟩

CHAPTER FIFTEEN

GRIEF DEFINED

⌒∞⌒

"Sorrow comes in great waves ... but it rolls over us, and though it may almost smother us it leaves us on the spot and we know that if it is strong we are stronger inasmuch as it passes and we remain."

ON SORROW

by

HENRY JAMES
(1843–1916)

The friendship between novelist Henry James and scholar Grace Norton, who was ten years his senior, spanned more than forty years. It was a close and confiding relationship, sustained primarily by their correspondence. In this brotherly and affectionate letter, James urges Norton to have the courage to do nothing, other than wait, until her grief subsides.

My dear Grace,

Before the suffering of others I am always utterly powerless, and the letter you gave me reveals such depths of suffering that I hardly know what to say to you. This indeed is not my last word—but it must be my first. You are not isolated, verily, in such states of feeling as this—that is, in the sense that you appear to make all the misery of mankind your own; only I have a terrible sense that you give all and receive nothing—that there is no reciprocity in your sympathy—that you have all the affliction of it and none of the returns. However—I am determined not to speak to you except with the voice of stoicism. I don't know *why* we live—the gift of life comes to us from I don't know what source or for what purpose; but I believe we can go on living for the reason that (always of course up to a certain point) life is the most valuable thing we know anything about and it is therefore presumptively a great mistake to surrender it while there is any yet left in the cup. In other words consciousness is an illimitable power, and though at times it may seem to be all consciousness of misery, yet in the way it propagates itself from wave to wave, so that we never cease to feel, though at moments we appear to, try to, pray to, there is something that holds one in one's place, makes it a standpoint in the universe which it is probably good not to forsake. You are right in your consciousness that we are all echoes and reverberations of the *same,* and you are noble when your interest and pity as to everything that surrounds you, appears to have a sustaining and harmonizing power. Only don't, I beseech you, *generalize* too much in these sympathies and tendernesses—remember that every life is a special problem which is not yours but another's and content yourself with the terrible algebra of your own. Don't melt too much into the universe, but be as solid and dense and fixed as you can. We all live together, and those of us who love and know, live so most. We help each other—even unconsciously, each in our own effort, we lighten the effort of others, we contribute to the sum of success, make it possible for others to live. Sorrow comes in great waves—no one can know that better than you—but it rolls over us, and though it may almost smother us it leaves us on the spot and we know that if it is strong we are stronger inasmuch as it passes and we remain. It wears us, uses us, but we wear it and use it in return; and it is blind, whereas we after a manner see. My dear Grace, you are passing through a darkness in which I myself in my ignorance see nothing but that you have been made wretchedly ill; but it is only a darkness, it is not an end, or *the* end. Don't think, don't feel, any more than you can help, don't conclude or decide—don't do anything but *wait.* Everything will pass, and serenity and *accepted* mysteries and disillusionments, and the tenderness of a few good people, and new opportunities and ever so much of life, in a word, will remain. You will do all sorts of things yet, and I will help you. The only thing is not to melt in the meanwhile. . . .

> Ever your faithful friend,
> Henry James

"I do not want to die without leaving a record of my belief that suffering can be overcome. For I do believe it."

ON OVERCOMING SUFFERING

by

KATHERINE MANSFIELD
(1888–1923)

Born in New Zealand, Katherine Mansfield lived most of her brief writing life in England. Her mastery of the short-story form puts her in the highest ranks. For the last five years of her life she suffered from tuberculosis, from which she died at thirty-five.

I should like this to be accepted as my confession. There is no limit to human suffering. When one thinks: "Now I have touched the bottom of the sea—now I can go no deeper," one goes deeper. And so it is forever. I thought last year in Italy, any shadow more would be death. But this year has been so much more terrible that I think with affection of the Casetta! Suffering is boundless, it is eternity. One pang is eternal torment. Physical suffering is—child's play. To have one's breast crushed by a great stone—one could laugh!

I do not want to die without leaving a record of my belief that suffering can be overcome. For I do believe it. What must one do? There is no question of what is called "passing beyond it." This is false.

One must submit. Do not resist. Take it. Be overwhelmed. Accept it fully. Make it part of life.

Everything in life that we really accept undergoes a change. So suffering must become Love. This is the mystery. This is what I must do. I must pass from personal love to greater love. I must give to the whole of life what I gave to one. The present agony will pass—if it doesn't kill. It won't last. Now I am like a man who has had his heart torn out—but—bear it—bear it! As in the physical world, so in the spiritual world, pain does not last forever. It is only so terribly acute now. It is as though a ghastly accident had happened. If I can cease reliving all the shock and horror of it, cease going over it, I will get stronger.

Here, for a strange reason, rises the figure of Doctor Sorapure. He was a good man. He helped me not only to bear pain, but he suggested that perhaps bodily ill-health is necessary, is a repairing process, and he was always telling me to consider how man plays but a part in the history of the world. My simple kindly doctor was pure of heart as Tchekhov was pure of heart. But for these ills one is one's own doctor. If "suffering" is not a repairing process, I will make it so. I will learn the lesson it teaches. These are not idle words. These are not the consolations of the sick.

Life is a mystery. The fearful pain will fade. I must turn to work. I must put my agony into something, change it. "Sorrow shall be changed into joy."

It is to lose oneself more utterly, to love more deeply, to feel oneself part of life—not separate.

O Life! accept me—make me worthy—teach me.

❧

"Grief remains one of the few things that has the power to silence us."

THE LIVING ARE DEFINED
BY WHOM THEY HAVE LOST

by

ANNA QUINDLEN
(1953–)

During Anna Quindlen's tenure as an editorial columnist at the New York Times, *the following column was the one that received the most reader mail.*

My great journalistic contribution to my family is that I write obituaries. First my mother's, twenty-two years ago, listing her accomplishments: two daughters, three sons. Then that of my father's second wife, dead of the same disease that killed his first one. Last week, it was my sister-in-law. "Sherry Quindlen, 41," I tapped out on the keyboard, and then it was real, like a last breath.

"When you write about me," she said one day in the hospital, "be nice." For the obit I could only be accurate.

338

The limitations of the form eliminate the more subjective truths: a good heart, a generous soul, who made her living taking care of other people's children. My brother's wife, the mother of a teenager and a toddler, who went from a bad cough to what was mistakenly said to be pneumonia to what was correctly diagnosed as lung and liver cancer, from fall to spring, from the day she threw a surprise fortieth birthday party for her husband to the day he chose her casket.

Only days after the funeral her two daughters were shopping together when a salesperson looked at them and said admiringly, "Your mother must have beautiful hair." "Yes, she does," said the elder, who has learned quickly what is expected of survivors.

Grief remains one of the few things that has the power to silence us. It is a whisper in the world and a clamor within. More than sex, more than faith, even more than its usher death, grief is unspoken, publicly ignored except for those moments at the funeral that are over too quickly, or the conversations among the cognoscenti, those of us who recognize in one another a kindred chasm deep in the center of who we are.

Maybe we do not speak of it because death will mark all of us, sooner or later. Or maybe it is unspoken because grief is only the first part of it. After a time it becomes something less sharp but larger, too, a more enduring thing called loss. Perhaps that is why this is the least explored passage: because it has no end.

The world loves closure, loves a thing that can, as they say, be gotten through. This is why it comes as a great surprise to find that loss is forever, that two decades after the event there are those occasions when something in you cries out at the continual presence of an absence. "An awful leisure," Emily Dickinson once called what the living had after death.

Sherwin Nuland, a doctor and professor at Yale, has become an unlikely best-selling author with a straightforward, unsparing, yet deeply human description of the end of life titled *How We Die*. In the introduction he explains that he has written the book "to demythologize the process of dying." But I wondered, reading on, if he was doing something else as well. He wrote, "My mother died of colon cancer one week after my eleventh birthday, and that fact has shaped my life. All that I have become and much that I have not become, I trace directly or indirectly to her death."

Loss as muse. Loss as character. Loss as life.

When the president talks of moving some days to the phone to call his mother, who died in January, he is breaking a silence about what so many have felt.

"The hard part is for those of us who've kept silent for decades to start talking about our losses," Hope Edelman writes in her new book, *Motherless Daughters.* Yet how second nature the silence becomes, so much a rule of etiquette that a fifteen-year-old knows when her loss is as raw as a freshly dug grave not to discomfit a stranger by revealing it in passing. All that she and her sister will become, and much they will not, will be traced later on to a time when spring has finally passed over the threshold of winter and the cemetery drives were edged with pink tulips, shivering slightly in a chilly April rain.

My brother and I know too much about their future; both teenagers when our mother died, we know that if the girls were to ask us, "When does it stop hurting?" we would have to answer, in all candor, "If it ever does, we will let you know."

The landscapes of all our lives become as full of craters as the surface of the moon. My brother is a young widower with young children, as his father was before him. And I write my obituaries carefully and think about how little the facts suffice, not only to describe the dead but to tell what they will mean to the living all the rest of our lives.

We are defined by whom we have lost.

"Don't let them forget me," Sherry said. Oh, hon, piece of cake.

❧

"The death of a parent requires us to ask yet again: Who am I? Who we are while our parents live is not, cannot be who we are once they are dead."

GRIEF

by

JULIUS LESTER

(1939–)

Julius Lester is a novelist who teaches at the University of Massachusetts in Amherst, Massachusetts. This essay was first delivered on National Public Radio's All Things Considered.

My father died in July of 1981. No event of my life before or since so totally destroyed me as that. I remember how empty the very universe felt and how surprised I was that my father had occupied that much space. I remember my despair that the vacuum his death created could never be filled. And there was my grief that I would never, ever again see the pride in his eyes for me, and I understood, slowly, that so much of what I had done in my life had been in the hope of evoking that pride.

Above all, I remember an incredible anger that my father had died. I was angry at him for dying, and what did it matter that he was eighty-four? He was my father and neither fathers nor mothers are supposed to die. I was also angry at myself. Deep down where unattended pain cries because it is being neglected, I was convinced my father died because I had not loved him enough. I hated myself for not loving with such purity that even Death would have retreated from the withering heat of my devotion.

However, if nature does not spite us, we know we will live to witness the deaths of our parents. We watch them age and find ourselves imagining their deaths and our lives in the world without them. Yet, when the time comes and we face that unending silence which death is, we understand it was impossible to prepare. There is no rehearsal that will make it easier to bear the loss of those who gave us life.

Unfortunately, we live in a culture which does not make space for grief. We live in a culture which does not permit us to acknowledge that grieving requires time and attention. When our personal universes are shattered, it requires patience and care to reconstruct them because that piece we called "mother" or "father" is no longer there. The death of a parent requires us to ask yet again: Who am I? Who we are while our parents live is not, cannot be who we are once they are dead.

I am sorry that President Clinton went from his mother's funeral to the summit meeting in Europe. I am sorry he will not give himself the necessary time and space to know how the loss of his mother will change his life. I am sorry he does not know that summit meetings come and go every five years, but the death of a mother is an event that happens only once, and it deserves to be honored and respected. I am sorry we do not live in a nation that would say to the president that we want him to take the time he needs to do the grieving he needs to do. He would be a better president if that could be so. But we are unable to tell ourselves and each other that it is all right to take the time to grieve. We would be better men and women if we did.

I am sorry that the president has to go through his days pretending as if nothing has happened, acting as if his life has not been changed in the most profound of ways. The death of his mother is not something he can "put behind him," as we Americans are fond of saying when tragedy strikes.

Grief ebbs but grief never ends. Death ends a life but death does not end a relationship. If we allow ourselves to be still and if we take responsibility for our grief, the grief becomes as polished and luminous and mysterious as death itself. When it does, we learn to love anew, not only the one who has died. We learn to love anew those who yet live.

⊙⟆⟆⟆⟆⊙

"[Mother's Day is] a day of appreciation and respect. I can think of no mothers who deserve it more than those who had to give a child back."

MOTHERS WHO HAVE LOST A CHILD

by

ERMA BOMBECK
(1927–1996)

Erma Bombeck was an American humorist whose widely read columns were both popular and profound. This Mother's Day column was one of the most often reprinted.

If you're looking for an answer this Mother's Day on why God reclaimed your child, I don't know. I only know that thousands of mothers out there today desperately need an answer as to why they were permitted to go through the elation of carrying a child and then lose it to miscarriage, accident, violence, disease, or drugs.

Motherhood isn't just a series of contractions. It's a state of mind. From the moment we know life is inside us, we feel a responsibility to protect and defend that human being. It's a promise we can't keep.

We beat ourselves to death over that pledge. "If I hadn't worked through the eighth month." "If I had taken him to the doctor when he had a fever." "If I hadn't let him use the car that night." "If I hadn't been so naive, I'd have known he was on drugs."

The longer I live, the more convinced I become that surviving changes us. After the bitterness, the anger, the guilt, and the despair are tempered by time, we look at life differently.

When I was writing my book *I Want to Grow Hair, I Want to Grow Up, I Want to Go to Boise,* I talked with mothers who had lost a child to cancer. Every single one said death gave their lives new meaning and purpose. And who do you think prepared them for the rough, lonely road they had to travel? Their dying child. They pointed their mothers toward the future and told them to keep going. The children had already accepted what their mothers were fighting to reject.

The children in the bombed-out nursery in Oklahoma City have touched more lives than they will ever know. Workers who had probably given their kids a mechanical pat on the head without thinking that morning are making calls home during the day to their children to say I love you.

This may seem like a strange Mother's Day column on a day when joy and life abound for the millions of mothers throughout the country. But it's also a day of appreciation and respect. I can think of no mothers who deserve it more than those who had to give a child back.

In the face of adversity we are not permitted to ask, "Why me?" You can ask but you won't get an answer. Maybe you are the instrument who is left behind to perpetuate the life that was lost and appreciate the time you had with it.

The late Gilda Radner summed it up well: "I wanted a perfect ending. Now I've learned the hard way that some poems don't rhyme and some stories don't have a clear beginning, middle, and end. Life is about not knowing, having to change, taking the moment and making the best of it without knowing what is going to happen next. Delicious ambiguity."

"The one thing that should never be said when someone dies is 'It is the will of God.' Never do we know enough to say that."

ALEX'S DEATH

by

REV. WILLIAM SLOANE COFFIN
(1924–)

Rev. William Sloane Coffin, former chaplain at Williams College and Yale University, is a prominent activist for social justice. Ten days after his son Alex died in a car accident, he delivered this sermon before his congregation at Riverside Church in New York City.

As almost all of you know, a week ago last Monday night, driving in a terrible storm, my son Alexander—who to his friends was a real day-brightener, and to his family "fair as a star when only one is shining in the sky"—my twenty-four-year-old Alexander, who enjoyed beating his old man at every game and in every race, beat his father to the grave.

Among the healing flood of letters that followed his death was one carrying this wonderful quote from the end of Hemingway's *Farewell to Arms*: "The world breaks everyone, then some become strong at the broken places." My own broken heart is mending, and largely thanks to so many of you, my dear parishioners; for if in the last week I have relearned one lesson, it is that love not only begets love, it transmits strength.

When a person dies, there are many things that can be said, and there is at least one thing that should never be said. The night after Alex died I was sitting in the living room of my sister's house outside of Boston, when the front door opened and in came a nice-looking middle-aged woman, carrying about eighteen quiches. When she saw me, she shook her head, then headed for the kitchen, saying sadly over her shoulder, "I just don't understand the will of God." Instantly I was up and in hot pursuit, swarming all over her. "I'll say you don't, lady!" I said.

For some reason, nothing so infuriates me as the incapacity of seemingly intelligent people to get it through their heads that God doesn't go around this world with his fingers on triggers, his fist around knives, his hands on steering wheels. God is dead set against all unnatural deaths. And Christ spent an inordinate amount of time delivering people from paralysis, insanity, leprosy, and muteness. Which is not to say that there are no nature-caused deaths—I can think of many right here in this parish in the five years I've been here—deaths that are untimely and slow and pain-ridden, which for that reason raise unanswerable questions, and even the specter of a Cosmic Sadist—yes, even an Eternal Vivisector. But violent deaths, such as the one Alex died—to understand those is a piece of cake. As his younger brother put it simply, standing at the head of the casket at the Boston funeral, "You blew it, buddy. You blew it." The one thing that should never be said when someone dies is "It is the will of God." Never do we know enough to say that. My own consolation lies in knowing that it was *not* the will of God that Alex die; that when the waves closed over the sinking car, God's heart was the first of all our hearts to break.

I mentioned the healing flood of letters. Some of the very best, and easily the worse, came from fellow reverends, a few of whom proved they knew their Bibles better than the human condition. I know all the "right" biblical passages, including "Blessed are those who mourn," and my faith is no house of cards; these passages are true, I know. But the point is this. While the words of the Bible are true, grief renders them unreal. The reality of grief is the absence of God— "My God, my God, why hast thou forsaken me?" The reality of grief is the solitude of pain, the feeling that your heart is in pieces, your mind's a blank, that "there is no joy the world can give like that it takes away" (Lord Byron).

That's why immediately after such a tragedy people must come to your rescue, people who only want to hold your hand, not to quote anybody or even say anything, people who simply bring food and flowers—the basics of beauty and life—people who sign letters simply, "Your brokenhearted sister." In other words, in my intense grief I felt some of my fellow reverends—not many, and none of you, thank God—were using comforting words of Scripture for self-protection, to pretty up a situation whose bleakness they simply couldn't face. But like God herself, Scripture is not around for anyone's protection, just for everyone's unending support.

And that's what hundreds of you understood so beautifully. You gave me what God gives all of us—minimum protection, maximum support. I swear to you, I wouldn't be standing here were I not upheld.

After the death of his wife, C. S. Lewis wrote, "They say 'the coward dies many times'; so does the beloved. Didn't the eagle find a fresh liver to tear in Prometheus every time it dined?"

When parents die, as did my mother last month, they take with them a large portion of the past. But when children die, they take away the future as well. That is what makes the valley of the shadow of death seem so incredibly dark and unending. In a prideful way it would be easier to walk the alley alone, nobly, head high, instead of—as we must—marching as the latest recruit in the world's army of the bereaved.

Still there is much by way of consolation. Because there are no rankling unanswered questions, and because Alex and I simply adored each other, the wound for me is deep, but clean. I know how lucky I am! I also know this day-brightener of a son wouldn't wish to be held close by grief (nor, for that matter, would any but the meanest of our beloved departed) and that, interestingly enough, when I mourn Alex least I see him best.

Another consolation, of course, will be the learning—which better be good, given the price. But it's a fact: few of us are naturally profound. We have to be forced down. So while trite, it's true:

> *I walked a mile with Pleasure,*
> *She chattered all the way;*
> *But left me none the wiser*
> *For all she had to say.*
>
> *I walked a mile with Sorrow*
> *And ne'er a word said she;*
> *But oh, the things I learned from her*
> *When sorrow walked with me.*
> —ROBERT BROWNING HAMILTON

Or, in Emily Dickinson's verse:

By a departing light
We see acuter quite
Than by a wick that stays.
There's something in the flight
That clarifies the sight
And decks the rays.

And of course I know, even when pain is deep, that God is good. "My God, my God, why hast thou forsaken me?" Yes, but at least, "My God, my God"; and the psalm only begins that way, it doesn't end that way. As the grief that once seemed unbearable begins to turn now to bearable sorrow, the truths in the "right" biblical passages are beginning, once again, to take hold: "Cast thy burden upon the Lord and He shall strengthen thee"; "Weeping may endure for the night but joy cometh in the morning"; "Lord, by thy favor thou hast made my mountain to stand strong"; "For thou hast delivered my soul from death, mine eyes from tears, and my feet from falling"; "In this world ye shall have tribulation, but be of good cheer; I have overcome the world"; "The light shines in the darkness, and the darkness has not overcome it."

And finally I know that when Alex beat me to the grave, the finish line was not Boston Harbor in the middle of the night. If a week ago last Monday, a lamp went out, it was because, for him at least, the Dawn had come.

So I shall—so let us all—seek consolation in that love which never dies, and find peace in the dazzling grace that always is.

CHAPTER SIXTEEN

LETTERS OF CONDOLENCE

⊙∭⊙

"One friend must in time lose the other."

Letter of Dr. Samuel Johnson (1709–1784) to the mother of a friend.

Dear Madam,

The grief which I feel for the loss of a very kind friend is sufficient to make me know how much you suffer by the death of an amiable son: a man, of whom I think it may be truly said, that no one knew him who does not lament him. I look upon myself as having a friend, another friend, taken from me.

Comfort, Dear Madam, I would give you, if I could; but I know how little the forms of consolation can avail. Let me, however, counsel you not to waste your health in unprofitable sorrow, but go to Bath, and endeavour to prolong your own life; but when we have all done all that we can, one friend must in time lose the other.

> I am, Dear Madam,
> Your most humble servant,
> Samuel Johnson

⊙∭⊙

"It is the will of God and nature, that these mortal bodies be laid aside, when the soul is to enter into real life. This is rather an embryo state, a preparation for living."

Letter of Benjamin Franklin (1706–1790) to Miss E. Hubbard, stepdaughter of Franklin's brother, John, on the occasion of his death.

February 23, 1756
Philadelphia

I condole with you. We have lost a most dear and valuable relation. But it is the will of God and nature, that these mortal bodies be laid aside, when the soul is to enter into real life. This is rather an embryo state, a preparation for living.

A man is not completely born until he is dead. Why then should we grieve, that a new child is born among the immortals, a new member added to their happy society? We are spirits. That bodies should be lent to us, while they can afford us pleasure, assist us in acquiring knowledge, or in doing good to our fellow creatures, is a kind and benevolent act of God. When they become unfit for these purposes, and afford us pain instead of pleasure, instead of an aid become an encumbrance, and answer none of the intentions for which they were given, it is equally kind and benevolent, that a way is provided by which we may get rid of them. Death is that way. We ourselves in some cases, prudently choose a partial death. A mangled painful limb, which cannot be restored, we willingly cut off. He who plucks out a tooth, parts with it freely, since the pain goes with it; and he, who quits the whole body, parts at once with all pains and possibilities of pains and diseases which it was liable to, or capable of making him suffer.

Our friend and we were invited abroad on a party of pleasure, which is to last forever. His chair was ready first, and he is gone before us. We could not all conveniently start together, and why should you and I be grieved at this, since we are soon to follow and know where to find him?

Adieu,
B. Franklin

❧

"Thirteen years ago I lost a brother, and with his spirit I converse daily and hourly in the spirit. . . ."

William Blake (1757–1827) to William Hayley on the death of his son.

Dear Sir,

I am very sorry for your immense loss, which is a repetition of what all feel in this valley of misery and happiness mixed. . . . I know that our deceased friends are more really with us than when they were apparent to our mortal part. Thirteen years ago I lost a brother, and with his spirit I converse daily and hourly in the spirit and see him in my remembrance, in the regions of my imagination. I hear his advice, and even now write from his dictate. Forgive me for expressing to you my enthusiasm, which I wish all to partake of, since it is to be a source of immortal joy, even in this world. By it I am the companion of the angels. May you continue to be so more and more; and to be more and more persuaded that every mortal loss is an immortal gain. The ruins of Time build mansions in Eternity.

☙

"It is strange, almost awful, that, when this great miracle has been performed for us, Nature gives no sign . . . yet perhaps a minute before the most immediate presence of God which we can conceive was filling the whole chamber. . . ."

Letter from American poet, critic, and editor of the Atlantic Monthly *James Russell Lowell (1819–1891) to Charles F. Briggs on the death of his little daughter, Blanche.*

20 August 1844.

My dear Friend—I did not get your letter of the 19th until yesterday, or you may be sure that I should have written sooner to assure you (if words are needful) of my fullest and tenderest sympathy. Maria sends hers also, and there are tears in the eyes of both of us.

I agree entirely with what you have said of Death in your last letter; but at the same time I know well that the first touch of his hand is cold, and that he comes to us, as the rest of God's angels do, in disguise. But we are enabled to see his face fully at last, and it is that of a seraph. So it is with all. Disease, poverty, death, sorrow, all come to us with unbenign countenances, but from one after another the mask falls off, and we behold faces which retain the glory and the calm of having looked in the face of God. To me, at least, your bereavement has come with softest step, and the most hallowed features, for it has opened a new channel for my love to flow toward you in. . . . The older I grow, the less am I affected by the outward observances and forms of religion, and the more confidingness and affection do I feel toward God. "He leadeth me in green pastures." Trust in Providence is no longer a meaningless phrase to me. The thought of it has oftener brought happy tears into my eyes than any other thought except that of my beloved Maria. It is therefore no idle form when I tell you to lean on God. I know that it is needless to say this to you, but I know also that it is always sweet and consoling to have our impulses seconded by the sympathy of our friends.

I could not restrain my tears when I read what you say of the living things all around the cast mantle of your child. It is strange, almost awful, that, when this great miracle has been performed for us, Nature gives no sign. Not a bee stints his hum, the sun shines, the leaves glisten, the cock-crow comes from the distance, the flies buzz into the room, and yet perhaps a minute before the most immediate presence of God which we can conceive was filling the whole chamber, and opening its arms to "suffer the little one to come unto Him."

God bless you a thousand times and comfort you, for He only can. I know not what I can say to your wife.

> Most lovingly yours,
> J.R.L. and M.W.
> I shall write again soon.

༄

"When not inconvenient to your heart, please remember us, and let us help you carry it, if you grow tired."

Letter from poet Emily Dickinson (1830–1886) to a friend.

Dear Friend, —Your touching suggestion . . . is a tender permission. . . .

We cannot believe for each other—thought is too sacred a despot, but I hope that God, in whatever form, is true to our friend. . . . Consciousness is the only home of which we *now* know. That sunny adverb had been enough, were it not foreclosed.

When not inconvenient to your heart, please remember us, and let us help you carry it, if you grow tired. Though we are each unknown to ourself and each other, 'tis not what well conferred it, the dying soldier asks, it is only the water.

> *We knew not that we were to live,*
> *Nor when we are to die*
> *Our ignorance our cuirass is;*
> *We wear mortality*
> *As lightly as an option gown*
> *Till asked to take it off.*
> *By His intrusion God is known—*
> *It is the same with life.*

Emily

⌒⟁⟁⟁⊃

"In this sad world of ours, sorrow comes to all; and, to the young, it comes with the bitterest agony, because it takes them unawares. The older have learned to ever expect it."

Letter of Abraham Lincoln to Miss Fanny McCullough on the death of her father.

EXECUTIVE MANSION
Washington, December 23, 1862.

Dear Fanny,

It is with deep grief that I learn of the death of your kind and brave Father; and, especially, that it is affecting your young heart beyond what is common in such cases. In this sad world of ours, sorrow comes to all; and, to the young, it comes with the bitterest agony, because it takes them unawares. The older have learned to ever expect it. I am anxious to afford some alleviation of your present distress. Perfect relief is not possible, except with time. You can not now realize that you will ever feel better. Is not this so? And yet it is a mistake. You are sure to be happy again. To know this, which is certainly true, will make you some less miserable now. I have experienced enough to know what I say; and you need only to believe it, to feel better at once. The memory of your dear Father, instead of an agony, will yet be a sad sweet feeling in your heart, of a purer, and holier sort than you have known before.

Please present my kind regards to your afflicted Mother.

Your sincere friend,
A. LINCOLN

※

"I have been so long waiting for death; I have unwrapped my thoughts from about life for so long, that I have not a filament left to hold by. . . ."

Letter of Robert Louis Stevenson (1850–1894) to his friend Charles Baxter on the death of his father. Within three months, Stevenson himself was dead.

Valima, September 1894

My dear Charles,

Well, there is no more Edmund Baxter now; and I think I may say I know how you feel. He was one of the best, the kindest and the most genial men I ever knew. I shall always remember his brisk, cordial ways and the essential goodness which he showed me whenever we met with gratitude. . . . He is another of the landmarks gone; and when it comes to my own turn to lay my weapons down, I shall do so with thankfulness and fatigue; and whatever may be my destiny afterwards, I shall be glad to lie down with my fathers in honour. It is human at least, if not divine. And these deaths make me think of it with an ever greater readiness. Strange that you should be beginning a new life when I who am a little your junior am thinking of the end of mine. But I have had hard lines; I have been so long waiting for death; I have unwrapped my thoughts from about life for so long, that I have not a filament left to hold by; I have done my fiddling so long under Vesuvius, that I have almost forgotten to play, and can only wait for the eruption, and think it long of coming. Literally no man has more wholly outlived life than I. And still it's good fun.

※

"Death is not unfriendly to the aged . . . the unfriendly thing is bereavement, the sharpest of privations."

Letter from Ambrose Bierce (1842–1914?) to his friend Lella Cotton on the death of her father.

April 14, 1904

My Dear Lella,

Your good father did, as you say, "live out his life." Death being as natural a thing as birth, is no evil when it comes after "length of days"—if it ever is. I do not know that it ever is. But of course we take counsel in this matter, not of our heads but of our hearts; and I know your heart is sore. Would that I could make its pain less. And poor Cottie—she is indeed bereft. But she too must soon be at rest, and I know that is to her a sweet and consoling thought. She must be sleepy for death; may it come to her as to one who "lies down with pleasant dreams."

I am enough older than you, my comrade, to know, better than you, that death is not unfriendly to the aged. I could myself meet it with a smile. No, the unfriendly thing is bereavement, the sharpest of privations. May you bear yours, now and hereafter, better than I have always borne mine, as is becoming to your better heart and disposition.

Please say to dear Cottie that she has my deep sympathy in her great loss.

God bless and comfort you both.

Ambrose Bierce

ᏳᏣᏍᎧ

"You have lost a father. Shall I dare tell you of the desolation of an old man who has lost a friend . . . ?"

From American novelist, critic, and editor William Dean Howells (1837–1920) to Clara Clemens on the death of her father, Mark Twain.

April 22, 1910

My dear Clara,

I found Mr. Paine's telegram when I came in late last night; and suddenly your father was set apart from all other men in a strange

majesty. Death had touched his familiar image into historic grandeur.

You have lost a father. Shall I dare tell you of the desolation of an
old man who has lost a friend, and finds himself alone in the great
world which has now wholly perished around?

We all join in sending you our helpless love.

Yours affectionately,
W. D. Howells

❦

"Because of them, I am ready to say 'Take it' more easily than before."

*Letter of British teacher and critic Sir Walter Raleigh (1861–1922) to Lady
Desborough, who lost two sons in World War I.*

Oxford, August 5, 1915

I know the ordinary consolations; they do not seem to me to be quite
real. But there is something quite real and consoling, if human nature
could take it without ceasing to be human; we cannot work it out,
that's all. But we couldn't do without Julian's life and Billy's. They are
not gone, we breathe them, they are the temper of the British Army at
its best. It would not matter even if they were not remembered, they
passed on the flame undimmed. The great things seem cold, but
they are there all the time, and Julian and Billy believed in them, and
had splendid lives. Anyhow, they have made life the little thing it is.
Because of them, I am ready to say "Take it" more easily than before.
What must it be for the people they fought alongside of? . . .

I go limping along. . . . And I am glad to have met and known such
soldiers.

(Walter Raleigh)

❦

**"It is not his business to say nice things about it, but to shout that
the 'voice of thy son's blood crieth unto God from the ground.' "**

*Letter of playwright George Bernard Shaw (1856–1950) to Mrs. Patrick
Campbell on the death of her son, killed in action in World War I.*

London, 7 January 1918.

Never saw it or heard about it until your letter came. It is no use: I can't be sympathetic; these things simply make me furious. I want to swear. I *do* swear. Killed just because people are blasted fools. A chaplain too, to say nice things about it. It is not his business to say nice things about it, but to shout that the "voice of thy son's blood crieth unto God from the ground."

No, don't show me the letter. But I should very much like to have a nice talk with that dear Chaplain, that sweet sky-pilot, that . . .

No use going on like this, Stella. Wait for a week, and then I shall be very clever and broadminded again and have forgotten all about this. I shall be quite as nice as the Chaplain.

Oh, damn, damn, damn, damn, damn, damn, damn, damn, DAMN.

And oh, dear, dear, dear, dear, dear, dearest!

G.B.S.

"There is a very great thing gone from my reach. [He] was the most honourable stopping place I've ever found. . . ."

Letter of T. E. Shaw (Lawrence of Arabia, 1888–1935) to the widow of novelist Thomas Hardy.

16.2.28

Dear Mrs. Hardy:

I'm afraid I wrote you a very poor letter, the day I heard that T.H. was gone. But just then the news struck me almost as a triumph. He had kept it up to the very end: and was through with an existence he had not highly valued. . . .

I've been reading *The Dynasts,* and I can feel that there is a very great thing gone from my reach. T.H. was the most honourable stopping place I've ever found, and I shall miss him more and more. I wonder if you will be like that: or if time will make the being alone easier for you. . . .

The biography is a very difficult thing. They will trouble you very much about that. Do not let these troubles go in too far. What he told you . . . that he'd done all he meant to do, absolves you from indefinite toil. He will defend himself, very very completely, when people listen to him again. As you know, there will be a wave of detraction, and none of the highbrows will defend him, for quite a long time: and then the bright young critics will rediscover him, & it will be lawful for a person in the know to speak well of him: and all this nonsense will enrage me, because I'm small enough to care. Whereas all that's needful is to forget the fuss for fifty years, and then wake up and see him no longer a battle-field, but part of the ordinary man's heritage.

Please do not answer all this: it's just me talking to you, as I used to do in Max Gate, while we waited for him to come down. I wish I hadn't gone overseas: I was afraid, that last time, that it was the last.

Yours sincerely,
T. E. SHAW

⁂

"All our affections, when clear and pure, and not claims to possession, transport us to another world; and the loss of contact, here or there, with those external beings is merely like closing a book which we keep at hand for another occasion. We know that book by heart. Its verses give life to life."

The following is excerpted from a letter the philosopher-poet George Santayana (1863–1952) wrote to his friend the Marchesa Iris Origo, whose only child had recently died.

May 1933
. . . We have no claim to any of our possessions. We have no claim to exist; and as we have to die in the end, so we must resign ourselves to die piecemeal, which really happens when we lose somebody or something that was closely intertwined with our existence. It is like a physical wound; we may survive, but maimed and broken in that direction; dead there.

Not that we ever can, or ever do at heart, renounce our affections. Never that. We cannot exercise our full nature all at once in every direction; but the parts that are relatively in abeyance, their center lying perhaps in the past or in the future, belong to us inalienably. We should not be ourselves if we cancelled them. I don't know how literally you may believe in another world, or whether the idea means very much to you. As you know, I am not myself a believer in the ordinary sense, yet my *feeling* on this subject is like that of believers, and not at all like that of my fellow-materialists. The reason is that I disagree utterly with that modern philosophy which regards *experience* as fundamental. Experience is a mere whiff or rumble, produced by enormously complex and ill-deciphered causes of experience; and in the other direction, experience is a mere peephole through which glimpses come down to us of eternal things. These are the only things that, in so far as we are spiritual beings, we can find or can love at all. All our affections, when clear and pure, and not claims to possession, transport us to another world; and the loss of contact, here or there, with those external beings is merely like closing a book which we keep at hand for another occasion. We know that book by heart. Its verses give life to life.

I don't mean that these abstract considerations ought to console us. Why wish to be consoled? On the contrary, I wish to mourn perpetually the absence of what I love or might love. Isn't that what religious people call the love of God?

⚮

"The golden bowl is broken indeed but it *was* golden. . . ."

From novelist F. Scott Fitzgerald (1896–1940) to his close friends Gerald and Sara Murphy, who had just lost the second of their three children within two years.

January 31, 1937

Dearest Gerald and Sara,

The telegram came today and the whole afternoon was so sad with thoughts of you and the happy times we had once. Another link binding you to life is broken and with such insensate cruelty that it is hard to say which of the two blows was conceived with more malice. I can see the silence in which you hover now after this seven years of struggle and it would take words like Lincoln's in his letter to the mother who had lost four sons in the war to write you anything fitting at the moment. The sympathy you will get will be what you have had from each other already and for a long, long time you will be inconsolable.

But I can see another generation growing up around Honoria and an eventual peace somewhere, an occasional port of call as we all sail deathward. Fate can't have any more arrows in its quiver for you that will wound like these. Who was it said that it was astounding how deepest griefs can change in time to a sort of joy? The golden bowl is broken indeed but it *was* golden; nothing can ever take those boys away from you now.

Scott

⊙ｍｍℭ

"Our task must be to free ourselves from this prison by widening our circle of compassion. . . ."

The following is from a letter Albert Einstein (1879–1955) wrote to the father of a nineteen-year-old girl who had lost her beloved younger sister and wanted to know what a scientist could tell her to comfort her, as she was not able to find solace in traditional religious concepts.

March 4, 1950

A human being is part of the whole, called by us "Universe," a part limited in time and space. He experiences himself, his thoughts and feelings as something separated from the rest—a kind of optical delusion of his consciousness. This delusion is a kind of prison for us, restricting us to our personal desires and affection for a few persons nearest to us. Our task must be to free ourselves from this prison by widening our circle of compassion to embrace all living creatures and the whole nature in its beauty. Nobody is able to achieve this completely but the striving for such achievement is in itself a part of the liberation and a foundation for inner security.

⊙ｍｍℭ

"Since he had to die at least he has gotten it over with."

Letter of Ernest Hemingway (1899–1961) to Charles Scribner Jr. on the death of his father, Charles Scribner Sr.

1952

I won't try to write to you how much he meant to me as a friend and as a publisher. He was the best and closest friend that I had and it seems impossible that I will never have another letter from him. It does not do any good to talk about it and there is nothing to say that makes it any easier. Since he had to die at least he has gotten it over with.

If there is anything practical I can do please let me know. . . . I will try and not worry you about finances nor about anything else. You don't have to write me letters nor have me on your mind in any way. I know what a terribly tough job you have now with Navy, Estate and the House of Scribner to look after. They shouldn't do that to any human being. Please take it as easy as you can and feel free to call on me in any way that I can be of help. . . . This is not a good letter, Charlie. But I still feel too sad to write a good one.

> Your friend,
> Ernest Hemingway

The Lord hath laid trials after trials on thee—as your fathers would have said. But don't think of your predicament on those terms.

From a letter of writer Thornton Wilder (1897–1975) to Robert Hutchins.

Ca. 1960

The Lord hath laid trials after trials on thee—as your fathers would have said. But don't think of your predicament on those terms. I— and Goethe—acknowledge a God but we don't anthropomorphize him. We call him "die Natur" and we know He, She, It embraces this vast process and has fashioned it with a million marvelous smaller processes which betray an intense concern for how the whole thing works—a concern that much resembles love. All Nature strives to bring every detail to its truest expression of its function. All Nature is working *for* you. Rise above immediate things and feel that, get-a-holt of that. Float in the teleological tide.

"God paints the picture in the frost, and the sun melts it away. Yet the picture had purpose and fulfilled its mission."

In Brother to a Dragon Fly, *about his mentally ill brother, Joseph, author Will Campbell writes of a Rabbi Schlager, who came to his brother's house the day after he had died and handed Joseph's wife, Josephine, a letter. She wept because she knew that her husband had been so rude to the rabbi, calling him terrible anti-Semitic names. Campbell remembered that as his brother got sicker, he did rave and rant about the Jews. "It was," he wrote, "out of character, like a cancer fighting with every benign cell around it for its own destructive survival. I didn't take it seriously. Apparently neither had the rabbi."*

From Rabbi Schlager's letter:

Through the valley of tears, let us search for light, for some word. Where else shall it be? It will be in the source of all solace—in Sacred Scripture! . . . "I am Joseph your brother" (Gen. 45:4). He represented many things to many people; but above all, with his genial personality and the generous instincts of a Christian and a gentleman, it was easy for him to build himself into the hearts of all who knew him. He lived in deeds, not years; in feelings, not figures upon the dial. He counted time by heart throbs, practicing daily his spiritual exercises. I saw daily that exercise of his heart—his reaching down and lifting someone up. I heard that heart pound with empathy toward all peoples and causes. Even in death he teaches us, reminds and points us to the enduring values that transcend it; showing the indestructibility of the human spirit, the urgency which the limitations of life's span impose on its travelers.

God paints the picture in the frost, and the sun melts it away. Yet the picture had purpose and fulfilled its mission. "I am Joseph your brother." He said it often to me. He was with us too short a while. But this mission is fulfilled. Might nature rise now and announce to the world, "This was a man, a brother, a friend, a valiant spirit." And might the still small voice echo in refrain, "I am Joseph your brother."

❦

"Why is it that so often there is a wonderful smile on the face of the one who has just passed away (?)"

Letter of writer Henry Miller (1891–1980) to a friend.

October 12th, '65

Dear friend—

Nobody knows anything about death. I like to believe that we do come back again and again until we have nothing more to learn. But I have no proof that this is the case. The fear of death is more the fear of dying, I think. We want to live forever. We are afraid of the unknown. Yet we came from the unknown. All is mystery—and the best we can do is to accept it. "Where were you when I laid the foundations of the earth," said the Lord to Job.

If there were no pain involved perhaps dying would be much easier. But why is it that so often there is a wonderful smile on the face of the one who has just passed away (?) Did he see glorious visions at the last moment? Did he realize that at last he had found peace? We do not know. But we can hope and dream and believe.

Ever yours,
Henry Miller

⌒〰〰〰〇

"You, the one who didn't die, change, enlarge your nature so that there is room for them too...."

Letter from New Yorker *editor in chief William Maxwell (1908–) to Faith Morrow Williams on the death of her brother, Stephen, in 1987.*

Dear Faith,

If you love someone with your whole heart it is unbearable to have them die. And because you can't bear it, you don't let it happen. Without even thinking about it you, the one who didn't die, change, enlarge your nature so that there is room for them too, and they go on living in you and through you. It is something I have experienced.

Love,
Bill

⌒〰〰〰〇

"When your dear one came to us from the night . . ."

On the night of December 21, 1988, the body of Frank Ciulla was found on the farm of the Connell family. Frank Ciulla was one of the 270 passengers who perished on Pan Am 103, which was blown apart by a terrorist explosion thirty-one thousand feet above the village of Lockerbie, Scotland. His daughters, Laurie Ann and Michelle Ciulla, read the letter they received from the Connells at the dedication of the Pan Am 103 Memorial Cairn at Arlington National Cemetery on November 3, 1995. Their introductory remarks and the letter follow.

Until the spring of 1992, my family and I knew almost nothing about my father's final hours. Like many of you, we tried not to concern ourselves with the details. But like many of you, we did. It mattered to us who the people were who found my dad. It mattered to us who took care of him, after his death. He mattered to us and no other justification was necessary.

I am not sure how it happened, but somehow in the spring of '92 our questions were answered. Somehow, by luck or by fate, we were told about the Connells, who own Minsca Farm in Waterbeck, Scotland, eight miles out of Lockerbie. The Connells had the answers we were looking for.

We traveled to Scotland for the first time in the summer of that same year and found there a human kindness we had begun to doubt still existed. Since today, above all, is about the ties that bind, we would like to share with you a letter we received from our dear friends, the Connells, shortly after our journey.

My Dears, Mary Lou and family,

I can hardly believe that I am writing to you. This is something that I had longed to do since 21st December, 1988. When your dear one came to us from the night, it was so unbelievable, haunting and desperately sad. You said that your visit altered the picture for you in many ways; this is just how it was for us too. Frank was a young man with a name but connected to nobody. Now at last we can match him with a loving family. Sometimes I would stop to think as the months went past, "I wonder how his loved ones are coping now, I wonder what they are doing?"

We were told maybe some of the relatives will never come; we were afraid that you'd come and not want to get in touch. . . . I was so thankful that you made the effort to come and ask all the questions you had always wanted to ask. You had at last found someone who could fill in those last hours, that piece that had always remained a mystery. It's the "not knowing" that can bring so much pain and bewilderment. We all have imaginations that can run riot in us, and I'm sure your dear souls must have had untold agonies wondering and worrying.

It was just wonderful to meet you face-to-face. We needed to talk to you all too. As you said, we will get to know Frank through you. He was never just "another victim" to us. For months we called him "Our Boy." Then we found out his name. He was "Our Frank." Please believe me we were deeply affected by his coming to us. We will never forget our feelings seeing him there, a whole-bodied handsome man, the life gone out of him in a twinkling. We were just past trying to grasp the whole thing.

Then to have to leave him there, but he was visited throughout the night by police and a doctor and we went back again in the morning. . . . He was a fellow man and he had come to us in the saddest way. So now through him we have you in our hearts, and please, we want you all to know that you are welcome here whenever you can come.

The Connell Family

⟢∞⟣

"You can always count on me and on this love."

The following letter was written by Robert Williams (1970–1995) to his mother, Martha, after his younger brother, Matthew (1972–1989), had been killed in an automobile accident when he was seventeen. Four years later, Robert was killed the same way. His own letter was read at his funeral.

11/18/91

Mom,

I have just been sitting here thinking about Matt and feeling very sad. But I also thought of what you were saying about being so busy when Matt was here and this just made me want to express my appreciation and feelings for you. I am here in this world and I love you as deeply as I know love. Whatever happens through the course of our lifetimes or if you are feeling deeply lonely, you can always count on me and on this love.

From my heart & soul,
Robert

☙

"But since there is always a light,
I'll be with you."

The following letter, in the form of a poem, was written by Katherine Sprinkel, when she was thirteen, to her seventy-seven-year-old former baby-sitter, Louise Burnett, after her niece died.

Dear Louise,

I just wanted you to know
That through all these times,
I'll think about you,
And I'll be with you.

Death may seize many around us
And so darkness seems to surround us,
But since there is always a light,
I'll be with you.

As everyone seems to fade away,
We cherish those who are with us,
For fear we'll be the only one left,
But I'll always be with you.

I just wanted you to know,
That through all these times,
I'll think about you,
And I'll be with you.

☙

CHAPTER SEVENTEEN

POETRY

⌒〰〰⌒

AFTER GREAT PAIN,
A FORMAL FEELING COMES

by

EMILY DICKINSON
(1830–1886)

After great pain, a formal feeling comes—
The Nerves sit ceremonious, like Tombs—
The stiff Heart questions was it He, that bore,
And Yesterday, or Centuries before?

The Feet, mechanical, go round—
Of Ground, or Air, or Ought—
A Wooden way,
Regardless grown,
A Quartz contentment, like a stone—

This is the Hour of Lead—
Remembered, if outlived,
As Freezing persons, recollect the Snow—
First—Chill—then Stupor—then the letting go—

⌒〰〰⌒

"About suffering they were never wrong. . . ."

MUSÉE DES BEAUX ARTS

by

WYSTAN HUGH AUDEN
(1907–1973)

About suffering they were never wrong,
The Old Masters; how well they understood
Its human position; how it takes place
While someone else is eating or opening a window or just walking dully
    along;
How, when the aged are reverently, passionately waiting
For the miraculous birth, there always must be
Children who did not specially want it to happen, skating
On a pond at the edge of the wood:
They never forgot
That even the dreadful martyrdom must run its course
Anyhow in a corner, some untidy spot
Where the dogs go on with their doggy life and the torturer's horse
Scratches its innocent behind on a tree.

In Brueghel's Icarus, *for instance: how everything turns away*
Quite leisurely from the disaster; the ploughman may
Have heard the splash, the forsaken cry,
But for him it was not an important failure; the sun shone
As it had to on the white legs disappearing into the green
Water; and the expensive delicate ship that must have seen
Something amazing, a boy falling out of the sky,
Had somewhere to get to and sailed calmly on.

"Crowned/with lilies and with laurel they go; but I am not resigned."

DIRGE WITHOUT MUSIC

by

EDNA ST. VINCENT MILLAY
(1892–1950)

I am not resigned to the shutting away of loving hearts in the
*   hard ground.*
So it is, and so it will be, for so it has been, time out of
*   mind:*
Into the darkness they go, the wise and the lovely. Crowned
With lilies and with laurel they go; but I am not resigned.

Lovers and thinkers, into the earth with you.
Be one with the dull, the indiscriminate dust.
A fragment of what you felt, of what you knew,
A formula, a phrase remains,—but the best is lost.

The answers quick and keen, the honest look, the laughter,
*   the love,—*
They are gone. They are gone to feed the roses. Elegant and
*   curled*
Is the blossom. Fragrant is the blossom. I know. But I do
*   not approve.*
More precious was the light in your eyes than all the roses
*   in the world.*

Down, down, down into the darkness of the grave
Gently they go, the beautiful, the tender, the kind;
Quietly they go, the intelligent, the witty, the brave.
I know. But I do not approve. And I am not resigned.

༄

"There is nothing left remarkable/Beneath the visiting moon."

FROM *ANTONY AND CLEOPATRA*

by

WILLIAM SHAKESPEARE
(1564–1616)

O, withered is the garland of the war,
The soldier's pole is fallen: young boys and girls
Are level now with men: the odds is gone,
And there is nothing left remarkable
Beneath the visiting moon.

൜

"Here doth lye/Ben Jonson his best piece of poetrie."

ON MY FIRST SONNE

by

BEN JONSON
(1572–1637)

Farewell, thou child of my right hand, and joy;
My sinne was too much hope of thee, lov'd boy,
Seven yeeres tho' wert lent to me, and I thee pay,
Exacted by thy fate, on the just day.

O, could I lose all father, now! For why
Will man lament the state he should envie?
To have so soone scap'd worlds, and fleshes rage,
And, if no other miserie, yet age?
Rest in soft peace, and, ask'd, say here doth lye
Ben Jonson his best piece of poetrie.
For whose sake, hence-forth, all his vowes be such
As what he loves may never like too much.

൜

"Underneath this stone doth lie
As much beauty as could die. . . ."

EPITAPH ON ELIZABETH L. H.

by

BEN JONSON
(1572–1637)

WOULDS'T thou hear what man can say
In a little? Reader, stay.

Underneath this stone doth lie
As much beauty as could die:
Which in life did harbour give
To more virtue than doth live.
If at all she had a fault,
Leave it buried in this vault.
One name was ELIZABETH,
The other, let it sleep with death:
Fitter, when it died, to tell,
Than that it lived at all. Farewell!

⟨∞⟩

"A violet by a mossy stone
Half hidden from the eye!"

SHE DWELT AMONG THE UNTRODDEN WAYS

by

WILLIAM WORDSWORTH
(1770–1850)

She dwelt among the untrodden ways
Beside the springs of Dove;
A maid whom there were none to praise,
And very few to love.

371

A violet by a mossy stone
Half hidden from the eye!
—Fair as a star, when only one
Is shining in the sky.

She lived unknown, and few could know
When Lucy ceased to be;
But she is in her grave, and O!
The difference to me.

꘎

"But O for the touch of a vanished hand. . . ."

BREAK, BREAK, BREAK

by

ALFRED, LORD TENNYSON
(1809–1892)

Break, break, break,
On thy cold grey stones, O Sea!
And I would that my tongue could utter
The thoughts that arise in me.

O well for the fisherman's boy,
That he shouts with his sister at play!
O well for the sailor lad,
That he sings in his boat on the bay!

And the stately ships on go
To their haven under the hill;
But O for the touch of a vanished hand,
And the sound of a voice that is still!

Break, break, break,
At the foot of thy crags, O Sea!
But the tender grace of a day that is dead
Will never come back to me.

꘎

"Though wise men at their end know dark is right. . ."

DO NOT GO GENTLE
INTO THAT GOOD NIGHT

by

DYLAN THOMAS
(1914–1953)

Do not go gentle into that good night,
Old age should burn and rave at close of day;
Rage, rage against the dying of the light.

Though wise men at their end know dark is right,
Because their words had forked no lightning they
Do not go gentle into that good night.

Good men, the last wave by, crying how bright
Their frail deeds might have danced in a green bay
Rage, rage against the dying of the light.

Wild men who caught and sang the sun in flight,
And learn, too late, they grieved it on its way,
Do not go gentle into that good night.

Grave men, near death, who see with blinding sight
Blind eyes could blaze like meteors and be gay,
Rage, rage against the dying of the light.

And you, my father, there on the sad height,
Curse, bless, me now with your fierce tears, I pray.
Do not go gentle into that good night.
Rage, rage against the dying of the light.

☙

"Where we live in the world
Is never one place."

MY GRANDMOTHER
IN THE STARS

by

NAOMI SHIHAB NYE
(1952–)

It is possible we will not meet again
on earth. To think this fills my throat
with dust. Then there is only the sky
tying the universe together.

Just now the neighbor's horse must be standing
Patiently, hoof on stone, waiting for his day
To open. What you think of him,
And the village's one heroic cow,
is the knowledge I wish to gather.
I bow to your rugged feet,
The moth-eaten scarves that knot your hair.

Where we live in the world
Is never one place. Our hearts,
those dogged mirrors, keep flashing us
moons before we are ready for them.
You and I on a roof at sunset,
Our two languages adrift,
Hearts saying, Take this home with you,
never again,
and only memory making us rich.

༄

"She who now bestows and now denies/Hath taken thee. . ."

CATULLUS' ODE TO HIS BROTHER
(CA. 84–CA. 54 B.C.)

By ways remote and distant waters sped,
Brother, to thy sad grave-side am I come,
That I may give the last gifts to the dead
And vainly parley with thine ashes dumb;
Since she who now bestows and now denies
Hath taken thee, hapless brother, from mine eyes.

But lo! these gifts, the heirlooms of past years,
Are made sad things to grace thy coffin—shell,
Take them, all drenched with a brother's tears,
And, brother, for all time, hail and farewell.

ᏻᎷᎭᎧ

"In my sorrows lay your head. . . ."

SWEET BROTHER, IF I DO NOT SLEEP

by

THOMAS MERTON
(1915–1968)

Sweet brother, if I do not sleep
My eyes are flowers for your tomb;
And if I cannot eat my bread,
My fasts shall live like willows where you died.
If in the heat I find no water for my thirst,
My thirst shall turn to springs for you, poor traveller.

Where, in what desolate and smokey country,
Lies your poor body, lost and dead?
And in what landscape of disaster
Had your unhappy spirit lost its road?

Come, in my labor find a resting place
And in my sorrows lay your head,
Or rather take my life and blood
And buy yourself a better bed—
Or take my breath and take my death
And buy yourself a better death.

When all the men of war are shot
And flags have fallen into dust,
Your cross and mine shall tell men still
Christ died on each, for both of us.

For in the wreckage of your April Christ lies slain,
And Christ weeps in the ruins of my spring:
The money of Whose tears shall fall
Into your weak and friendless hand,
And buy you back to your own land:
The silence of Whose tears shall fall
Like bells upon your alien tomb.
Hear them and come: they call you home.

"Roaming—without a name—without a chart
The unknown garden of another's heart."

TO THE MEMORY
OF ARTHUR GREEVES

by

C. S. Lewis
(1898–1963)

That we may mark with wonder and chaste dread
At hour of noon, when, with our limbs outspread
Lazily in the whispering grass, we lie
To gaze out fully upon the windy sky—
Far, far away, and kindly, friend with friend
To talk the old, old talk that has no end,
Roaming—without a name—without a chart
The unknown garden of another's heart.

ᏫᏫᏫ

"Though the heart be still as loving. . ."

WE'LL GO NO MORE A-ROVING

by

George Gordon Lord Byron
(1788–1824)

So, we'll go no more a-roving
So late into the night,
Though the heart be still as loving,
And the moon be still as bright.

For the sword outwears its sheath,
And the soul wears out the breast,
And the heart must pause to breathe,
And Love itself have rest.

Though the night was made for loving,
And the day returns too soon,
Yet we'll go no more a-roving
By the light of the moon.

ᕙᗯᕗ

"That there's some corner of a foreign field
That is for ever England."

THE SOLDIER

by

RUPERT BROOKE
(1887–1915)

If I should die, think only this of me;
That there's some corner of a foreign field
That is for ever England. There shall be
In that rich earth a richer dust concealed,
A dust whom England bore, shaped, made aware,
Gave, once, her flowers to love, her ways to roam,
A body of England's, breathing English air,
Washed by the rivers, blest by suns of home.

And think, this heart, all evil shed away,
A pulse in the eternal mind, no less
Gives somewhere back the thoughts by England
given;
Her sights and sounds, dreams happy as her day;
And laughter, learnt of friends; and gentleness,
In hearts at peace, under an English heaven.

ᕙᗯᕗ

"And Paradise was opened in his face."

OF ALL THIS NUMEROUS PROGENY

by

JOHN DRYDEN
(1631–1700)

Of all this numerous progeny was none
So beautiful, so brave, as Absalon. . . .
Early in foreign fields he won renown
With kings and states allied to Israel's crown.
In peace the thoughts of war he could remove,
And seemed as he were only born for love.
Whate'er he did was done with so much ease,
In him alone 'twas natural to please;
His motions all accompanied with grace,
And Paradise was opened in his face.

ⓖⱳⱥ

"Born of the sun they traveled a short while towards the sun, And left the vivid air signed with their honor."

I THINK CONTINUALLY OF THOSE
WHO WERE TRULY GREAT

by

SIR STEPHEN SPENDER
(1909–)

I think continually of those who were truly great.
Who, from the womb, remembered the soul's history
Through corridors of light where the hours are suns,
Endless and singing. Whose lovely ambition
Was that their lips, still touched with fire,
Should tell of the spirit clothed from head to foot in song.

And who hoarded from the spring branches
The desires falling across their bodies like blossoms.

What is precious is never to forget
The delight of the blood drawn from ageless springs
Breaking through rocks in worlds before our earth;
Never to deny its pleasure in the simple morning light,
Nor its grave evening demand for love;
Never to allow gradually the traffic to smother
With noise and fog the flowering of the spirit.

Near the snow, near the sun, in the highest fields
See how those names are feted by the wavering grass,
And by the streamers of white cloud,
And whispers of wind in the listening sky;
The names of those who in their lives fought for life,
Who wore at their hearts the fire's centre.
Born of the sun they traveled a short while towards the sun,
And left the vivid air signed with their honor.

᷐ᦸᦸᦸ

"And soonest our best men with thee do go. . . ."

DEATH, BE NOT PROUD

by

JOHN DONNE
(1572–1631)

Death, be not proud, though some have called thee
Mighty and dreadful, for thou art not so;
For those whom thou think'st thou dost overthrow
Die not, poor Death; nor yet canst thou kill me.
From rest and sleep, which but thy picture be,
Much pleasure; then from thee much more must flow;
And soonest our best men with thee do go—
Rest of their bones and souls' delivery!

Thou'rt slave to fate, chance, kings, and desperate men,
And dost with poison, war, and sickness dwell;
And poppy or charms can make us sleep as well
And better than thy stroke. Why swell'st though then?
One short sleep past, we wake eternally,
And Death shall be no more: Death, thou shalt die.

※

"Among these winters there is one so endlessly winter...."

BE AHEAD OF ALL PARTING

by

RAINER MARIA RILKE
(1875–1926)

Be ahead of all parting, as though it already were
behind you, like the winter that has just gone by.
For among these winters there is one so endlessly winter
that only by wintering through it will your heart survive.

Be forever dead in Eurydice—more gladly arise
into the seamless life proclaimed in your song.
Here, in the realm of decline, among momentary days,
be the crystal cup that shattered even as it rang.

Be—and yet know the great void where all things begin,
the infinite source of your own most intense vibration,
so that, this once, you may give it your perfect assent.

To all that is used up, and to all the muffled and dumb
creatures in the world's full reserve, the unsayable sums,
joyfully add yourself, and cancel the count.

※

381

"That's what the silence meant: *you're not alone.*"

YOU WILL NEVER BE ALONE

by

WILLIAM STAFFORD
(1914–1993)

You will never be alone, you hear so deep
A sound when autumn comes. Yellow
pulls across the hills and thrums,
or the silence after lightning before it says
its names—and then the clouds' wide-mouthed
apologies. You were aimed from birth:
you will never be alone. Rain
will come, a gutter filled, an Amazon,
long aisles—you never heard so deep a sound,
moss or rock, and years. You turn your head—
that's what the silence meant: you're not alone.
The whole wide world pours down.

ᏯᎷᎾ

**"I was real once.
I was very real."**

FLESH OF MY FLESH

by

BARBARA BOGGS SIGMUND
(1939–1990)

Children of my children's children
And beyond;
Now, well into
The tragi-
   comic
      slide
Of my flesh into decay,
I yearn for you.

I long for:
Lush, languid babies
   laughing in the sunlight;
Gawky, gap-toothed children,
   gamboling into life;
Adolescents, sprouting breasts
and beards,
   with equal mix of secret shame
   and pride;
Lovers not quite willing to believe
   in your astounding luck;
Newly-minted parents,
   wonder-filled and worshipful
   with awe.

Not for me
The all too certain maladies
Of
   your
      flesh.
The sleepless nights,

The screams of rage and pain,
The heart-stopping
> *sickness*
>> *and*
>> *accidents.*
I did that once and more,
Paying just dues
To Life
For her great gift to us.
But for you who will be born
When my flesh is almost finished,
Or dissolved,
I lust only for the joy.

And if perchance
One of you,
Courteous, or curious, or both,
Should visit at my cool,
indifferent grave,
It is my passion
That you know
That as I write to you:
> *I fiddle with the texture of my hair*
> *And gaze upon a limpid grove*
> *Of trees*
> *And feel the after-glow of a*
>> *warm and sunny day,*

Just as you do, my darlings,
Just exactly
> *as*
>> *you*
>> *do.*

I write to you, ghostly little loves,
Present only in the loins and longings
Of your ancestors,
Not to lecture you
That you are dust

And unto dust you will return,
(Though lectures I have heard)
Nor to ask that you should theorize
On spiritual and fleshly love,
(Though theories I do know)
Nor even to tell you that life is good,
(For there are some of you
who think that,
And others who do not)
But simply to let you know,
(Though why I care I do not know)
That just as real as is the drop of sweat
Now running down my side,
In whose existence you will scarce
believe,
I was real once.
I was very real.

﹙ﾟﾟ﹚

"I also say it is good to fall. . . ."

FROM "SONG OF MYSELF"

by

WALT WHITMAN
(1819–1892)

With music strong I come, with my cornets and my drums,
I play not marches for accepted victors only, I play marches
*   for conquered and slain persons.*

Have you heard that it was good to gain the day?
I also say it is good to fall, battles are lost in the same spirit
*   in which they are won.*
I beat and pound for the dead
I blow through my embouchures my loudest and gayest for
*   them.*

Vivas to those who have failed!
And to those whose war-vessels sank in the sea!
And to those themselves who sank in the sea!
And to all generals that lost engagements, and all overcome
  heroes!
And the numberless unknown heroes equal to the greatest
  heroes known!

~

"God's joy moves from unmarked box to unmarked box."

DON'T GRIEVE

by

RUMI
(1207–1273)

Don't grieve. Anything you lose comes round
in another form. The child weaned from mother's milk
now drinks wine and honey mixed.

God's joy moves from unmarked box to unmarked box,
from cell to cell. As rainwater, down into flowerbed.
As roses, up from ground.
Now it looks like a plate of rice and fish,
now a cliff covered with vines,
now a horse being saddled.
It hides within these,
till one day it cracks them open.

Part of the self leaves the body when we sleep
and changes shape. You might say, "Last night
I was a cypress tree, a small bed of tulips,
a field of grapevines." Then the phantasm goes away.
You're back in the room.
I don't want to make anyone fearful.
Hear what's behind what I say.

Ta dum dum, taa dum, ta ta dum.
There's the light gold of wheat in the sun
and the gold of bread made from that wheat.
I have neither. I'm only talking about them,

as a town in the desert looks up
at stars on a clear night.

❧

"I am content to live it all again...."

FROM "A DIALOGUE OF SELF AND SOUL"

by

WILLIAM BUTLER YEATS
(1865–1939)

I am content to live it all again
And yet again, if it be life to pitch
Into the frog-spawn of a blind man's ditch,
A blind man battering blind men;
Or into that most fecund ditch of all,
The folly that man does
Or must suffer, if he woos
A proud woman not kindred of his soul.

I am content to follow to its source
Every event in action or in thought;
Measure the lot; forgive myself the lot!
When such as I cast out remorse
So great a sweetness flows into the breast
We must laugh and we must sing,
We are blest by every thing,
Everything we look upon is blest.

❧

"And for all this, nature is never spent. . . ."

GOD'S GRANDEUR

by

GERARD MANLEY HOPKINS
(1844–1889)

The world is charged with the grandeur of God.
It will flame out, like shining from shook foil;
It gathers to a greatness, like the ooze of oil
Crushed. Why do men then now not reck his rod?
Generations have trod, have trod, have trod;
And all is seared with trade; bleared, smeared with toil;
And wears man's smudge and shares man's smell: the soil
Is bare now, nor can foot feel, being shod.

And for all this, nature is never spent;
There lives the dearest freshness deep down things;
And though the last lights off the black West went
Oh, morning, at the brown brink eastward, springs—
Because the Holy Ghost over the bent
World broods with warm breast and with ah! bright wings.

"My body of a sudden blazed. . . ."

FROM "VACILLATION"

by

WILLIAM BUTLER YEATS
(1865–1939)

My fiftieth year had come and gone,
I sat, a solitary man,
In a crowded London shop,
An open book and empty cup
On the marble table top.

While on the shop and street I gazed
My body of a sudden blazed;
And twenty minutes more or less
It seemed so great my happiness,
That I was blessed and could bless.

CREDITS

Johann Sebastian Bach by William F. Buckley: Reprinted from *Happy Days Were Here Again: Reflections of a Libertarian Journalist*, ed. Patricia B. Bozell, by permission of Random House, Inc. © 1993 by William F. Buckley Jr.

Pierre Auguste Renoir by Jean Renoir: Reprinted from *Renoir, My Father* by permission of Little, Brown and Company. © 1958 by Jean Renoir.

William Butler Yeats by Wystan Hugh Auden: "In Memory of W. B. Yeats" reprinted from *W. H. Auden: Collected Poems*, ed. by Edward Mendelson, by permission of Random House, Inc. © 1940 and renewed © 1968 by W. H. Auden.

Flannery O'Connor by Thomas Merton: "Flannery O'Connor: A Prose Elegy" reprinted from *Raids on the Unspeakable* by permission of New Directions Publishing Corporation and Laurence Pollinger, Ltd. © 1964 by The Abbey of Gethsemani, Inc.

Wystan Hugh Auden by Hannah Arendt: Reprinted from "Hannah Arendt: Remembering Wystan H. Auden" in *W. H. Auden: A Tribute*, ed. Sir Stephen Spender, by permission of Simon & Schuster Inc. © 1974 by George Weidenfeld & Nicolson, Ltd.

John Hersey by Bernadine Connelly: Reprinted by permission of the author.

William Stafford by Kim R. Stafford: "My Father's Place" reprinted from *Hungry Mind Review* (Winter 1993–1994) by permission of Kim Stafford.

Lawrence of Arabia by Sir Winston Churchill: Reprinted from *Winston S. Churchill: His Complete Speeches*, Vol. VI, 1935–1942, ed. Robert Rhodes James, by permission of Curtis Brown, Ltd., London, on behalf of the Estate of Sir Winston S. Churchill. © by Winston S. Churchill.

Astronauts Virgil Grissom, Edward White, and Roger Chaffee by Eric Sevareid: Delivered on *CBS News*, January 31, 1967. Reprinted by permission of Harold Matson, Inc. © 1967 by Eric Sevareid.

Yitzhak Rabin by Noa Ben-Artzi Philosof: "Goodbye to a Grandfather: We Are So Cold and So Sad," translated and transcribed by *The New York Times* (November 7, 1995). Reprinted by permission of *The New York Times*. © 1995 by The New York Times Company.

Abraham Lincoln by Carl Sandburg: Speech before Congress on February 12, 1959, reprinted from *Looking Forward* by permission of the Estate of Carl Sandburg, c/o Maurice C. Greenbaum, Esq., New York. © 1959 by Carl Sandburg.

John Fitzgerald Kennedy by Sean Quinlan: Reprinted from *America* magazine (December 14, 1963) by permission of America Press, Inc., 106 West 56th Street, New York, NY, 10019, in the absence of Sean Quinlan. © 1963.

Adlai Ewing Stevenson by Richard Goodwin: Reprinted from *The Sower's*

"A Valedictory to the Unknown Soldiers of World War II" by James O'Neill: Reprinted from *Washington Daily News* (May 30, 1958) by permission of Scripps Howard News Service. © 1958.

"Days of Remembrance" by Elie Wiesel: Reprinted as delivered in the Rotunda of the United States Capitol on April 30, 1984, by permission of Georges Borchardt, Inc. for the author. © 1984 by Elirion.

Rev. Henry Ward Beecher by Sinclair Lewis: Reprinted from the preface to Henry Ward Beecher: An American Portrait by Paxton Hibben (The Reader's Club/Reader's Digest, 1942) by permission.

William Jennings Bryan by H. L. Mencken: Reprinted from *The American Mercury* (October 1925) by permission.

Nadezhda Mandelstam by Joseph Brodsky: Reprinted from *Less than One: Selected Essays* by permission of Farrar, Straus & Giroux, Inc. © 1986 by Joseph Brodsky.

Marilyn Monroe by Diana Trilling: Reprinted from *Claremont Essays* (New York: Harcourt Brace and World, 1964) by permission of the author. © 1964 by Diana Trilling.

Ambrose Bierce by Florence King: Reprinted from *The Wall Street Journal* (January 31, 1996), A13, by permission of the author. © 1996 by Florence King.

Sister Beatrice of Jesus, OCD, by Sister Robin Stratton, OCD: Carmelite Sisters of Baltimore, Maryland. Reprinted from funeral booklet by permission of the author.

Laurie Lee on His Mother, Annie Lee: Reprinted from *Edge of Day* by permission of The Hogarth Press, London. © 1959 by Laurie Lee.

Richard Selzer on His Mother, Gertrude Selzer: Reprinted from *Down from Troy: A Doctor Comes of Age* by permission of William Morrow & Company, Inc. © 1992 by Richard Selzer.

Betsy McCully Cooper on Her Mother, Eloise McCully Simmons: Previously unpublished. Reprinted by permission of Betsy McCully Cooper.

Charles Trueheart on His Father, William C. Trueheart: Reprinted from *Washington Post Magazine* (May 1993) by permission of the author. © 1993 by Charles Trueheart.

Michael Saltz on His Father, Jerome Saltz: Delivered September 1, 1994, previously unpublished. Reprinted by permission of Michael Saltz.

Julie Houston on Her Mother, Rutheda Hunt d'Alton: Reprinted from *Parents* (September 1988) by permission of the author. © 1988 by Julie Houston.

Marie Harris on Her Mother, Marie Murray Harris: Reprinted from *The Granite Review* (published as "Only in Memory"), and as republished in *The Party Train: An Anthology of North American Prose Poetry* (Minneapolis: New Rivers Press) by permission of the author.

"A Eulogy to My Unknown Father" by Rosa Ordaz: Previously unpublished. Reprinted by permission of Rosa Ordaz.

Catherine A. MacKinnon on Her Father, George E. MacKinnon: Delivered May 5 and 8, 1995. Previously unpublished. Reprinted by permission of Catherine MacKinnon. © 1995, 1996 by Catherine MacKinnon.

David R. Cook on His Mother, Nelle Reed Cook: Previously unpublished. Reprinted by permission of David Cook.

Susy Clemens by Mark Twain: Reprinted from *Mark Twain's Autobiography, Volume II* by permission of HarperCollins Publishers, Inc. © 1924 by Clara Gabrilowitsch, renewed © 1952 by Clara Clemens Samossoud.

Mary White by William Allen White: Reprinted from *Emporia Gazette* (Emporia, Kansas: May 1921) by permission of Barbara Allen White.

INDEX